THE DUST BOWL

THE DUST BOWL

Men, Dirt, and Depression

Paul Bonnifield

UNIVERSITY OF NEW MEXICO PRESS

Albuquerque

Library of Congress Cataloging in Publication Data

Bonnifield, Mathew Paul, 1937-
  The Dust Bowl.

  Bibliography: p. 217
  Includes index.
    1. Great Plains—History. 2. Great Plains—
  Economic conditions. 3. Great Plains—Climate.
  4. Depressions—1929—United States. 5. Droughts
  —Great Plains—History. 6. Agriculture—Great
  Plains—History. I. Title.
  F595.B73   978   78-55706
  ISBN 0-8263-0485-0

Designed by Barbara J. Hoon

THE DUST BOWL

Preface

Shortly after arriving as a new faculty member at Panhandle State University in Goodwell, Oklahoma, I took my wife, Ellen, and the children to visit No Man's Land Historical Museum. There we met the curator, Joan Kachel, who was bubbling with enthusiasm about the history of the Oklahoma Panhandle and the southern Great Plains. During our visit she led us into a small room filled with newspapers and other documents. Soon I found myself leafing through some of the material describing the 1930s. From this simple beginning, interest in the dust bowl, its people, the dust storms, and the depression grew to a point of deep fascination for myself and my family.

Soon after I began the research, it became apparent that our traditional ideas of life in the dust bowl needed to be overhauled and sharply modified. The intense greed and cynical attitude of the farmers toward the soil, which traditional works express and government reports of the period assert, simply had to be reevaluated. I expected to find vast numbers of documents describing deep poverty, mass migration, and extreme suffering. Again it was necessary to restate the conditions with a new perspective. At each corner I found something new and different from what I had been led to believe. Ultimately the story of the heartland of the dust bowl is the chronicle of hardworking, stouthearted folks who withstood the onslaught of nature at its worst, while living through a devastating depression and facing government idealism. It was the people who lived in the heartland of the dust bowl who fought the battles to save the land. They were the ones who suffered the casualties. To them should go the credit for the victory—a victory that helps feed a hungry world and heat our homes.

This book attempts to approach the numerous questions presented by the dust bowl from several angles, among which are the nature of the climate, the causes of the severe wind erosion, the strength of the region's economy, the role played by government agencies, and the character of the people who resided in the area.

When a person sets out to research and write a book, it is necessary to rely on numerous people. Without the continual support and encouragement of Dr. Harold Kachel and his wife, Joan, I would have stopped working long ago. The people of the heartland of the dust bowl were most cooperative. Old-timers willingly and frankly opened themselves to my questions. Mr. and Mrs. W. D. Ross, Mr. and Mrs. Bill Kraft, Mrs. Emma Love, and Mr. Gordon Grice were especially helpful. The editors and staff at local newspapers were most agreeable and found ways to provide me a place to work undisturbed even though I often arrived on press day. At area museums and libraries and Grasslands offices I was treated very cordially. Most of all I would like to thank my wife, Ellen, and my two children, Heather and Juanita. They tolerated a great deal from me and continued to help in every way. At one point in the research I became so involved that the two girls (who are small) dated all events from the dust bowl. Ellen has helped in a million ways. She has been research director, critic, typist, and loving wife.

Contents

Illustrations

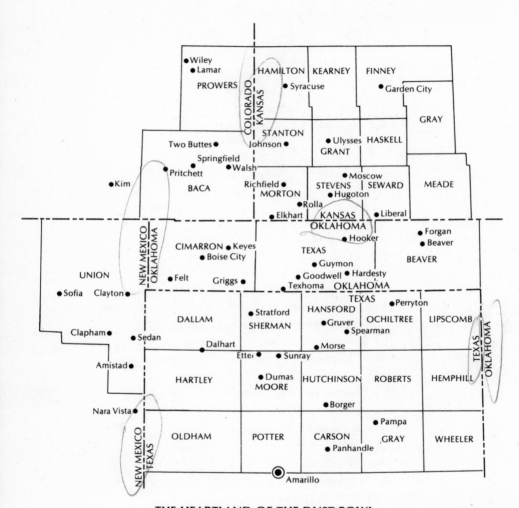

THE HEARTLAND OF THE DUST BOWL

1

Early Dust and Climate

The gale came blowing from the south on March 3, 1935. Dirt leaped into the air and pounded everything it struck. At his home on the north edge of Guymon, Oklahoma, Vernon L. Hopson was standing by a window watching the storm when a fifty-five-gallon oil drum came jetting past the window. The next day he looked out the same window and was amazed to see a 120-foot, steel oil derrick, which had been in operation before the storm, lying flat against the earth. The same storm broke off fifty telephone poles between Guymon and Goodwell, Oklahoma.[1]

That storm was followed by another and yet another. In late March the major wire services were arousing national concern for the health of children who were sick and dying from dust pneumonia in Baca County, Colorado. Hundreds of residents in the Kansas counties of Stanton, Morton, Stevens, and Grant, dreadfully ill with measles and dust pneumonia, were being treated at emergency hospitals. As the storms continued to rage, many residents fled the stricken land until the blow was over.[2]

The sun rose in a pleasant blue sky on April 14. The wind was soft and gentle, from the southwest, and the air was clean and healthy, a pleasant respite from the dirt storms of the previous months. It was a day for a drive in the country, a day for a fishing trip to Two Buttes Lake, a day for a rabbit drive northwest of Hooker, Oklahoma. It was also a day for a roller. About

1

four o'clock in the afternoon, the rabbit hunters were ready to corral thousands of jackrabbits when a black rolling cloud engulfed the men and beasts. Immediately everything turned black. All the hunters could do was sit down, pray, cough, pray, choke, and pray, while horses and rabbits squealed, ran, and floundered among them.[3]

Mrs. Emma Love, who was at Hooker visiting her parents while her husband participated in the rabbit drive, stood and admired the approaching storm as only an artist could. She was thrilled by the mauves of the cloud. At the top of the storm were plumes that danced in the sunlight and emblazoned the colors of the rainbow across the sky before plunging savagely toward the ground.[4]

At the little farming community of Griggs, Oklahoma, one woman watched the mighty cloud and feared that the Lord was returning to gather his flock. When the storm struck Pampa, Texas, Woody Guthrie began writing his famous song "So Long, It's Been Good To Know You." When Guthrie began the song, he thought the end of life was near. The storm continued, submerging everyone in its path in darkness and an unforgettable experience.

After the storm was over, the Associated Press reporter at Guymon, Robert Geiger, wrote: "Three little words—achingly familiar on a Western farmer's tongue—rule life today in the dust bowl of the continent. . . . If it rains." The following day the Washington *Evening Star* carried Geiger's story and soon the phrase "dust bowl," which had been born in the hard humor of America's Next Year People and repeated by Geiger, was on the lips of everyone.[5]

Since Geiger popularized the term dust bowl, the phrase has become synonymous with drought, migration, Great Plains relief, and severe wind erosion during the 1930s. Although the term remains in wide usage, the dust bowl and its story remain shrouded in mystery. No one during the late 1930s or since has agreed on the actual boundary that determined when a person or region was in the dust bowl. Geiger's report located the center of the dust bowl at Guymon, Oklahoma. During the spring of 1935, columnists, feature writers, and newspaper reporters located the heartland of the dust bowl in the five-state area of the northern Texas Panhandle, northeastern New Mexico, southeastern Colorado, southwestern Kansas, and the Oklahoma Panhandle. Arthur H. Joel's soil conservation reconnaissance in 1936 further defined the heartland of the dust bowl to consist of twenty counties; Joel did not, however, include New Mexico in his study.

In terms of wind erosion, national publicity, federal relief, and common history, the heartland of the dust bowl consisted of Cimarron, Texas, and Beaver counties, Oklahoma; Union County, New Mexico; Prowers and Baca counties, Colorado; Morton, Stevens, Seward, Stanton, Grant and Hamilton counties, Kansas; and Dallam, Hartley, Sherman, Moore, Hansford, and Ochiltree counties, Texas.

While the protracted drought and the dirt storms of the 1930s swept the heartland of the dust bowl, well-meaning and intelligent men sought to determine the cause of the maladjustment in the region's agriculture and the cause of the tremendous loss of vital national resources through wind erosion. The generally accepted theory expressed by most experts argued that there was no wind erosion until the buffalo grass was turned under by the plow; that selfish, greedy men sought quick wealth by raising wheat despite wise council given by scientists and government farm leaders. The spark that set off the great plow up, continued the theory, was the high price of wheat during World War I. In the mad race to achieve quick wealth, dust bowl farmers abandoned stock raising and other crops and turned to a single-crop agricultural system. To stop the advancing deserts the government had to apply heroic measures to right the wrongs to the soil and establish a permanent, stable agricultural economy in the stricken region. Allotment, resettlement, soil conservation, and land-use programs were attempted in order to achieve the necessary ends.

Since the dust bowl era, historians have generally been content to accept the newspaper accounts and government reports of the period at face value. Vance Johnson's *Heaven's Tableland* comes close to deifying the Soil Conservation Service. And Fred Floyd's dissertation, "A History of the Dust Bowl," speaks very highly of the Soil Conservation Service. But these works, which are nearly thirty years old, leave several questions unanswered.

"The disaster that overtook the Great Plains," wrote Theodore Saloutos, "has been recounted in dramatic fashion by columnists,

Figure 1. A roller approaching Guymon, Oklahoma, on March 17, 1923. Courtesy of No Man's Land Historical Museum, Goodwell, Oklahoma.

feature writers, and others; hence it would be belaboring the obvious to repeat what others have stated."[6] Yet, Morris L. Cooke, director of the Water Section of the National Resources Board, which forged the long-range plan for meeting the challenge of agricultural maladjustment, "called a luncheon meeting of the nation's top editors (newspapers, magazines, and books) at the Engineers' Club in New York. There his guests and the committee members thrashed out dozens of problems concerning the presentation of the proposed report."[7] In light of the fact that leading editors were working closely with the committee, it might be useful to reexamine the events that have been recounted in "dramatic fashion."

Saloutos continued his analysis of the disaster by saying:

> The makers and the administrators of New Deal farm programs and policies inherited in the Great Plains one of the most maladjusted agricultural regions in the country, along with the worst depression and some of the most devastating drought and dust storms in history. Fortunately, they recognized that the problems were more deeply rooted than

Figure 2. The most famous roller descending on the people at the rabbit drive near Hooker, Oklahoma, on April 14, 1935. Courtesy of Mrs. Emma Love, Goodwell, Oklahoma.

Figure 3. This roller is all but forgotten. The picture was taken on June 4, 1937, at Goodwell, Oklahoma. Courtesy of Mrs. Emma Love, Goodwell, Oklahoma.

the destructive work of the elements. Efforts to realign the physical and human resources of the region so as to maximize production and minimize destruction posed new problems of communication and education, of winning over those who feared basic changes, and of resolving conflicts between local and state authorities, on the one hand, and federal authorities on the other.[8]

But what methods were used to realign the physical and human resources of the region so as to maximize production and minimize destruction? What happened to the people who were realigned in order to conform to a government policy? Did the federal policy makers recognize the deep-rooted problem, especially concerning the impact of technology on the Great Plains?

Synthesizing the efforts and statements of the Great Plains Committee to cope with the disaster, Saloutos set out to tell

> the story of the sustained efforts of the various agencies to help: to cushion the effects of commercial, one-crop farming on small scale producers who lacked the necessary capital, technical equipment, and managerial abilities; to consolidate local units of government and realize economies; to discourage the spread of "suit-case" farming and the inevitable loss of interest in rural community affairs; to redirect the farming practices of marginal and submarginal producers who persisted in employing methods more suitable to the humid areas; to keep the range from being overstocked with cattle; to make better use of land in relation to water; and to prepare the farmers for the cycles of dry years and bad harvests that often followed the cycles of wet years and good harvests.[9]

How did the New Deal policy makers meet the challenge of providing credit, technical equipment, and managerial abilities? How were local governments consolidated? What was accomplished to discourage "suit-case" farming? How did the agencies improve farming methods? What was their range land program? How did the New Dealers prepare farmers to meet the weather cycles? In terms of humanity, what happened to the small-scale producer?

In a federal publication, "Our National Grasslands: Dustland to Grassland," by Keith A. Argow, the dust bowl and its residents were described as "a dead land—populated by defeated people who were plagued by drought and depression. No one had much hope for it, . . ." Was it a dead land and the people without much hope?

After the roller of April 14, 1935, the editor of the *Panhandle Herald* wrote: "In this vicinity, the rolling of the clouds, and their fiery aspects [were] most spectacular and hundreds of citizens took snapshots of the effects as they approached. It was awe inspiring, but was not as resplendent in color effects as was the famous storm on St. Patricks' Day in 1923."[10] The editor of the *Hooker Advance* claimed that the April 14 roller was the third to strike the Oklahoma Panhandle. The first was on May 2, 1904. Mrs. Maude Yates, who was among the first homesteaders arriving in the Oklahoma Panhandle, recalled that in 1904 the noon train was stranded at Texhoma for nearly twelve hours before the storm lifted enough that it could safely continue its journey. While the train was stranded in town, one passenger nearly died from fright and suffocation. But that was not the first severe dirt storm to rage across the semiarid land.[11]

The story of the semiarid Great Plains begins in those ages long ago when the heartland of the dust bowl was a swampland ruled by dinosaurs. The footprints left in the mud by the dinosaurs in present Cimarron County all point in the same direction. No doubt the great reptiles were traveling to some destination, but where, and what sent them on their errand? Were they migrating from some natural disaster and desperately seeking a safe refuge? These questions are unanswerable. But the migration of the dinosaurs introduces us to the soil—a soil formed through the ages of settlement from seas and lakes and swamps, a soil with fine granules.

After the age of the great reptiles came that of the massive glaciers, which terminated in the vastness of the southern Great Plains. As the mountains of ice receded, gigantic hills of caliche were deposited. As the caliche weathers, it turns to fine particles of soil. The ice age was followed by a period of great lakes and rivers that left a smooth, silt-covered floor, a floor that became the tableland of the Great Plains.

While the ice still dominated the land, man hunted game in the region. The discovery of Folsom points in fossil remains located on a tributary to the Cimarron River establishes man's presence in the five-state region as long ago as the Pleistocene Age. Early basketmakers and farmers worked the soil and provided for their families some 10,000 years ago. The farming society on the Cimarron disappeared some 3,500 years ago, but man did not abandon agriculture in the region. The remains at the Stamper site near Optima, Oklahoma, contain stores of maize and cotton raised by the inhabitants. The extensive irrigation ditches in Beaver County, Oklahoma, still remind us of those early farmers, who saw their society destroyed by floods on the upper Cimarron River.[12]

The early remains of the first settlers indicate that man could not agree on the proper way to live on the southern Great Plains. The nomadic hunting cultures viewed the region as a climate best suited to grazing. Herds of buffalo, antelope, and other animals grazed the land, while men followed them in search of food, clothing, and tools. It was a hard life. The hunters were always on the move and never had a large cache to carry their families through lean periods. The farmers preferred a more sedentary life with a permanent home, but cropping the land was heavy toil.

Cropping or grazing the short-grass country depends upon the whims of nature. The Great Plains at its best or at its worst is ruled by the wind and the sun. The Sand Hills of Nebraska stand as silent monuments of a terrific dust bowl in antiquity. Fanning out to the east and south from the Sand Hills are broad expanses of loess soil, whose very name speaks of its birth—born of the wind. Reaching well to the south of the Arkansas, Cimarron, Beaver, and Canadian rivers, as well as the area's creeks, are rolling sand hills formed by the wind. These hills of sand, sandy loam, and loamy sand soils bear testimony to the many sand storms that have swept the country for aeons.[13]

Nature has attempted to restrain the waywardness of the sun and wind. The sand hills and dunes often become dams which prevent the precious rain from escaping to the streams and abandoning the plains before it has completed its task of aiding the thirsty soil. The level tableland is filled with playas (small lakes or buffalo wallows), which collect life-giving moisture. Large expanses of level land and rolling hills slope away from streams and prevent the water from escaping. In some counties in the heartland of the dust bowl, as much as 80 percent or more of the land surface does not drain to a stream. Thus the rainfall must stay near the spot where it falls. But the sun and wind often quickly evaporate the moisture into the air.[14]

The soils of the dust bowl record their rich heritage. The hardland, clay soil that recalls the days when water ruled the land, forms broad bands of "wheat land." Richfield Soil Series forms along the Colorado-Kansas border and extends in an irregular line to the south and east across the Oklahoma Panhandle. In Texas, Richfield Soil is replaced by the Pullman Soil of Ochiltree and Hansford counties. Scattered across the hardlands are extensive hills formed by blow dirt and glacial deposits. In Beaver County, Oklahoma, there are extensive drainages and rolling sand hills. In Dallam and Hartley counties, Texas, and parts of Cimarron County, Oklahoma, the land has extensive rolling terrain. Union County, New Mexico, is a mixture of plains, foothills, and mountains. Although it does not have the remains of ancient volcanoes, Baca County, Colorado, is similar to northeastern New Mexico and the plains of Kansas. Thus the country is a mixture of extremes.

The soils of the eighteen counties that formed the heartland of the dust bowl vary widely in texture, structure, and parent material. The names of the soil series suggest the differences in the soil and their location. A soil map reads like a map of place names: Dumas, Sunray, Dalhart, Richfield, Kim, Wiley, Ulysses, and Gruver are a few of the major soil series that were named after towns. Sherm, Dallam, and Baca soils denote the counties for which the soil series have been named.

Each of the soils responds differently to wind, rain, and sun. Generally, the sandier the soil, the more readily it absorbs water. And because the sandy soil particles are larger (having fewer sides to hold moisture) more of the moisture is available to plants than in clay soil. The result is that plants can start more readily in sandy soil than in clay soil. Sandy soils, however, dry more quickly than clay soils and thus tend to start blowing earlier than clay soils.

In dry weather clay soil will crack, leaving open mouths facing the sky, ready to trap any moisture sent from the clouds. But moisture on the lips of the cracks often closes the soil before it has drunk deeply of the precious liquid. The result is the loss by drainage of life-giving moisture during dry years. During hard

rains, which are common on the high plains, clay soil packs
tightly and the absorption of moisture is much too slow to trap
the needed water.

Plants, animals, and men that survive on the semiarid lands
must adjust themselves to the soil. Some soils are better at
catching water; others are designed to hold moisture. Within a
small area the soils change often and quickly, and each soil re-
quires its own special care if it is not to be a victim of the wind
during droughts. It was on the question of how to take advantage of the moisture in the soil that most scientific research was
done before the dirty 1930s.

The weather patterns on the southern plains appear to be
cyclical. Periods of wet years intermingled with dry years are followed by the reverse. During the wet cycles, grasses that require more moisture for survival spread from their safer haven to
dangerous areas. When a dry cycle begins, these grasses are
quickly killed, leaving large patches of soil exposed to the wind.
Scientists have observed as much as 40 percent of the native
grass being killed in a single year, and during extended periods
of drought, 100 percent of the grass died in large areas.[15]

A shortage of water is not the only weapon in the alliance of
sun and wind. Tender new blades of buffalo grass easily succumb
to the forces of wind erosion. After a rain, buffalo grass quickly
sends stolons to reclaim the barren soil. But in the open land
removed from the colony, the young grass often falls victim to
the dust the wind hurls as it ebbs and flows across the earth.
The struggle is constant.[16]

When the two antagonists are left to themselves, the struggle is
nearly equal. First one and then the other is ahead. But the sun and
wind have other allies. Without ice, snow, and rain, more grasshopper, grassworm, and other insect eggs hatch. The insects mass in
great hordes and march across country. Their path is marked by exposed soil. The population of rabbits and rodents also increases during dry cycles. These animals, as well as buffalo or cattle, overgraze
the grass. The weapon of last resort for the wind and sun is fire.
Grass fires started by nature or man have been known to burn more
than a million acres. The infinite number of combinations of elements render the Great Plains a ready victim of dust storms when
conditions are right. It was some combination of these elements that
caused the terrific dirt storms before any plow broke the sod.[17]

The winds and the mountains control the moisture in the region where the five states of Colorado, New Mexico, Texas, Oklahoma, and Kansas approach each other. Moist winds from the Gulf of Mexico blow inland across Texas and swing to the east. On the outer limits of the reach of the southwest winds lies the land of the five-state area. The limits of the reach of gulf moisture are illustrated by the average precipitation received in four of the northern Texas Panhandle counties. Beginning in the northwest corner of the panhandle and moving east, the average precipitation is 16.25 inches in Dallam County, 16.55 inches in Sherman County, 22.00 in Hansford County, and 21.13 in Ochiltree County. The northeastern flow of moisture is also visible by comparing the average precipitation at Dumas, Texas, Hooker, Oklahoma, and Liberal, Kansas. These communities are on a northeast-southwest line. The average precipitation is 18.95 inches at Dumas, 18.24 inches at Hooker, and 19.38 inches at Liberal. Just to the west of a line connecting the three communities is Goodwell, Oklahoma, where the average rainfall is nearly an inch less than Hooker's average.[18]

At the western tip of the Oklahoma Panhandle rises Black Mesa. The mesa runs east and west until it joins the main range of the Rockies. On the southern side of the mesa at Kenton, Oklahoma, average precipitation is nearly an inch greater than at Boise City, Oklahoma, only a few miles to the east. On the northern side of the mesa, precipitation drops sharply. In northwestern Baca County, Colorado, the average precipitation is just over twelve inches. In the southeastern part of the county, which is out of the shade of the mesa, precipitation averages over seventeen inches.[19]

Moisture-bearing winter storms from the Pacific Northwest often leave a blanket of snow across the plains of northern Colorado and Kansas but begin to swing to the east before crossing the Arkansas River. Between the flows of moisture from the gulf and the Pacific is a rough triangle of very low precipitation. From Stanton County, Kansas, to the north, south, and east average precipitation increases. It is to the east of Stanton County that the Pacific and gulf storms merge. To the west is a zone near the Baca and Prowers county line where precipitation decreases. The 12 inches of precipitation in northwestern Baca County is in the zone with Stanton County that averages 15.73 inches of precipitation.[20]

With some exceptions, the only winter storms to reach the five-state area consist of cold and dry artic weather that slides down the eastern edge of the Rockies. These fronts bring little moisture, and, by the time they cross the Arkansas River, much of the cold has been removed.

The sun during periods of drought takes advantage of the nature of the soil. The soil holds heat more easily than the atmosphere. At the beginning of tests in 1934 the soil three inches below the surface was cooler than the atmosphere four inches above the soil. But the temperature of the soil at a depth of three inches eventually surpassed atmospheric temperature and soared to 140–50 degrees, while the maximum atmospheric temperatures ranged between 96 and 111 degrees. Soils reaching these temperatures soon become very dry and most of the soil life is killed or retarded. As a result, several inches of earth are readied for a flight to some distant port or nearby dune.[21]

Through the centuries the southern Great Plains was claimed by several Indian tribes and European nations. The Louisiana Purchase gave the United States a claim to the land. "One of the uses President Jefferson hoped to make of the Louisiana Purchase was to develop an Indian colonization zone on its western margins beyond the pressure and influence of the American settlement."[22] The government leaders, including Jefferson, believed that moving the Indians west would provide for humane treatment of the native Americans and simultaneously establish a better land-use policy. The humid areas to the east would be used for extensive cultivation by yeoman farmers, and the more distant zone would be suitable to the Indian way of life. The reports of Zebulon M. Pike in 1810 and Stephen H. Long in 1823 described the Great Plains as deserts and compared them to the sandy, windswept, and eroded deserts of Arabia. While inspecting land in 1830 for the resettlement of the Delaware Indians in Kansas, Isaac McCoy noted the severity of the drought and the dust and smoke in the air.[23] The Plains was viewed as unfit for farming and civilization. These reports and others added fuel to the argument for resettling the Indians to the west and for maintaining the short-grass regions for grazing. Although the federal government was removing Indians earlier, the Indian Removal Act of 1830 marked the legislative enactment of a new resettlement and land-use policy.

The research of James C. Malin on dust storms before the turn of the century leaves little doubt that very severe dirt storms occurred in Kansas before any plow turned the short-grass sod or longhorn cattle overgrazed the range. The first white settlers to the humid area of eastern Kansas in 1854 noted the drought conditions and the dirt blowing in on them. In January 1855, three months before the normal blowing season, the editor of the *Kansas Free State* at Lawrence commented: "The strong south winds that we experience here are our greatest annoyance. They frequently last for several days, and are loaded with the black dust from the burnt prairie, which penetrates every corner of our houses, and makes every one who is exposed to it as 'sooty' as a collier."[24] During the blowing season of March and April, the settlers of Kansas suffered through several days of intense dirt storms.

The extent of the drought beyond the limits of Kansas was recorded in the reports of the missionaries and Indian agents to the Choctaws in southeastern Indian Territory. And in 1854, J. H. Wright traveled with his family from Missouri to the Red River and back. "All along our route," recalled Wright, "was the dreary picture of the drouth fields of stubble, leafless trees and dust white roads. . . . There was no relieving spectacle anywhere along the whole 700 miles of our homeward journey."[25] The drought of 1854 was so severe that a man in Elliottville, Indiana, delayed a trip to Pleasant Run, Texas, because "the dust and scarcity of water would kill our horses."[26]

During the protracted drought of the 1850s and 1860s, numerous dust storms were reported. Some of the storms carried dirt several miles east of the Great Plains. Professor Fairchild at Oberlin College, Ohio, recorded a black snow on February 7, 1855. And on April 5, 1860, Syracuse, New York, had a black rain. Two days earlier Fort Scott, Kansas, had experienced one of its worst dust storms.[27]

The worst year of the drought was 1860. The Choctaws appropriated "the sum of $134,512.40 to be expended . . . in the purchase, shipment and distribution of sixty-five thousand bushels of corn among the Choctaw people."[28] After the drought, whenever the weather was dry and the dirt storms began to blow, Kansas farmers compared conditions to 1860. In 1863, reports arrived in eastern Kansas that "the present season is said to be the dryest ever known of the plains. Owing to the drying up of the Platte River and its tributaries, large numbers of stock have died for the want of water above Fort Kearney [*sic*]."[29]

The decade of the 1870s was again one of severe drought. In 1872 one Kansas editor recalled the Civil War and noted how well men from the Union and the Confederacy were getting along at the various cattle shipping towns. But

> the effect of the "late unpleasantness" may yet daily be witnessed upon our streets. Men of both sections have forgotten and forgiven all, but the winds are on it strong. At present advices the south (wind) stands three days ahead and real estate is going rapidly northward, as are, also, a hat now and then. Zephyrs are our strong point—they lift ten pound boulders and two year old mule colts off the ground—the squawking flocks overhead may be geese, may be jackasses.[30]

The editor went on to advertise the following:

> Real estate for sale at this office, by the acre or bushel. We have no disposition to infringe upon the business of our friends down street, but owing to the high winds and the open condition of our office, and not being ready for interment just yet, necessity compels us to dispose of the fine bottom land now spread over our type and presses.[31]

A prolonged and severe drought struck the nation in 1873 and did not end until 1881. In the fall of 1873, the *Monthly Weather Review* reported that "in the later part of November, vast prairie fires occurred in the far West, and several dust storms, filling the air with fine and unpalpable particles, . . . and sometimes are finally precipitated with water, forming the celebrated 'black rain.' "[32] Between 1873 and 1881, many sources reported prairie fires, grasshopper plagues, and dust storms. It was a time when nature was in a foul mood.

During the early 1870s, hunters slaughtered buffaloes while the army rounded up the Indians and drove them to reservations. The Great Plains, which stretches from Canada to Texas and from the Rocky Mountains to the 100th meridian, was nearly empty of men and large herds of grazing animals. The buffalo grass had yet to feel the killing edge of the plow; but, terrific dirt storms swept the virgin land.

In spite of the rigors of the elements, frontiersmen continued to push west. At the Point of Rock on the Cimarron River along the old Santa Fe Trail, Bates and Beals moved a herd of live-stock onto summer range in 1877. After resting their cattle a few months, the stock was moved further south to the Canadian River north of present Amarillo, Texas. The Bates and Beals L-X cowboys were the first to make a temporary settlement in pres-ent Morton County, Kansas. Two years later the Beaty Brothers drove a herd of cattle to the Point of Rock and constructed a rude two-room cow camp. The ranch became the first settlement in that part of Kansas. In the 1870s and early 1880s ranches dominated the dust bowl region, but the first ranchers did not remain master of the domain for long.[33]

The western construction of the railroads made it possible for the open-range cattle industry to operate, but those same rail-roads attracted homesteaders. During the 1870s the Santa Fe Railroad built a line along the Arkansas River and west towards the Pacific. The Denver and Fort Worth Railroad had completed construction on its line across northeastern New Mexico into the Texas Panhandle, and the Rock Island Railroad constructed a line that fostered Liberal, Kansas, in 1888. In a general way these railroads framed the region that later became known as the heartland of the dust bowl.

With the advancement of railroads, and the promise or dream of more railroads from 1886 to 1889, homesteaders and town builders flooded southwestern Kansas, southeastern Colorado, and No Man's Land—later the Oklahoma Panhandle. John and Harriet Jefferson were among the first settlers to arrive at the new community of Richfield, Kansas. It had been a long, dif-ficult, and dangerous trip west for the Jeffersons. In the pre–Civil War years, John, wanting to be a free man rather than chained to a plantation system, escaped from his slave master in Kentucky and headed west. In Clay County, Missouri, he and Harriet were married. In 1886 they were in southwestern Kan-sas ready to make a new home on free land. After pausing a few days in Richfield, the Jeffersons moved to northwestern Morton County, where they staked their claim. Here the family built a small dugout for a home, built a rock corral, dug a well, and planted a crop. Over the years the pioneers were able to raise an orchard and till the land. In time the dugout, with its invincible sand fleas, was replaced by a frame home. Building a new life in a new land was a grueling task, and through the years, which witnessed depressions, blizzards, droughts, dust storms, and plagues, the Jefferson children and grandchildren grew to maturity. Hard times and difficult elements were a normal part of their lives by the time the depression and drought of the 1930s stalked the land.[34]

While the Jeffersons were establishing their roots in Morton County, John A. and Amanda C. Bell were starting a new life for their family in Stevens County. Their homestead and tree claim was near Hugoton, Kansas. Shortly after arriving in Stevens County, John Bell purchased a broomcorn seeder and a thresher.[35] These two vital implements made it possible for the settlers to raise a cash crop.

The Bells, the Jeffersons, and others came to make a new home, and with hard work and preseverance they accomplished their task. But the majority of the new settlers were simply speculators and town folks who wanted to capitalize on the railroads. The advancement of railroads to Englewood, Meade, and Liberal, Kansas, attracted over 6,000 settlers to the public domain in No Man's Land. Along the Jones-Plummer Trail and the Tuttle Trail, Beaver City, Gate City, Neutral, and dozens of other communities were founded. In 1887 representatives from the strip met in Beaver City and organized Cimarron Territory. Congress failed to recognize the territory, and in 1890 No Man's Land was combined with the Unassigned Lands to form Oklahoma Territory.[36]

Town boomers believed the D. M. & A. Railroad would soon connect southwestern Kansas towns with the Colorado coal fields and other points. With the railroad would come fantastic prices for lots, businesses, and farms. To attract the railroad, in 1887 Richfield began construction of a magnificent stone courthouse and brick church. While Richfield was building a courthouse for Morton County, rival factions in Stevens and Grant counties warred over the location for their respective county seats. The number of towns platted and the bitter rivalry between town site promoters as compared to the number of homesteads actually settled on and sod plowed clearly establishes that the vast majority of the settlers were speculating on the railroad and were not in the area to build new homes.[37]

By 1889 the prospects for the future were dimmed. The often talked about railroad was not coming to the region. By 1890 the exodus from southeastern Colorado, southwestern Kansas, and the Oklahoma Panhandle was in full swing. People were heading for their old homes or chasing a new rainbow in a new region. By the mid 1890s, only a few hardy families remained in the high, windswept plains, and little of the land had been plowed.

At old Tascosa in the Texas Panhandle, pioneers were leaving because of the elements and economic depression. The early years of the 1880s were hard but not as harsh as the years after 1885. The combination of blizzards and droughts in 1886–87 brought an abrupt end to the heyday of the open-range cattle industry. The price of live cattle plunged very low and victims of blizzards, wolves, and droughts were plentiful on the range. Unemployed cowboys, ranch hands, and freighters were everywhere. In towns across the plains, storekeepers had large inventories of goods they could not move. At Tascosa in 1889, the Canadian River was dry. The sand was dry to depths which made it difficult to dig for water. Along the banks of the dead stream, and on the plains beyond, great circles of barren soil marked the path of the grasshoppers. It was so dry and water and grass so scarce that no trail herds from New Mexico made the trip to Tascosa for shipping.[38]

The lean year of 1889 extended its reach through 1890 and 1891. On March 29, 1890, the wind "just naturally blew and blew and blew, and blowed and blowed and blowed, and swept the country all up in one great big continuous sweep." For two days dust from the plains and sand from the river bottom rasped the community and its residents. Through every crack poured a choking cloud of dust. Nothing was safe and no one was sure of the outcome. This was the high plains at its worst.[39]

In April 1895, settlers on the Great Plains were introduced to a new terror—the snuster. A snuster is a combination of snow and dirt driven by strong, cold winds. The railroads east from Denver were blocked and the "men at work cleaning the way were obliged to wear coverings for their faces, and the sand cutting even through the cloth like a knife and lacerating the shovelers in a horrible fashion."[40]

At Johnson City, Kansas, the editor of the *Journal* wrote:

> The worst storm ever witnessed by our oldest residents
> passed over the western part of this country and eastern
> Colorado, April 5th and 6th. It was a combination of snow,
> and sand, which was blown across the prairie at a terrific
> speed uninterrupted for 40 hours.
>
> The Cimarron, North Fork, Little North Fork, San Ar-
> royo, Horse Creek and Butte were strewn for miles with
> the dead carcasses. The storm came so suddenly that few
> people got their stock in. Thousands of dollars worth of
> stock, that required 8 and 9 years of hardship and economy
> for our farmers to accumulate, was lost.[41]

The snuster took its toll not only of Stanton County livestock,
but of people. Three children, ranging in age from eight to thir-
teen, had gone to gather the stock as the storm approached, but
the storm engulfed them. Two were found about three miles
from home. Another, who was forced to walk with a crutch, was
found about a half mile from home. The children were not the
first, nor would they be the last victims of the harsh climate.[42]

Severe weather, difficulties of pioneering, and lost dreams for
the future defeated many of the settlers—but not all of them.
The remaining settlers adapted to the new conditions and continued their business. Although the general migration was out-
bound during the 1890s, a few hardy souls moved in to continue
the task of opening the country. In 1891 Jacob Berends moved
his family to a homestead along the Cimarron River north of
Gate, Oklahoma. Berends was a master craftsman. His talent
kept the machinery and windmills vital to that region operating.
On one occasion a major gear to a steam tractor simply wore
out. Without the tractor, the threshing machine could not do its
task. Distance and cost prohibited the purchasing of a new gear.
Berends used the worn gear for a pattern and made a mold in
the sand. He built a furnace from a washtub over the mold,
melted scrap iron, and cast a new gear.[43]

Berends's feat with the tractor gear was only one of his
numerous accomplishments. With the new auto era after the
turn of the century he saw the advantage in a four-wheel-drive
vehicle. In 1911 he began developing a four-wheel-drive system.
With handmade parts, Berends successfully equipped an old Rio

car with four-wheel drive. Although he received the first patent, Berends failed to gain financial support for further development. But his ingenuity and adaptability reflected the people's willingness to accept new methods and ideas necessary to meet the challenge of the Great Plains. With the dawning of the twentieth century a new era began in the heartland of the dust bowl.

2

The Good Years

A reporter for the *Oklahoma Farmer-Stockman* was interviewing a Texas County, Oklahoma, homesteader while the wild winds of 1935 raised havoc across the land. The old-timer recalled how his first crops failed and he was nearly starved out, "but when it turned, it turned quickly and was awful good."[1] Things turn quickly on the high plains, and they are either awful or good or "awful good."

By 1905 the long dry years and the depression of the 1890s were over. For the next thirty years the region experienced a very wet cycle. For example, at Boise City, Oklahoma, the average precipitation was 19.7 inches annually between 1909 and 1930. During nine years of the wet cycle, 1914 to 1923, the average annual precipitation was nearly 28 inches. One gets a glimpse of how striking those years were by comparing them to the overall average from 1909 to 1957, which was 16.81 inches. From 1930 to 1957 total annual precipitation reached the average of the earlier wet cycle on only eight occasions.[2] It was during the years 1900 to 1930 that farmers settled the heartland of the dust bowl and developed their dryland farming methods. The farming methods were more in tune with a wet cycle than a drier period. This was an important factor in the devastation caused during the 1930s.

Accompanying the return of rainfall at the turn of the century was the growth of railroads. In 1900 the Rock Island began construction on its line from Liberal, Kansas, across the Oklahoma and Texas panhandles into New Mexico. Soon new communities fostered by the railroad began to flourish along the line. With the developments came a wave of homesteaders, home seekers, and speculators.[3]

It was a long journey for Alex and Mary Kraft to their new home near Optima, Oklahoma. Their grandfathers had been part of a resettlement and land-use policy whereby German farmers were sent to Russia to teach improved farming. The stay in the foreign land was a grueling experience. The Russians insulted and threatened the foreigners, and government officials made life unbearable. Mary Rexius was very small when her father died, and the family was left alone to fend for itself. During these difficult years of the 1880s, an American agent promoting settlement in Kansas recruited colonies of Germans from Russia. These people first settled in Kansas, where they worked as field hands, followed the harvest, and homesteaded. Mary, as a girl of nine, earned her own living by cooking for harvest crews. In time, she was able to change occupations and became a skilled nurse. While working as a nurse, she married Alex Kraft. By the turn of the century, the couple had a growing family to consider, and the lure of new land and a new life brought the young family to the high plains of Oklahoma.[4]

Their first home in the new land was uninviting. It was only a small granary in which it was necessary to place the chairs on the bed during the daytime so Mrs. Kraft would have room enough to move about to do her work. And work there was. While Alex labored on the railroad, Mrs. Kraft and the children milked several cows and raised pigs and chickens. The money from the sale of butterfat, eggs, fryers, and pigs provided the family income while Alex's wages were saved. Every means of economizing was practiced; soap was homemade as was clothing and furniture.

By 1911 the homestead was the Kraft's private property and the awful times were over. Soon the farm was traded for a livery barn in the booming town of Hooker, Oklahoma. The livery business was good, but the family continued to practice strict economy. Nothing was wasted; all the produce from the family garden was either eaten immediately or canned for later consumption. The habit of being frugal and resourceful was deeply ingrained and strictly followed.

By a stroke of luck, and not farsightedness, Alex decided to trade the livery barn for three quarters of land on Wild Horse Lake just before the car and garage replaced the horse and buggy. He purchased an additional two quarters and moved his family to the lake in 1919. When the family arrived in the spring, the winter wheat that had already been planted looked sick and dying. Alex decided to plow the ground and prepare it for summer crops, but before he was half through, it began to rain and the seemingly dead wheat started to grow. At harvest time he had a fine wheat crop. From 1919 to the 1930s conditions were good for the Krafts. By 1928 the folks who started life as humble peasants were able to build a large $10,000 home. The years between 1905, when the family first arrived in Texas County, and 1931 were boom times for the Krafts, but the remaining years of the 1930s tested their mettle.[5]

Similar, though not identical events happened to thousands of pioneers in the five-state area of Texas, Oklahoma, Kansas, Colorado, and New Mexico. So many people of German descent settled near Liberal, Kansas, and Hooker and Tyrone, Oklahoma, that German was a commonly spoken language in daily activities. In Beaver County, several immigrants from Austria found refuge from their oppressive government and an unacceptable social system based on land ownership. At Oslo in Hansford County, Texas, the Norwegians began a new life. From Kentucky came pioneers who did not see any possibility of getting a farm in their old home area. Settlers from Georgia and Texas came to find new homes and a new society. Although several settlers came from distant places, the vast majority of the pioneers came from areas adjacent to the short-grass plains. These settlers had some knowledge of dryland farming and settling a new region.

The settlement of the southern plains after the turn of the century was a story of rapid land occupation by devoted farmers as well as by land speculators. Prospective settlers had several choices for obtaining land. In New Mexico and Oklahoma, good farms were available to homesteaders. In Kansas and Colorado a few good homesteads were available and extensive acreages of tax lands or very cheap land could be acquired. In Texas, farms of all sizes were sold. Numerous developers, speculators, railroad companies, and settlers popularized the region across the nation. For farmers accustomed to paying high prices for land, the opportunities offered on the southern plains were attractive.[6]

The settlement of the region took many forms. Several people planned only to stay until their homesteads or land purchases were sold at advantage. Others came to make permanent homes. In Texas, where land was purchased and large tracts available, settlers revealed their understanding of the climatic hazards of the region. "Quarter section farming dominated in the eastern third of the Panhandle, while the western two-thirds leaned toward one section units."[7]

To encourage settlers, and to prove the agricultural merits of the region, several experimental farms were established. The Standard Land Company had an experimental farm near Stratford, Texas. The Capitol Freehold Land and Investment Company, organized to dispose of the vast holdings of the XIT Ranch, had several demonstration farms. The Santa Fe Railroad, the XIT, and Farm Land Development Company created model farms at Bovina and Farwell, Texas, and employed Hardy Webster Campbell as director of the farms. Campbell had established a reputation for scientific dryland farming and his system was highly respected by many farmers. "Even more significantly," believes Garry L. Nall, "the Capitol Syndicate cooperated with the United States Department of Agriculture in establishing the Panhandle's first experiment station at the company's headquarters at Channing in 1903."[8] Farmers' institutes, sponsored by the Department of Agriculture, organized community efforts to improve and promote Great Plains farming. Often, highly respected agricultural experts, such as J. W. Carson from Texas A & M, would instruct community gatherings on methods of Great Plains agriculture. Soon after settlement began, the Office of Dry Land Agriculture began a research station at Dalhart, Texas. The results of government publicity encouraged settlers to plow the sod and take up homesites. "The United States Department of Agriculture further encouraged farm development in the Panhandle by making arrangements with the commissioners' court in Potter, Randall, Carson, and Oldham counties for sending a demonstration agent in 1913."[9]

Despite the glowing resports from private and public sources,

Figure 4. Etta Wilson turning the virgin sod near Texhoma, Oklahoma. Courtesy of Texhoma Genealogical and Historical Society, Texhoma, Oklahoma.

Figure 5. Celebrating the opening of a stream crossing near Texhoma, about 1912. Courtesy of Texhoma Genealogical and Historical Society, Texhoma, Oklahoma.

Figure 6. The C. R. Moore family and home (a half-dugout) at Grand Valley, Oklahoma, April 1, 1917. Courtesy of No Man's Land Historical Museum, Goodwell, Oklahoma.

settlement often resulted in failure for individuals. A contrast to the success story of Alex and Mary Kraft was the story of Leonard L. Cloninger and Pearl Hamilton. The opening of new land for settlement at Nara Visa, New Mexico, brought the Cloninger and Hamilton families to the region. Len Cloninger and his brothers, Roy and R. E. (Bob), traveled with a group of settlers from Hughes Springs, Texas. Roy filed a claim while Len found work at the pumping station on the Rock Island, and Bob went to work at a store. During the first months of settlement the future appeared bright. But the change in climate from the humid lands to the near desert conditions around Nara Visa, combined with the hard work of pioneering, soon made many people easy victims to disease. A typhoid epidemic took its toll among the pioneers. During the 1910 epidemic, Roy Cloninger died. Len Cloninger decided to remain a railroad employee rather than stake a claim on some lonesome tract of land.

The Hamilton family left their home, friends, and comforts in West Virginia to join the Nara Visa settlement because of Mrs. Hamilton's health. In the new community, James W. Hamilton began a grocery business. During the first years, the store prospered and the future looked good. Mr. Hamilton's daughter, Pearl, filed on a half section of land in 1913. Being inexperienced at filing, she chose one quarter that was on school land. When the mistake was discovered, Pearl naively selected a lawyer to defend her interests and settle the matter. The lawyer collected his fee in advance and left the country while the client lost both quarters of land. Mr. Hamilton's grocery business started to decline, and he eventually sold the store and left the area. Pearl married Len Cloninger, and within two years the young couple, like others, moved away. Nara Visa's climate proved too dry for farming even during the wet cycle. By 1913 many people were beginning to look elsewhere for the promise of tomorrow.[10]

In 1900 in Beaver County settlement fever was fired by the promise of free land and railroads to provide transportation and accessible markets. By 1912 the Wichita Falls and Northwestern ran its first passenger train to Gate, Oklahoma. Long before the tracks actually reached the county, the lure of free land attracted hundreds of people. Among the settlers was a colony of Mennonites, who, like the Krafts, began their migration from Russia as the result of promoters sent from American business firms. The first wave of Mennonites to Kansas brought Turkey Red Wheat, which in time became the backbone of the southern plains economy. The early wheat pioneers in Kansas, following their dream for a better tomorrow, came to the Oklahoma Panhandle and brought with them their farming methods and crops.[11]

The excitement in Texas and Beaver counties stirred activities in more remote areas. Morton County, Kansas, which had been hard hit by the depression, drought, and dirt storms of the 1890s, began to take on new vigor in 1905. That year the county sold 400 quarter sections of grassland for one dollar per acre. The tax sale was immediately followed by a rush of homeseekers and homesteaders. Soon every available tract of land was claimed, but due to the lack of an accessible railroad, farming development was slow, and few people actually lived on their land.[12]

The editor of the *Richfield Monitor*, E. C. Wilson, and other old-timers vividly recalled the drought of the 1890s. To avoid similar drought conditions again, and to attract permanent settlers, irrigation was promoted and two artesian wells were dug. Although water enough to irrigate between thirty and eighty acres was obtained, few settlers were attracted. What good was a crop when the harvest could not be marketed at a profit? The region needed a railroad more than irrigation water. "Few prayers," recalled an old-timer, "were ever addressed to the Throne of Grace as fervently by the settlers as were those that some railroad company might be moved to build their railroad into Morton County."[13]

In 1912 the Santa Fe Railroad began building a branch line southwest from Dodge City, Kansas, along the old Dry Fork of the Santa Fe Trail. As the railroad advanced, there was a flourish of new towns, including Santanta, Moscow, Feterita, Rolla, Wilburton, and Elkhart. Soon Elkhart was a major broom-corn shipping center with a population varying between two and three thousand. But older communities like Richfield still remained isolated. The rails ran through the sandy land (old blow dirt) south of the Cimarron River. It was not until roads and bridges across the river were built in the 1920s that extensive farming began on the hard lands to the north.[14]

Homesteading and homemaking in the five-state region was a hard calling. Fires, floods, blizzards, and disease were constantly testing the mettle of the pioneers. During the years from 1905 to 1932, numerous grass fires swept the land. Each fire meant disaster unless it was brought under control quickly. In 1910 a fire started about noon in southwestern Cimarron County, Oklahoma; by midnight the flames had traveled over forty miles and destroyed the vegetation on nearly 200,000 acres. Homesteads in the wake of the fire were burned out and families lost most of their possessions. It was a hard blow to the many settlers who still depended primarily on livestock raising to earn a living. After the fire, several pioneers became discouraged and left the country.[15]

On May 1, 1914, a flash flood roared down the Cimarron River. At the 81 Ranch, Thomas Woodson (Wood) Walsh, his wife, Mae, and their two children were just sitting down to eat when they heard a roar like a freight train. Mae went to the door and discovered water already there. The family quickly retreated to the barn, which was located on higher ground. Walsh's neighbors at the Point of Rock Ranch were not so lucky. Two children drowned. The flood also destroyed many fine alfalfa fields along the stream.[16]

The blizzards of 1918–19 were extremely hard on men and livestock on the southern high plains. Thousands of cattle died in the blizzards or from starvation when feed ran out. The high drifts and the distance prevented men from getting feed to stock even when hay and grain were available. The effects of the blizzard, followed by very low market prices, bankrupted several large ranches.

While the blizzards swept the plains, the flu epidemic took its toll. The amount of suffering caused by the flu epidemic was immeasurable. Emergency hospitals were organized at several locations to aid the suffering. At Elkhart over forty patients were forced to wait agonizingly several days for the arrival of medicine that was on a train stuck in a snow drift a few miles from town. Out on the farms, where help could not be had at any price, families suffered through the storms and epidemic on raw nerve and home remedies. For some pioneers, courage and determination were not enough to prevent death.[17]

Despite the hardships, the overall development of the region reflected progress and prosperity. In the northern Texas Panhandle large ranches dominated the land until 1919. That year the Santa Fe reached the new town of Perryton in Ochiltree County. The following year the road was extended to the new town of Spearman in Hansford County. With the railroad came the vital means of transportation and communication. Being assured of a means of marketing their crops, farmers hurried to settle the new land, which could still be purchased at a low figure.[18]

The Santa Fe had hardly completed the Shattuck (Oklahoma)-Spearman branch when it began construction of a line from Santanta, Kansas, through the new lands of Grant and Stanton counties, Kansas, into Baca County, Colorado. The Stanton-Pritchett (Colorado) line was completed in 1927. Along the new line booming communities flourished. The decade of the 1920s witnessed phenomenal growth in Haskell, Grant, and Stanton counties, Kansas, with 93-percent, 184-percent, and 137-percent increases respectively. Haskell County was located where the branch line started and Stanton County was the last Kansas county to get rail service on the line. Baca County also saw a flurry of development with new towns and settlers.[19]

While these railroads were under construction, other lines

were being built. The Beaver, Meade, and Englewood completed its line from Forgan to Hooker in 1925 and in 1931 built into Keyes, Oklahoma. At the time the B M & E was reaching Hooker, the Rock Island was busy constructing a road from Dalhart, Texas, east to the new town of Sunray, Texas. This line was extended in 1930 to make a junction with another Rock Island branch and the Santa Fe, which was extended from Spearman to Etter, Texas. While the open lands of the Texas Panhandle were being connected with rail service, the Santa Fe in 1925 extended its Dodge City-Elkhart branch to Felt, Oklahoma. And in 1926 the Rock Island began construction of a line from Amarillo, Texas, to Liberal, Kansas, where it arrived in 1930. At the junction of the Liberal-Amarillo branch, the Sunray-Dalhart branch, and the Santa Fe-Rock Island intersection, the town of Morse was created in November 1930. The more important town to the north, Gruver, Texas, was started in 1927.[20]

The last flurry of railroad construction was in 1930–32. During these years the Santa Fe built a line from Amarillo to Boise City, Oklahoma, and extended its line from Felt, Oklahoma, to Colmar, New Mexico. A line from Boise City through Springfield to Las Animas, Colorado, was planned and eventually built in 1936–37. The Santa Fe built a large roundhouse and fuel dock at Boise City. When one looks at a map of present viable communities in the heart of the dust bowl, the vast majority of them were settled after 1900 and a significant number were born during the 1920s. The area was still in the pioneering phase of settlement when the depression of the 1930s struck the region.[21]

Settlement and railroad building had added to the area's booming economy during the 1920s. Homesteaders who were on places too small to be financially profitable, or too far from marketing centers to profit from the sale of grain, found corn in liquid form sold well during prohibition. The counties immediately bordering the five state lines (Dallam, Union, Baca, Morton, and Cimarron) became major producers of whiskey for the Dallas and Denver trade. In the broken land around Black Mesa there were numerous stills. At the height of the trade in the early 1930s, moonshiners were shipping nearly 50,000 gallons of white lightning per week and hundreds of farmers were active. Among the more enterprising moonshiners it was common to clear a $1,000 profit per week.

There was an unwritten agreement between local law en-
forcement officers, who were not in the pay of outlaws, and
bootleggers. When an officer came upon a still that was in operation, the moonshiner's lookout would fire shots ahead of the
officer. The officer would take cover and wait until the moonshiners had time to flee, then he would destroy the still and
conclude his investigation. When a moonshiner was arrested, the
fine and sentence were light. Under this arrangement, officers
were able to remain honest, if not zealous, and moonshiners
were able to operate.[22]

Arrangements were not always as humane and understanding
as that between bootleggers and local lawmen. The following
examples suggest that there was a vicious criminal element in
the region during this booming settlement period. A young Baca
County man shot his father while the elderly man sat peacefully
by his fire. And a father in Ochiltree County hired two men to
kill his small sons. The father was later killed by the hired gunmen when he refused to pay them for their employment. Two
men were killed in a Lamar, Colorado, bank robbery and a hos-
tage and a doctor were later murdered by the robbers. In 1930
at least one revenue agent, Ray Sutton, and possibly two of his
informants were murdered. (When the agent's skeleton was
found in Union County in 1936, there were two other skeletons
in the watery grave.) While being held for trial on charges of
robbing the First National Bank of Texhoma in 1931, Bob "Big
Boy" Brady was wounded in an attempted jail break. Later
Brady was killed in a gun fight as he attempted his third prison
escape. An elderly man, who did not hear the Elkhart bank robbers, was shot in the back side for not obeying orders. Later the
robbers had a falling out that left one shot through the chest and
another through the leg. [23]

While gunmen were taking their toll, cunning men swindled
or embezzled thousands of dollars from innocent citizens. One of
the more repulsive crimes occurred in Baca County where a boy
was held in peonage for several years, while a local rancher
exploited him of wages and land. On learning of the plight of the
young man, local citizens took steps to see that justice was
achieved in the courts.[24]

The pioneering story of the dust bowl includes the advancement of two frontiers. One was rural, based on agriculture. The other was urban, based on oil and gas exploration and development. Wildcatters came with the first wave of settlers in the twentieth century. In 1906 F. W. (Bob) Gilman drilled in Wheeler County, Texas. Four years later another test well was drilled in the county; however, nothing came of the test until the 1920s. As early as 1912, the Land Office of the State of Oklahoma contracted for the surveying of their 210,000 acres of state land in Cimarron County. The Land Office divided their property into four tracts and called for bids as a result of Dr. R. L. Lunsford's survey. By 1917 the Segregated Oil and Gas Company and the Empire Gas and Fuel Company were drilling two test wells in the county. Associated with the Segregated Oil and Gas Company was C. M. Hopgood, who was also drilling a well in northern Potter County, Texas, for the Amarillo Oil Company.[25]

The Amarillo Oil Company came about as the result of geological work done by Charles N. Gould and promotion by M. C. Nobles. Their first well, Masterson No. 1, near John Ray Butte, struck an extraordinary natural gas flow in December 1918. Shortly after striking gas at Masterson No. 1, the company drilled another well and expanded their leases, for it was believed that natural gas, a waste product of the oil industry, heralded the approximate location of oil. The amount of natural gas struck at Masterson No. 1, and the news of the discovery of the vast Burkburnett Oil Field in 1917, spurred the company on to seek a fabulous deposit of black gold.[26]

The advance in the automotive industry and the use of petroleum products, joined with a fear that the nation did not have enough oil to take advantage of the new technology, drove crude oil prices extremely high during World War I. Investors who hoped for handsome profits made large sums of money available for exploration, and regions that had never been seriously considered before were tested for oil. One of the remote territories extensively tested was the five-state area of the future dust bowl.[27]

In 1919 at least three test wells were drilled in northeastern New Mexico. After the Ute Creek test struck gas and oil, the Standard Oil Company's rig burned after striking gas, and the Snorty-Gobbler test found traces of oil in the water well before beginning actual drilling, one of the editors of a Clayton, New

Figure 7. The tin elevators that flourished during the 1920s, until they were replaced by giant concrete elevators in the 1930s, helped open the way for large-scale commercial farming on the southern Great Plains. Courtesy of Texhoma Genealogical and Historical Society, Texhoma, Oklahoma.

Figure 8. Fordsons were among the most popular tractors that helped end the use of muscles to power farm equipment. Courtesy of the Texhoma Genealogical and Historical Society, Texhoma, Oklahoma.

Figure 9. The James #1 near Texhoma, Oklahoma, was one of the first wells in the Hugoton Field. Picture was taken July 15, 1920. Courtesy of the Texhoma Genealogical and Historical Society, Texhoma, Oklahoma.

Mexico, paper proclaimed: "This proves conclusively that the whole country is underlaid with an oil field."[28]

At Texhoma, Oklahoma, in 1919, A. H. Stores, Frank A. Sewell, Edgar Coons, and J. L. Williams organized the Texhoma Oil and Gas Company, which later changed its name to the Home Development Company, and completed the Allison No. 1 and Allison No. 2 in 1922 and 1926. In both wells, millions of cubic feet of natural gas were discovered. While the Texhoma men were testing the subsoil five miles north of their community, another group from Guymon, Oklahoma, organized the Beaver Oil and Gas Company. The company spudded in a well near the mouth of Coldwater Creek in early January 1920. The Beaver Company well struck natural gas, which ignited and burned the drilling rig. At Liberal, Kansas, local investors started at least three wells in 1919. One of the wells was never completed; another reported a strong flow of oil and gas; and in 1922 the Boles No. 1 struck a mammoth flow of natural gas.[29]

In Ochiltree County, Texas, oil promotion began as early as 1912 but nothing was accomplished until 1917, when S. J. Allen organized a continuous block of seventy-five sections of land located primarily in Beaver County, Oklahoma. The Empire Gas and Fuel Company, which failed to drill deep enough, made several tests but did not strike anything. Later, much of the lease produced large quantities of oil and gas.[30]

After the original surge of oil exploration in the heart of the dust bowl, drilling paused. All that had been discovered were mammoth gas wells; little local market existed for the product and it was too expensive to transport the fuel long distances. During the pause, the Amarillo interests began developing markets for their product. Soon a gas line from the gas field reached the city, and the U.S. Zinc Company built a smelter nearby. In 1922 the Cannon Gasoline Company built an extraction plant north of Amarillo. After striking helium in one of the test wells, the federal government built a helium plant in Potter County in 1928.[31]

In 1926 the strikes of oil in Hutchinson and Carson counties, Texas, set off another wave of exploration and development. Overnight, new towns were large booming communities and older towns were small cities. Where empty plains had dominated Hutchinson County, twenty-eight towns sprang to life. The developers of Borger, Texas, sold over a million dollars worth of lots in one year. At one time, the Santa Fe Railroad was handling more material at Panhandle, Texas, than at any station except Chicago. It was in response to the oil developments that the northern Texas Panhandle counties were crisscrossed with railroads.[32]

In 1927, just to the east of Hutchinson County, in Moore County, A. D. Morton struck oil on the Jones Lease fourteen miles northwest of Dumas, Texas. Within a week of the discovery, the sleepy community of Dumas (with a population of 250) was a beehive of activity. At the site where the Apache Refining Company chose to build a plant, the city of Sunray was born.[33]

The Magnolia-Ramsey people decided to look for oil again on the Oklahoma state lands in 1926. By February 1927, the test well was showing a strong flow of oil, when, as the editor of the *Morton County Farmer* related, "Finding of oil in a well north of Boise City has sort of been held up this week by the cold weather and the fact that the rig burned down before they 'shot' the well."[34] The company was not discouraged; a new rig was brought in and drilling began near the old well. The test was not successful, but in the spring of 1930 another test well was drilled; it was given up in December of that year.[35]

Near Hugoton, Kansas, R. M. (Bob) Crawford assembled a thirty-five-thousand-acre tract of oil and gas leases. The Independent Oil and Gas Company in May 1927 struck gas in Crawford No. 1. Those residents not aware of the presence of natural gas became so a few weeks after its discovery when the well shot flames so high in the air that they could be seen for miles. The well flamed out of control until Tex Thornton placed five quarts of nitroglycerin in the well and extinguished the blaze. Shortly after the Crawford well was struck, the Hitch Well, Grandy Well, and the Ham Well began producing natural gas.[36]

Eleven prospect wells were drilled in Texas County in 1926, and some forty companies spent approximately two million dollars annually for leases. Of the eleven tests, seven proved to produce high-grade natural gas. In 1928 a well north of Guymon set all records of gas production to that date. On August 20, 1931, the Safranko Well was producing 22,208,000 cubic feet of natural gas.[37]

During the years 1925–31, some gas and oil exploration or leasing was done in all of the eighteen counties which make up the heart of the dust bowl. The Hugoton and Panhandle gas fields proved to be the largest known natural gas fields in the world. Technology advanced during those years so that long transmission lines could be built, and natural gas was no longer a waste product of the petroleum industry.[38]

Long distance natural gas transmission lines were constructed from the fields between 1927 and 1931. The Amarillo promoters joined with men in Denver, Colorado, and built a pipeline to Colorado cities. Work was also done on pipelines from Amarillo to Lubbock, Texas. In 1929 Arthur K. Lee and A. J. (Gus) Hardendorf formed the Argus Production Company and the Argus Pipe Line Company to develop the Hugoton Field. Soon many communities were heating with natural gas. At festivities celebrating the arrival of natural gas in Dodge City, Kansas, Governor Clyde M. Reed declared Hugoton the gas capital of the Southwest.

No sooner had the Argus interests completed the line to Dodge City than they began planning further expansion. Al-

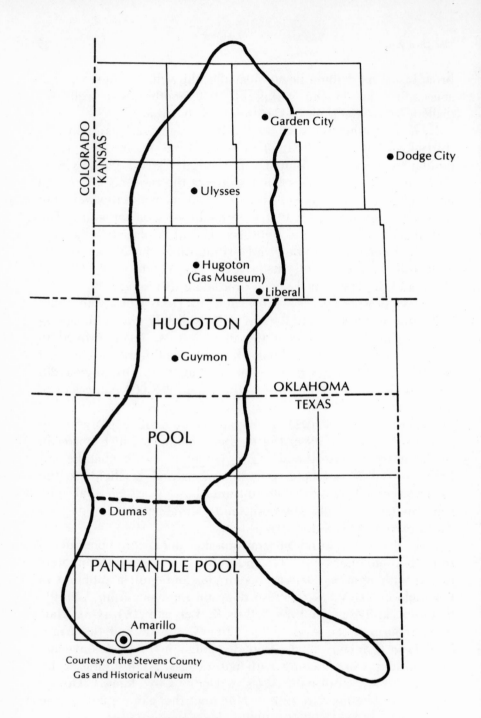

COLORADO
KANSAS

● Garden City

● Dodge City

● Ulysses

● Hugoton
(Gas Museum)
● Liberal

HUGOTON

● Guymon

OKLAHOMA
TEXAS

POOL

● Dumas

PANHANDLE POOL

Amarillo ⊙

Courtesy of the Stevens County
Gas and Historical Museum

THE HUGOTON AND PANHANDLE
NATURAL GAS POOLS

though the depression gripped the nation, Argus united with the Missouri Valley Pipe Line Company to construct natural gas lines to Omaha, Nebraska, and Davenport, Iowa. In May 1930, the two companies merged part of their interests by creating the Northern Natural Gas Company. Northern controlled approximately 850 miles of line in 1930; a year later the company built 1,031 miles of line and drilled 76 wells in southwestern Kansas and the Oklahoma Panhandle. With the residue after organizing Northern Natural Gas Company, the Argus, Missouri Valley, and other companies continued to develop their properties until they were united in 1935 under Republic Natural Gas.

A third major gas company was born in Seward County in 1929 when a group of local promoters met with several eastern investors. The result of the meeting was the organization of the Missouri-Kansas Pipe Line Company. In 1930 the company started the ambitious forty-million-dollar project of building a pipeline from the Panhandle and Hugoton fields to Indianapolis, Indiana. In addition, several new wells were drilled in Texas and Kansas. In 1932, the Missouri-Kansas Pipe Line Company was reorganized into the Panhandle Eastern Pipe Line Company.[39]

The year the depression began (1929), Kansas officially recorded only four gas wells in the southwestern part of the state. In 1931 the record showed 140 wells in the Kansas section of the Hugoton Field. Farmers received royalty or lease money for millions of acres. In addition to the Hugoton Field, there were extensive oil and gas leases in Moore, Ochiltree, Dallam, and Hartley counties, Texas. Further leases were in Cimarron and Beaver counties, Oklahoma, Union County, New Mexico, and Baca County, Colorado.[40]

After the depression struck the rest of the nation, the heartland of the dust bowl experienced its greatest boom and modernization. In the years 1929–31, each of the major communities undertook extensive building and development: streets were paved with brick, water systems were expanded and modernized, sewers were built or improved. The businessmen built new structures and expanded their inventory. For recreation, golf courses and swimming pools were provided. To take advantage of modern transportation, highways were started and airports completed. During this period, several smaller towns and farm communities received electrical power and telephone service.

Nation's Business map of business activities listed the two pan-handles as part of the most prosperous areas in the nation. For the people who lived in the area those were the good years. Proudly, on February 21, 1931, the *Boise City News* boasted, "Refuse State Aid: Cimarron and Texas Counties Turn Down Drouth Relief Dole."[41] Time would make a mockery of the proud declaration.

3

Causing the Dust Bowl

The boom years were over when the wife of an Eva, Oklahoma, farmer penned, "We were more than glad to welcome this messenger of spring [a blue bird], for the winter of our discontent has been long and stormy and persistent."[1] The depression, marked by swirling clouds of dust, brought cries of torment and anguish from the farmers on the dry plains. America's Next Year People asked how and why these evils dominated the heartland of the dust bowl.

Before the first whites even settled the five-state area, the agricultural merits of the Great Plains were being debated. Explorer Stephen Long in 1819 proclaimed that the land was part of the Great American Desert. Following the same theme more than a century later, Under-Secretary of Agriculture Rexford G. Tugwell prophesied that "within 300 years the eastward march of the desert will bury St. Louis in oblivion under a blanket of sand."[2] Numerous commentators of the nineteenth and twentieth centuries divided the nation into agricultural zones. The Great Plains grassland was viewed as an area fit for livestock raising and very limited farming.

Opposing the desert school of thought were the followers of Hamilton Perkins Cady, a professor at the University of Kansas, who believed that the rainfall in Kansas was gradually increasing. The higher average precipitation was expressed in the belief that cultivation improved climatic conditions for farming.[3]

The third school of thought on the prospect of Great Plains agriculture was expressed by the father of "scientific dry land farming," H. W. Campbell. Campbell and his followers believed that the semiarid region could be successfully farmed if agricultural methods were adopted to the climate. Beginning in the 1880s, he started a series of studies in "scientific dry farming." After the turn of the century, the Department of Agriculture accepted Campbell's theory and began a series of studies in dryland farming at extension experiment stations. Support for the three arguments ebbed and flowed with the changes in weather, market, and personal prejudices.

Campbell's system of scientific farming was more an accumulation of farming methods that had evolved on the "dry lands" than original research. Very soon after the farmers arrived in Kansas, it was recognized that new farming methods were necessary to crop the land. At public forums, in newspapers, and in private conversations, Kansans discussed the problems of tillage, i.e., depth, direction, pulverization, implements, and so forth. Fundamental to the question was conserving moisture. To improve tillage a host of new implements were developed and old ones put to new uses. Farmers also debated what crops were best suited to the climate. As settlement moved west, corn was abandoned in favor of wheat, and hard winter wheat replaced soft wheat. Because of the price discrimination against winter wheat, farmers were slow in adopting the crop. Once winter wheat was accepted as a cash crop, several serious attempts were made to improve the wheat strains and better adapt them to the climate. With the development of wheat farming in the semiarid region, a new system of harvesting evolved. The end result was an extensive effort to adapt agriculture to the land and climate. Many farmers "hailed [Campbell's system] as the savior of agriculture on the Plains." His advocates believed that Cambell's method "proved that drifting soils could be made practically stationary."[4]

"The real difficulty in the semi-arid belt," argued Campbell, "is not a lack of rainfall, but the loss of too much by evaporation, and this can be largely controlled by proper cultivation, at least sufficiently to secure a good growth of crops every year."[5] Proper cultivation to conserve moisture included several methods of scientific farming. Early in his career, Campbell advocated placing a dust blanket on the soil. The "dust mulch," it was assumed, would insulate the soil and prevent evaporation. Tests showed that the dust mulch actually increased evaporation and wind erosion. To correct this mistaken concept, Campbell advocated "soil mulching," i.e., leaving minute, well-pulverized lumps of soil that would not restrict plant growth but would be large enough to provide insulation and reduce soil percolation. The soil was properly worked when "the particles seem most readily to separate, not simply into dust; but these minute lumps made from slightly moist soil when dry will never blow."[6]

To encourage water absorption, farmers "dragged" their fields after each rain. This would break the crust on the surface and form minute lumps. Later rains would be more readily absorbed and percolation reduced. The dragging of the fields also kept down weeds, which consumed moisture. Of course, the whole process left a neat, tidy-looking field that appealed to the pride of the "good" farmers.

Summer fallowing (not planting to crop) land was another method of scientific farming. To use this method a farmer required enough land to leave part of his crop acreage fallow and still produce sufficient income to tide him over until the fallowed land was planted and harvested. As a result, farmers tended to plow more acres than they expected to plant in a single crop year. The concept behind fallowing land was to store one year's precipitation in the soil to add to the following year's crop. Since some weeds consumed all the available plant moisture for a rod's distance, it was necessary to keep the land free from weeds by working it at least twice in the fall and four times through the spring and summer (before fall planting to winter wheat). Summer fallowing did increase the available plant moisture and the harvest; but, fallowing required several turnings and stirrings of the soil, which broke down the soil structure and burned more organic matter. Fallowing was widely used in dry years when there was not enough soil moisture to assure a good start of wheat at planting time. The result was a tendency to have extensive areas of bare, fallowed soil when it was most likely to erode. The farmers who prided themselves in keeping clean, tidy fields compounded the problem by leaving nothing to break the wind.[7]

In dryland farming, with the emphasis on preserving moisture, the problems associated with tillage were of prime importance. In 1906 the experiment station at Fort Hays, Kansas, began a series of studies for the Division of Dryland Agriculture of the United States Department of Agriculture. The Fort Hays station and several similar stations were to "study crop adaptation, the effect of different cultural methods, cropping systems, and fertilizer practices upon crop production, and the adaptation of various practices to farming in this area."[8] Scientists experimented with depths of tillage and subsoiling to make the soil more permeable and able to store the maximum amount of moisture. In these experiments, different implements were used to ascertain their efficiency for cropping and water preservation. All these studies helped preserve soil moisture and increase crop production. But, the sad fact is that most of the studies were primarily designed to prove or disprove Campbell's system of scientific dryland farming. The work failed to generate new approaches or new ideas; the result was a continuation of debates between factions of the same school (those interested in preserving water) and a lack of recognition of the problems of wind erosion. Nowhere in the array of scientific work done by eminent scholars of the day was there a complete study of the dangers of wind erosion or the methods of prevention of wind erosion once the force of the wind had started a field moving.

The nearest thing to such a complete study was done at Colby, Kansas. During a series of drought years, 1910–14, the soil near Colby in Thomas County began to erode severely. Before it was over, thousands of acres were blown away and in some areas the top six inches of soil were removed, exposing the plow pan. The associate agronomist of the Division of Dryland Agriculture at the Kansas Agricultural Experiment Station at Colby, J. B. Kuska, in 1914 began a project of listing the county in rows at right angles to the wind. The rough surface of the lister rows provided miniature windbreaks and protection for young plants. The land was planted to corn or other crops to provide a cover for the soil. "For at the time," wrote Kuska, "it looked as though even these efforts might be unsuccessful. Whether or not the efforts would have been successful of themselves will always remain a question. At about this time nature came to the rescue," and it began raining.[9] Apparently no follow-up study was made to determine the cause and control of wind erosion.

The following year, 1915, L. E. Call and A. L. Hallsted published the results of their extensive study on "The Relation of Moisture to Yield of Winter Wheat in West Kansas." The study made only two brief references to wind erosion. Under the heading "The Soil," the scientists noted: "The soil blows easily when the surface is made smooth by packing rains or by cultivation." Under the heading "Alternate Cropping and Summer-Fallowing" appears: "Late in the fall, or the last time it [experiment plot] was cultivated, a shovel cultivator was used for the purpose of leaving the surface of the soil ridged to prevent blowing and to keep it in good condition to receive moisture."[10] In these brief statements the problems of depth to till, of soil moisture content, or of desirable size of clodding were not considered important enough by the scientists to rate discussion. Preventing wind erosion, however, depended upon a series of interlocking processes. The all-important question of what to do if wind erosion began on a field was totally ignored by the scientists. Call and Hallsted's failure to grasp the implication of wind erosion after the Colby Blowout is hard to explain. More surprising was the same oversight by the entire scientific community. Wind erosion was not seen as a threat by agricultural scientists. Even the highly respected scientists, E. C. Chilcott, John S. Cole, and H. H. Finnel failed to sound a loud alarm about the dangers of wind erosion or to advocate studies on prevention of wind erosion.[11]

As head of the Soil Erosion and Moisture Conservation Investigations, Bureau of Chemistry and Soils, United States Department of Agriculture, Hugh Hammond Bennett wrote an article entitled "Land Impoverishment by Soil Erosion" for the 1931 Biennial Report of the Kansas State Board of Agriculture. In the article on soil erosion, the nation's foremost exponent on preventing erosion did not mention the dangers of wind to the soil; he apparently was unaware of the danger although western Kansas ran a high risk of devastating wind erosion. Even more astounding was Bennett's failure to caution his readers, in light of the reports and photographs taken by the United States Department of Agriculture Weather Bureau, about a roller, which struck Big Springs, Texas, September 14, 1930. The black blizzard had its origins near the southwestern Kansas state line. But nature's warning went unheeded by the experts.[12]

Although the Agricultural Adjustment Act of 1933 (which established the Agricultural Adjustment Administration) had provisions to prevent erosion, the federal government made no effort
to prevent wind erosion on allotment land in the heartland of
the dust bowl during the 1933–34 crop year. At the time the
allotments were made, the region was suffering its second consecutive year of erosion. Records at the Panhandle A & M College Experiment Station show 1933 as one of the worst years for
dust storms.

As late as the 1934 publication of the *Yearbook of Agriculture*,
the Department of Agriculture had not fully grasped the problem of wind erosion. Under the section "Soil-Erosion Studies,"
the editors describe methods of controlling water erosion only.
This oversight by scientists and the government cost dearly. The
first conservation methods were a combination of Campbell's efforts to conserve moisture and of water-erosion prevention
methods.[13]

At Panhandle A & M College, established in 1910 to improve
educational levels of farm children and to further the science of
dryland farming, several experiments were conducted. In 1930,
H. H. Finnell, who became nationally known for his battle
against the blowing dirt, published the result of his study on
"Saving Moisture With Level Terraces." In his findings, Finnell
noted: "The advantages of limited rainfall are too great to arouse
much legitimate desire for achievement of any far-reaching climatic modification of the Great Plains, even if it were possible."
Among the advantages were *"freedom from severe erosion* and
leaching of the soils, . . ."[14] (italics added). Three years later
Finnell was not saying anything about freedom from erosion, for
erosion was all around him.

The failure of the scientists to recognize the threat of wind
erosion was shared by farmers. While chairman of the 1914
International Dry-Farming Congress, which met at Wichita,
Kansas, W. I. Drummond assembled an illustrious group of
speakers, exhibits, and demonstrations to improve farming
methods. After the meeting a Ness County, Kansas, farmer remarked, "We know all those things. . . . We simply take
chances, winning in good seasons, and losing when it fails to
rain, or if the wind blows out our crops."[15]

The farmers did take unnecessary chances and in general were careless about protection against wind erosion. But, "the Plains farmers," noted Drummond, "themselves learned nearly everything about the prevention of soil blowing and the conservation of soil moisture that is now being taught and demonstrated by the agricultural colleges and experiment stations."[16]

As the wet years began to end in the late 1920s, it was the farmers who first recognized the danger and began experimenting with new methods and implements to prevent wind erosion. Near Rolla, Kansas, in 1927, Wade Benton began experimenting with a modified spring-tooth harrow to stop wind erosion and encourage moisture preservation, and his effort was encouraged and advertised by the *Morton County Farmer*. At the same time, near Arriba, Colorado, Charles T. Peacock began a series of experiments with a chisel and damming machine. There were others who were experimenting or attempting to develop irrigation. But the new experiments were few and scattered over a vast area.[17]

Although the dust storms of the 1930s vividly emphasized the failure of scientific dryland farming to meet the challenge of wind erosion, while highlighting the immense gulf between agricultural improvement for raising a crop and methods for controlling wind erosion, most of the farmers, scientists, and government officials of the pre–dust bowl assumed they were adapting agriculture to the new land. In 1926 the president of the Kansas State Historical Society, J. W. Berryman, noted that agriculture in southwestern Kansas had developed along lines suited to the soil. The rougher land was used for grazing while level lands were used for farming. Berryman's comments were supported by the United States Department of Agriculture Soil Survey of Texas County, Oklahoma. The soil survey, which in part was made as the result of the national land-utilization movement, noted that the flat hard lands were primarily wheat land; the gently rolling land was diversified between wheat and row crops; the more undulated sandy soils were dominated by grazing and row crops; and finally, the broken land was used exclusively for pasture. Farmers had also experimented with various crops (ranging from producing watermelon seeds for commercial markets to cotton, sorghums, broomcorn, Sudan grass, and wheat). Gradually the crops most adapted to the soil and climate were used on the various farms. H. H. Finnell probably came the closest to identifying the reason Great Plains farming failed to be adequately prepared for the drought of the 1930s. He noted that "agriculture [was] not yet fully developed, in other words, still in the trial stage."[18]

Let us turn now from scientific dryland farming and address ourselves to another question concerning the causes of dust storms and wheat price depression. It has generally been argued by scholars that the high price for wheat during World War I caused the demise of diversified farming and encouraged the great plow up of land for wheat. At the outset it should be recognized that prices for all the basic Great Plains crops increased dramatically during World War I. Thus, wheat did not exhibit a unique price characteristic.

In a study on winter wheat production at Fort Hays and neighboring counties, John S. Cole and A. L. Hallsted compared the acreage of wheat land to all other crops. Their study showed that in Ellis County, Kansas, winter wheat planting in 1897 occupied 73.6 percent of the total crop land. Twenty-three years later, in 1920, winter wheat was planted on 73.7 percent of the land. Further studies indicated that the neighboring counties had followed a similar mixing of wheat to all other crops. The major shift in the five counties considered by the study was the gradual increase in the total number of tilled acres but not in the ratio of wheat to other crops.[19]

Under the headline, "Wonderful Crop in Panhandle Country," the *Guymon Herald* presented its outstanding farmer for 1919. Gottlieb Wurner, who farmed near Optima, Oklahoma, "raised 5,540 bushels of wheat, 3,461 bushels of maize, 392 bushels of cane seed, 586 bushels of kafir corn, 400 bushels of barley, and 600 bushels of oats."[20] Clearly Wurner was a diversified farmer. In Texas County, Oklahoma, in 1920, there were 370,083 cultivated acres. On the cultivated land, 153,026 acres were in sorghums and 201,290 acres in wheat. The other cultivated acres were in broomcorn and small grains. The remainder of the county's 1,321,600 acres were in native grass. That year Texas County had more native grasslands than any other Oklahoma county. In 1924, Texas County produced 2,903,053 bushels of wheat and 1,748,750 bushels of sorghums. For the same period the combined production in Sherman and Hansford counties, Texas, were 957,745 bushels of wheat and 377,902 bushels of sorghums. As late as 1926 the editor of the *Texhoma Times* was encouraging the subdivision of the large ranches in the two Texas counties.[21]

In 1920 the war-boom wheat prices dropped dramatically. At harvest time, wheat was nearly $2.50 per bushel, but by December, wheat had declined to $1.55; and by the harvest of 1921, wheat brought only 90 cents per bushel. Wheat remained near the dollar figure from the harvest of 1921 until the harvest of 1924 when the price rose to over $1.50 per bushel. Although the wheat price fluctuated between the harvests of 1924 and 1928, it remained near relative retail prices of nonfarm goods.[22]

Since the ratio of wheat to all other crops did not shift during the war, and the wartime boom ended before the great plow up began, it is necessary to look elsewhere for the cause of the great plow up.

Historically the livestock business on the Great Plains was unstable. The famous drought and blizzard of the mid 1880s ended the traditional open-range cattle industry. And the blizzards of 1918–19 killed thousands of cattle. The market also crashed to a low of $4.15 per hundred pounds in 1924. That same year wheat prices were improving. From 1919 to 1928 beef remained well below the relative retail price of nonfarm goods. Among agricultural men in the five-state area, the depressed cattle industry encouraged the adoption of wheat farming; the bankrupt ranches of the Texas Panhandle were broken up and sold for farms.[23]

Until the end of World War I, broomcorn was one of the basic crops in the heartland of the dust bowl. The crop was relatively reliable although it required a tremendous amount of hand labor and much of the crop was lost to smut, or crooked, weak, green, or overripe heads. So long as the price remained high and stable, farmers profited from the crop. In 1919 the market fell and the farmers cut back production. In the United States some 352,000 acres of broomcorn were raised in 1919; a year later 275,000 acres were raised, and in 1921, only 207,400 acres were harvested. In Oklahoma during those same years farmers continued to decrease acreage from 231,000 to 128,000 acres of broomcorn. Despite the decreased acreage the market remained fragile. Among consumers, vacuum cleaners, dust mops, and fiber brooms were replacing broomcorn. If the farmers were to remain in business, they would have to turn to another crop.[24]

The sorghums of maize, kafir, and feterita were also basic crops in the heartland of the dust bowl. Sorghums were primarily used for feed and had to compete on the open market with corn. There was a tremendous amount of waste in using sorghums, which passed through an animal undigested; sorghums had to be cracked before they were used, whereas corn could be used whole. Therefore, feeders sharply discriminated against sorghums. Sorghums also had to be picked by hand before threshing, and after threshing were extremely difficult to keep from heating.[25]

If the sorghums could not be marketed successfully, farmers reasoned that they should feed the grain to hogs and market the crop in that manner. Apparently many farmers in the Oklahoma and Texas panhandles invested heavily in hogs in 1920–21. But the crop of 1922 was small, which left the farmers with the loss of putting in the sorghums plus having several animals they could not feed. Thus the pigs were also sold at a loss. Consequently, sorghum farmers were looking for another crop.[26]

"I think," wrote C. W. Maxey of the *Oklahoma Farmer-Stockman*, "we should prepare to grow more wheat and less kafir. These western plains are proving to be well adapted to wheat and failure seldom occurs where proper methods are employed. Wheat is the universal bread grain of the whole world and indications are that there will not be any too much wheat grown for years to come . . . "[27] Tests run by the Kansas State Board of Agriculture in 1919 showed that the western region of the state cleared $1.89 per acre of wheat, while the central and eastern regions lost money per acre. Wheat was the only farm crop Great Plains farmers could successfully raise and use to compete with other agricultural regions.[28]

But wheat had its disadvantages in the heartland of the dust bowl. Raising a good crop did not assure that it would be harvested. During the big wheat crop years of 1921, 1924, and 1926, there was stiff competition between farming areas and communities to attract field hands. Shortly before the harvest began in 1921, Texhoma, Oklahoma, sent agents into Texas to recruit men. The harvest in the Texhoma country had hardly begun when men from Liberal, Kansas, appeared and began spiriting away field hands. And so it went with every good crop. During poor crop years, farming towns were filled with unemployed and often desperate men. Also, as long as it was necessary to feed and care for large numbers of draft animals, farmers had to raise feed crops and maintain pastures. Until the labor and feed problems were solved, high plains farmers were forced to raise many crops.[29]

The primary cause of the great plow up was the mechanization revolution of high plains agriculture during the 1920s. The development of the tractor, the combine, the one-way plow, and the truck made the great plow up possible and determined what crops were planted. In 1915 there were approximately 3,000 tractors in Kansas; just five years later the Kansas farmers boasted owning 17,177 tractors, but that was only a start. In 1925 there were 31,171 tractors in the state. By the start of the depression, Kansas farmers were using 66,275 tractors. Even the depression did not stop the increase in tractors. In 1935 the figure stood at 71,000 tractors, while in 1940, farmers were using 95,139 tractors. Most of the tractors were on the Great Plains. The tractors, especially during the 1920s, replaced teams of horses and made it possible to farm land previously reserved for pasture. Accompanying the use of the tractor was the use of the combine. Again using Kansas data, the number of combines in 1925 was 4,700. Five years later, 24,239 combines were used in the harvest, and by 1940 farmers were using 42,800 combines for the harvest.[30]

In 1928 a *Panhandle Herald* reporter commented:

> When one sees a combine and tractor manned by one person sitting in the shade of a large umbrella, cutting a swath of wheat twenty feet wide, and not shaking down so much of the grain as the old ten-foot harvester did, and the clean grain falling into the wagon bed along side the combine, as compared with the header driver, four barge men and two stackers not to mention the threshing crew, which are obviated by the wonderful new machine, one realizes its advantage, and the labor and expense saved.[31]

When the Texas County farmers began the 1926 wheat harvest they were still depending on headers, header barges, and man power to reap the crop. The size of the crop and the market, however, encouraged farmers to invest in tractors, combines, and trucks. That crop brought more than ten million dollars to the county. The success of new implements encouraged other farmers to adopt the new method. With the next big crop, farmers plunged into wheat farming implements. At Texhoma over $360,000 was spent for implements, and combines were delivered by the train load. At Stratford, Texas, the McCormick dealer set a national record for tractor sales. During June and July, Texas County bought more trucks than any county in the nation. At Texhoma, "men and boys hoped to secure work during the harvest, and while some [were] finding work others [were] being disappointed because of advent of the combine decrease[d] the use of man power." Although the crop was nearly ten million bushels, the county agent, B. F. Markland, did not find it necessary to contact state and federal employment agents to secure field hands.[32]

The reporter for the *Panhandle Herald* continued his observation of the harvest:

> A marvelous number of new auto trucks swept by us, and they carried loads both to and from the market. Going in they were loaded with wheat, and coming back they were loaded with new disc plows and machinery to be used in following the combines and headers in preparing the land for next years crop, and were trailed in many instances with new drills to plant the coming crops.[33]

The new machines were a relief to the farmer, and they were a blessing to the farmer's wife. The farmer's wife, who faced an eighteen-hour, parboiled harvest day, was pleased to see a tractor and combine replace the harvest crew and the threshing crew. While the men worked in hundred-degree weather with a breeze to cool them, the women toiled over a hot stove fixing meals. Harvest time for the women meant "feeding a dozen hungry faces three times a day, with an early breakfast and late supper. . . . Six or seven pies to bake daily in a hot oven; on the go from 5 o'clock in the morning to 11 at night; prepare one meal, clean things up to ready for the next; work, work, work."[34]

The truck, which replaced the slow, faithful team at hauling grain to market at the new elevators located along the tracks, made it possible for the farmer to handle more grain in the same period of time. The use of the truck increased at a phenomenal rate. In 1920 Kansas farmers used 3,900 trucks; by 1930, farmers used 33,700 trucks; and in 1940, 42,600 trucks were owned by farmers. The combination of new trucks and new railroads made it possible for farmers in more remote areas to market their crop.[35]

The early combines were inadequate for harvesting most sorghums. Men who desired to take advantage of the new technology, with its wonderful, labor-saving aspects, began raising more wheat. Once the investment was made in wheat-harvesting equipment, a farmer could not quickly change to different crops; neither could he afford not to raise wheat until the equipment had depreciated. As more and more farmers became locked into the system, the total production of wheat increased—until the price came crashing down to twenty-five cents per bushel in 1931.

The tractor and the combine revolutionized harvesting, but wheat farming struck a bottleneck in tillage. At Plains, Kansas, Charles Angell put his mind and labor to the task of solving the problem of tillage. In 1923 he patented the Angell one-way disk plow. Although the one-way plow came in various lengths, the most popular was ten feet. With the new plow farmers could till many times more acreage in a much shorter time. The plow was ideal for the soil and climate and farming methods of the pre–dust bowl. After the Ohio Cultivator Company purchased the rights to manufacture the one-way plow in 1926, a large supply for farmers was assured. And between 1926 and 1930, the one-way became the most widely used plow in the region of the dust bowl.[36]

In 1927, in Moore County, Texas, W. J. Morton, Jr., and a hired man were working twenty-four head of mules in a vain effort to kill the weeds on some summer fallow land. Upon visiting the farm, W. J. Morton, Sr., found the mules jaded and the men worn. The older man decided it was time to try a tractor and one-way plow. The one-way plow proved to be an excellent weed killer, and for tilling the soil it was faster than conventional implements. The disks of the one-way plow left a pulverized, smooth soil which needed no disking or harrowing.[37]

On the disks of the one-way plow rest many of the faults that caused the farm depression and the dust bowl, although as late as 1937 some farm experts were still recommending the use of the one-way plow to stop wind erosion.[38] This plow made it pos-

Figure 10. Marketing broomcorn at Texhoma, Oklahoma. Courtesy of the Texhoma Genealogical and Historical Society, Texhoma, Oklahoma.

sible to turn many more acres than previously. With this imple-ment, farmers soon were able to work the soil down into the smooth, pulverized form accepted as a good farming method in that day. In tilled soil, the organic material burned more rap-idly, much as a stoked fire burns more hotly. This stoking en-couraged tremendous wheat crops, but it helped break down the soil structure. Since most of the plowing occurred within a few years before the drought of the 1930s, the soil and soil life had not adjusted to the new environment. Thus, the soil was highly vulnerable to wind erosion when the depression and drought years began.

Hindsight allows us to see the weaknesses in the farming sys-tem and gauge the vast distance between ability to raise a crop and knowledge to prevent severe wind erosion, but in the 1920s the shortcomings were not apparent. Farmers, scientists, and government officials believed that the combination of technol-ogy, land value, and climate were in harmony during the roaring decade. There were dry years, like 1925, and in January 1926 the soil was dry and the wheat looked sick. By March many acres appeared barren and lifeless. Then it began to rain—just a

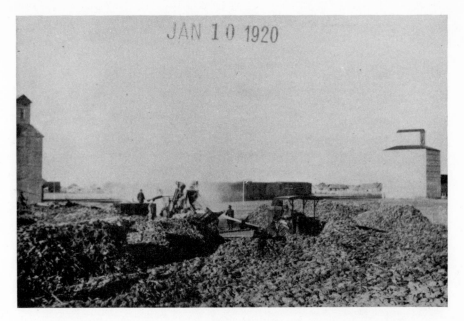

Figure 11. Maize was often hand picked and hauled to the elevator for threshing. Courtesy of the Texhoma Genealogical and Historical Society, Texhoma, Oklahoma.

Figure 12. After the crop was stacked, the threshing crew forked the grain and straw into a separator from which the grain was hauled to bins for storage until it could be taken to market. From header to market required handling the grain five times. Much of the labor was hand work. Courtesy of Gerald Davison, Texhoma, Oklahoma.

Figure 13. The revolution in harvesting was nearly complete when farmers began loading grain directly from the combine into wagons. Only two men were required—whereas sixteen men were used on the header, header barge, and threshing crew. Courtesy of the Texhoma Genealogical and Historical Society, Texhoma, Oklahoma.

Figures 14, 15, 16. The changing world of bringing grain to market is illustrated in figures 14, 15, and 16. Note the bedrolls in figures 14 and 15. They speak of the time required to reach the marketing center. Courtesy of the Texhoma Genealogical and Historical Society, Texhoma, Oklahoma.

Figure 15.

Figure 16.

little. But the lifeless soil began to turn green. By harvest time
in 1926 the five-state area had a bumper crop. Several fields
produced sixty bushels per acre. Never before or since has so
much wheat been produced on an acre of dry land. With a little
rain, in spite of the drought, a tremendous crop was harvested
and the price per bushel was near the relative retail price. Ed
Tucker was able to purchase two new tractors, a new combine, a
new truck, and some land with his profits from that crop. Hundreds of other farmers boasted similar profits.[39]

That was only one year. The authors of the *Soil Survey of
Texas County, Oklahoma,* E. G. Fitzpatrick and W. C. Boatright, noted that the county suffered from "partial failure of
wheat crop . . . about 1 year in every 4."[40] A farmer could afford
to gamble on a short crop every fourth year if he had a good
crop every few years. In Texas County, farmers had bumper
wheat crops in 1921, 1924, 1926, 1928, and 1931. Each of these
years followed a drought year and had less than average precipitation. At the same time, land prices were low and the new
technology was especially suited to the level plains. Thus, a
wheat crop could be raised in the heartland of the dust bowl for
half the cost of raising the same crop in more humid areas.
Many farmers were sure they had found the crop, the scientific
dryland farming system, and the technology best suited to the
land and the people.

During the booming years of agriculture, oil and gas development, and urban improvement, the warning signs of the late
1920s went unheeded. The new farm technology was a tremendous savings on labor, but what happened to the men displaced
by tractors, trucks, combines, and one-way plows? Over one-half
the farmers either sold or leased their land. Back in 1910 the
most common farm size in Texas County was 160 acres, and the
average farm had 247.3 acres. In 1930 the most common farm
size was 320 acres, and the average farm was 570 acres. The
small farmers who used tractors could plant their winter wheat
quickly in the fall, and being freed from the need to cultivate
weeds, they could seek other employment until it was necessary
to harvest the crop. Thus, they were able to combine farming
with industrially related employment. The system worked as
long as the price for wheat was sufficiently high and outside
employment was available. But when the depression came, these

small farmers were marooned on farms that provided only a subsistence.[41]

The culmination of technology, production costs, farming methods, and optimism combined with confidence moved farmers to plant more wheat. The increased wheat production soon began to flood the already bulging market. The threat of oversupply did not delay the planting of wheat. W. J. Morton, Sr., voiced the thoughts of many farmers when he stated: "If any money is made [from wheat], it will have to be on the quantity raised and not on the quality or the price it brings. A person will have to be able to raise so much more that he can afford to take a lower price."[42] By 1930, the wheat market was crumbling, but the plow up did not slacken. A farmer near Springfield, Colorado, confidently claimed, "there is nothing in the wheat situation to cause alarm. . . . We can produce wheat here cheaper than any other section of the United States, and since somebody has to raise wheat . . . we will be staying in the game."[43] In May 1930, with great assurance, the Springfield *Democrat-Herald* reported that Baca County was the largest wheat-producing county in the state, with 150,000 acres under cultivation (there are 1,641,600 acres in Baca County). The state agricultural statistician, H. L. Collins, observed that "Baca [had] less wheat winter killed and blown out than the other counties, thus giving evidence of Baca's up to date dry farming system."[44]

With a recklessness indicative of pioneers willing to risk everything in the game of making a new home in a strange land, the high plains farmers gambled on wheat as the pot of gold at the rainbow's end. After the Agricultural Marketing Act of 1929, which was supposed to stablize wheat at a good price, cleared Congress, farmers began planting with abandon. The *Kansas State Board of Agriculture Biennial Reports* statistics demonstrate the degree of this abandon (Table 3.1).

The southwestern Kansas farmers were only part of the plow up that was occurring in the eighteen counties of the five states. In Baca County the average wheat acreage for the three years 1930–32 increased by nearly fifty thousand acres. But the wild race to outrun disaster resulted in "hard times."

The most severe drought recorded in the nation's history to that date gripped the land in 1930. The worst of the drought affected the east and northern plains. In the winter wheat coun-

TABLE 3.1
Acres Planted in Wheat in Six
Kansas Counties, 1929–31

County	Year	Wheat Acreage	County	Year	Wheat Acreage
Hamilton	1929	16,641	Stanton	1929	60,972
	1930	37,274		1930	83,102
	1931	103,787		1931	160,330
Morton	1929	33,030	Stevens	1929	131,050
	1930	33,009		1930	131,204
	1931	112,735		1931	166,989
Seward	1929	139,195	Grant	1929	114,001
	1930	138,279		1930	150,712
	1931	169,880		1931	196,242

try, the drought did not set in until after the crop was well developed; as a result there was a good crop. In March the local wheat price was ninety cents per bushel. By harvest time the price had dropped to sixty-eight cents per bushel. But the farmers were not yet unduly alarmed. In the winter of 1930–31 the high plains was swept by blizzards that killed several people and destroyed large numbers of livestock. Those snows filled the ground with moisture, which started the wheat growing. By harvest time there were vast stacks of wheat. Elevators were filled and granaries loaded, and several county roads were blocked with mountains of wheat. Texas County, the number-one wheat county that year, produced more than twelve million bushels of wheat. By way of comparison, the average wheat surplus for the entire state of Kansas from 1923 to 1928 was 12,593,000 bushels. The record dryland crop of 1931 has been beaten only once in the entire history of Texas County. The 1931 wheat crop was a wonderful crop, but it brought only twenty-five cents per bushel. The wheat surplus was so great that at harvest time in 1932 the local markets were paying only thirty cents per bushel. With prices so low, no farmer could long remain in business unless he could find other employment to tide him over. But the depression was curbing the boom in railroads and gas and oil development. A farmer could muse optimistically that he had a lot of wheat to eat; and before times got better, he ate a lot of it. [45]

The decrease in acreage reported in the *Biennial Reports*

gives us an idea of the impact of low prices and surplus on farmers (Table 3.2).

TABLE 3.2
Acres Planted in Wheat in Six
Kansas Counties, 1931–32.

County	Year	Wheat Acres	County	Year	Wheat Acres
Hamilton	1931	103,787	Stanton	1931	160,330
	1932	47,915		1932	109,468
Morton	1931	112,735	Stevens	1931	166,989
	1932	59,463		1932	51,302
Seward	1931	169,880	Grant	1931	196,242
	1932	86,044		1932	27,915

There were similar rates of abandonment in the remaining counties of the five-state area.

In the spring of 1932, vast tracts of land lay empty, except for
tumble weeds. With the March winds, the weeds snapped their
stems and began rolling across the high plains. Behind, the plants
left a mellowed soil ready to blow. Out of the thirty-one days in
March, twenty-two were dirty. The tumble weeds gathered in
the fence rows, where the dirt soon buried them. But the farmers still saw a fading ray of hope. Not all the land was bare that
spring, and in large areas the wheat prospects looked good until
May. It was not until the end of May that the *Morton County
Farmer* reported, "Wheat Prospects Blown by Winds. Turn Yellow as the Dry Breezes Sap the Moisture from Soil; . . . Two
weeks ago there was a fair prospect for many wheat fields."[46] At
harvest time the *Texhoma Times* reported, "Wheat Harvest is
Not Good."[47] Although some row crops and feed were raised that
summer, the ground was too dry for planting in the fall. Then in
late September it began raining and the *Boise City News* boldly
proclaimed, "Drought Broken Here By General Rainfall."[48]
Some farmers began planting, but many waited on more rain. A
major disaster was just around the corner.

On a small corner of the leeward side of a field, a particle of
soil, broken loose by the wind, struck a cluster of soil particles
like a cue ball striking the racked balls. The avalanching effect of
soil erosion gathered force as it moved across the field. By the
time the effects of one tiny wind-driven soil particle reached the
opposite side of the field, a mighty force was assembled to as-

sault the neighboring abandoned field. Soon a dirt storm was
burning any living plant, while the soil around the plant's roots
was joining the race across the stricken land.

Early in the spring, farmers might have stopped the dirt
storms, but times were hard. "We cannot afford expensive mistakes," wrote Caroline Henderson, "and are trying to proceed
cautiously, . . . [We] require a lot of close accounting to prove
which involves the greatest loss."[49] Many farmers made the fatal
mistake of saving their limited capital for a later date; it was
hoped that the rains would return and settle the dust. The
technology of planting and harvesting a crop was far in advance
of methods of controlling wind erosion. During the eight years
from 1932 to 1940, the realm of the dust bowl paid dearly for
the false economy and failure to understand how to control wind
erosion.

4

1930s Weather

The history of the heartland of the dust bowl is a story of extremes. The depression drove farm prices to devastatingly low levels while the weather tormented the residents of the region. Severe depression and extremes in weather were accompanied by plagues of rodents and insects. Although the period is known for its dust storms, the era began with a flood.

The dry spell, which threatened the row crops and the planting of the winter wheat crop, ended when heavy rains hit the Oklahoma Panhandle in September 1930. During one cloudburst, streams became raging torrents. In Texas County, fifteen bridges were washed out. The Beaver River cut a new channel while washing out 400 feet of the north approach to the Putram Bridge near Texhoma. All the major streams in the county were ravaged by flood. The streams had just regained their normal flow when "one of the strongest and most thoroughly disagreeable winds of years swept across Cimarron County."[1] Northwest of Boise City, Oklahoma, I. H. House lost a grain storage building with seventy-five to eighty bushels of wheat in the granary. C. O. Taylor, who lived south of Boise City, lost a storage building that contained a plumbing plant. Many structures in the county were severely damaged by the storm. In the sandy-row crop land west of the community, many tons of surface soil were lost. A week later Cimarron County received 2.66 inches of rain in a cloudburst. Boise City was flooded and the dry lake east of

61

town filled to capacity. The storm turned roads and highways into impassible rivers of mud. Many farmers who planned to exhibit or attend the county fair were thwarted in their effort. The September weather was a prelude to the decade.[2]

During the night of November 19, the north winds brought a blizzard sweeping across the southern Great Plains. W. L. Clark and William Westfall were travelling from Cimarron, Kansas, when, only a quarter of a mile from Boise City, their car became stranded in a drift. The men waited in the car until their gas was gone, then they attempted to walk into town. Within a few yards of the car, Westfall, who was getting on in years, collapsed and had to be carried back to the car. The remainder of the night was spent huddled around a small fire the men built in the car. A wooden apple box and several documents furnished fuel. When the men were rescued the following day, they were near death from the cold and the fumes of the fire. Clark and Westfall were lucky. Howard Rhodes, an early day cowboy and homesteader north of Lamar, Colorado, lost his life in the storm. Rhodes was looking after his stock when the storm caught him and his horse. Both were found frozen.[3] This was only the first killer blizzard of that season.

The early morning of March 27, 1931, was a pleasant spring day. The weather had been wonderful for several days and there were no signs that disaster was near at hand. The school bus for the Pleasant Hill school district in Kiowa County, Colorado, gathered the children and carried them to the school. By the time the bus arrived a gentle snow was falling and the children hurried from the bus to play in the snow before school started. Soon the wind began blowing and the children scurried inside. Since it had been warm when the children left home, many did not have warm clothing. With the change in the weather, bus driver Carl Miller and the school officials agreed that the children should be returned home as soon as possible. With the twenty children, including his own daughter Mary, Miller began his fatal trip. Soon he was lost in the blinding storm; the bus stalled and would not start. Miller desperately attempted to find some landmark that would lead to safety. When night came, he built a fire in the bus and burned the wooden interior and anything else he could find. By morning the condition of the children was critical. Leaving some of the older children in charge,

Miller walked into the storm to find help. His frozen body was found several miles from the bus.

While the older children shared their clothing with the littler ones and labored to keep them moving, Andy Reinhart, H. A. Untiedt, and Dave Stonebraker began a search for their children. A few hundred yards from the Reinhart home the men found the bus. As quickly as possible, the living and dead children were moved to the Reinhart home. Several of the still living children were in critical condition.

When word of the disaster reached Dr. Hubert at Tribune, Kansas, and Dr. Casburn at Holly, Colorado, a rescue party was organized at once. Several carloads of men from Holly shovelled drifts and pushed and towed cars until they forced their way to the Reinhart home. Word was sent to Dr. N. M. Burnett at Lamar that speedy hospitalization was needed for some of the children. Since the storm was now spent and flying was possible, Jack Hart began flying children from the Pleasant Hill farming community to Lamar. The owners of the hospital instructed the pilot to have all the children brought to the hospital at once, and the parents were not to worry about the expense.[4]

From all over the area people began giving of themselves and their treasures to aid the stricken families. Unity and community marked their efforts to lessen the blows of disaster. Although the tragic events at the Pleasant Hill School were the most spectacular of the blizzard, that area was not the only scene of hardship and cooperation. Motorists were stranded at many points across the five-state area, and many people spent harrowing hours struggling to assist the helpless, or helplessly awaiting aid or death. From the storm emerged a new sense of brotherhood.

The fall rains of 1930 and the winter storms that followed brought hardship and disaster, but they nourished the wheat crop. In July 1931, farmers harvested the biggest crop they had ever seen. The elevators and farm granaries were filled with golden wheat. Along roadsides and in fields, farmers piled their wheat. But in spite of the bumper crop, farmers were going broke. Wheat was worth only two bits a bushel at the local markets. Many farmers abandoned their fields, especially the speculative farmers who had other sources of income. During the remainder of the summer, the weather continued hot and dry. With the approach of fall, farmers wondered if they should plant wheat as they watched the feed crop burn in the fields. Then in late September it began raining. Many farmers took new hope.

The fall rain was not sufficient to carry much of the crop through to harvest. During the winter, precipitation was deficient; then the strong winds of March began seriously eroding the soil. At Texhoma, there were twenty-two dust storms in March and drifts built up in the fence rows north and west of town. In late March a blizzard from the north dropped the temperature below freezing, and the storm destroyed the fruit crop for the second year in a row. In April strong winds laden with dust returned and at Texhoma broke out several windows in the school.[5]

Through April and May rains were scattered and did not supply enough moisture to assure a good crop. In June it began to rain, but the rains came in torrents. On June 4 Elkhart, Kansas, was hit by a small tornado, which did extensive damage to five houses in town. Further damage was done to fields along a strip nearly two miles wide and ten miles long. Following the Elkhart tornado on the night of June 12, severe thunder storms struck the five-state area. In Baca County, Colorado, over eight inches of rain fell in a short time. Streams flooded and bridges washed out. One bridge floated fifty miles to Johnson, Kansas. All the streams in the area overflowed. Coldwater and Frisco creeks reached new heights, and the Beaver River rose to the level of the May 1914 flood. Near Griggs, Oklahoma, and Campo, Colorado, hail destroyed most of the crop.[6]

Vance Johnson, in *Heaven's Table Land,* and other sources as well, argue that the floods that accompanied the drought were the result of poor farming practices and that the hard rains were a normal climatic condition of the dust bowl. Hard summer rains were normal, but the fact that 80 percent or more of the land in several counties drained into *playas* and not streams, and that the stream drainages were generally virgin grasslands, suggests that the rains were harder than normal.

The drought, dirt storms, winds, cloudbursts, and hail storms took their toll on the 1932 crop. Most of the farmers cut their crop, although the average yield was only about five bushels per acre. A few farmers near Hooker, Oklahoma, and Liberal and Elkhart, Kansas, cut some wheat fields that averaged nearly thirty bushels per acre. The elevators at Texhoma handled

225,000 bushels of wheat, well below average but better than none at all. Despite the short crop, the market failed to respond by rising. Locally, farmers received only thirty cents per bushel for their wheat in July and thirty-six cents per bushel in August.[7]

The summer was drier than usual and many of the row crops failed to fill out; but near Rolla, Kansas, many farmers and businessmen looked to the broomcorn harvest for relief. The crop was fair and many men received a few days employment during the harvest. But the price of broomcorn was discouraging.[8]

The *Morton County Farmer* for September 16 reported, "Wheat Acreage Will Be Cut Here if No Rain Comes Soon."[9] Farmers throughout the dust bowl were reluctant to plant a crop. When winter descended on the region, many fields were abandoned and bare.

On January 21, 1933, "without warning one of the worst dust storms in years hit the Panhandle."[10] Great clouds of dust restricted visibility and hid the sun. The storm did extensive damage to the drought-weakened wheat. Then on February 7, a cold wind from the north dropped the temperature 74 degrees in 18 hours, to a record low of 14 degrees below zero at Boise City. The temperature did not rise above zero for several days. Stockmen were required to double the feed to the livestock, which severely taxed the small supply of feed. In the fields the winter wheat crop froze while the ice pulverized the soil. Across the entire Great Plains, similar conditions existed.

The drought, depression, dust storms, and freezing temperature did not dampen the humor of the people. Someone at Amarillo claimed that the city was the coldest in the nation. He swore "a Confederate veteran statue there finally laid his gun down and stuck his hands in his pockets."[11]

After the cold wave left, the region's wheat was winter-killed and the soil was well pulverized. The dust bowl was ready for a major disaster. Soon the winds began to blow and so did the dust. By late April, "windblown fields appear[ed] like snow drifts."[12] By the year's end, the Panhandle A & M Experiment Station at Goodwell, Oklahoma, recorded seventy days of severe dust storms. The weather observer at Texhoma, L. E. Job, reported 139 dirt storms.[13]

Figure 17. The Broomcorn factory at Liberal, Kansas, was one of the many buildings destroyed by the killer tornado of May 22, 1933. Courtesy of Mrs. Lee King, Goodwell, Oklahoma.

Figure 18. The famous roller of April 14, 1935, near Liberal, Kansas. Courtesy of Mrs. Lee King, Goodwell, Oklahoma.

Figure 19. A Texas County, Oklahoma, farm which shows little damage caused by the dust bowl. The picture was taken on a noncooperator farm in the Pony Creek Project on May 27, 1938. Courtesy of the Texas County Soil Conservation District Office, Guymon, Oklahoma.

Figure 20. A farm severely damaged by wind erosion. Courtesy of the Texas County Soil Conservation District Office, Guymon, Oklahoma.

To many residents it seemed as though the very heavens had turned against them when, "a bursting projectile from an other world sprayed its meteoric fragments over the [South] Plains." At approximately 6:00 A.M. on March 24, a falling star lit the sky as it thunderously roared along toward its collision course with the earth in northeastern New Mexico.[14]

When the windy months of March and April were finally over, a hope for quieter times rose among the stricken folks. But, the dirt did not stop blowing. The dawn was clear and bright at Liberal, Kansas, on May 22. By midmorning the most destructive dust storm to date raced across the Plains. About 5:30 that afternoon, rain and hail mixed with mud, began falling. People along the streets raced for shelter from the hail as a killer tornado descended on the town. The tornado left 4 people dead, 750 more homeless, and the downtown area in wreckage.[15]

The dust-bowl weather in May was extreme. Two weeks before the tornado struck Liberal, "the heaviest rains that had ever been witnessed" drenched Gruver, Texas.[16] The rain poured for nearly eighteen hours, flooding farms and community. Bridges, railroads, and gas mains were washed out. Never had the people seen such weather. Even the great flyer, Charles A. Lindbergh, who had beaten the Atlantic in his famous crossing, was forced to abandon the skyways to the flying dirt when he attempted to cross the Texas Panhandle on May 6.

May's weather was only an exercise for later activities. The dust bowl received a terrific dust storm on July 14. John Minter was helping erect a house on a farm a few miles from Stratford, Texas, when the storm suddenly struck. The winds destroyed the building and badly injured Minter. Meanwhile at Perryton, Texas, hurricane-force winds did extensive damage to nearly every building in town, while tearing down the telephone and power lines. "The Oklahoma-Texas Wheat Pool Elevator of 250,000 bushel capacity . . . was almost demolished."[17] The roof of one of the hotels was removed, which allowed nearly six inches of rain to fall into the upper floor of the building.

Nature was not through. At Texhoma on September 2, a small tornado struck the town, doing extensive damage to several buildings including the hotel, which was unroofed and filled with water. The natural gas regulator house north of town was destroyed and thousands of cubic feet of gas dangerously poured into the air.[18]

The weather also took its toll on the crops. In early May, A. P. Emprie left Dodge City for a wheat inspection trip of southwestern Kansas. He found some wheat in Ness, Stanton, and Hamilton counties, although it was weak. Stevens, Haskell, and Seward county crops were the worst hit. At one point in Seward County he saw a road grader buried to the control wheels. The harvest of 1933 was the poorest and most demoralizing harvest of any during the entire decade of the "Dirty Thirties." By fall the row crops had failed and stockmen were stacking Russian thistles to get through the winter. Those families who could not find enough feed, even thistles and soap weed, were forced to sell their milk cows, with the accompanying loss of the cream check.[19]

At Christmas time, Bill Kraft returned to the family farm near Wild Horse Lake. He found a wasteland of dunes. When Bill questioned his mother about the disaster, she replied, "You're in the dust bowl; didn't you know? It's been that way a long time."[20] Accompanying the drought were plagues of rabbits and grasshoppers. As early as 1930, grasshoppers and spiders had injured the wheat crop in Cimarron County. By the fall of 1933, they had spread to Grant County, Kansas, where "grasshoppers are eating [the] young wheat."[21]

The proliferation of the rabbit population was both a blessing and a curse to the area. The rabbits did furnish meat for many depressed families. But the rabbits also ate everything in sight. In 1931, Hooker residents killed and shipped over 5,000 rabbits to relief agencies in Kansas City. The shipment did not reduce the problem. It was not unusual for the hunters in a rabbit drive to kill 2,000 rabbits in a section or two of land. During the winter months, rabbit drives were common across the southern High Plains.[22]

The year 1933 was the worst year of that hard decade. Business conditions were at their lowest point. The oil and gas development had stopped and leases were being dropped. The crop was virtually a total failure and brought only forty cents per bushel. Government relief programs were promised but did not start until 1934. And Secretary of Interior Harold Ickes was reported to have advised the residents of the Oklahoma Panhandle to abandon their homes. All the people had was hope. And hope for a better next year was old and powerful medicine. It was their unfailing optimism that earned the plainsmen the title of "America's Next Year People."

Nationally, 1934 was a year of severe dust storms, with their origins primarily in the northern states. High winds sweeping across Nebraska in mid November 1933 deposited dirt from New York to Georgia. In Iowa, the storm was one of the worst (if not the worst) ever experienced in the state. The storm took some lives and did extensive property damage. The Weather Bureau called this "the first great storm"[23] and claimed, "The second of these was on April 9–12, 1934, with dust noted from the Dakotas to Florida." Two more storms, which originated in the Dakotas, were recorded before the famous storm of May 9–12, 1934. At Topeka, Kansas, the worst storms were reported on April 11 and 23. It is worth noting, since several Kansas counties were included in the famous dust bowl, that the Weather Bureau's report does not mention Kansas in the May 9–12 dust storm. The weather reporting station at Minneapolis, Minnesota, however, stated: "April greatly favored dust storms, with unusually dry, windy weather prevailing during most of the months. Soil moisture was rapidly depleted, much new seeding was blown out of the ground, soil from plowed fields drifted badly." The report went on to state that the dust storms of May 9–10 [12] were the most severe. In Wisconsin "there were fresh to strong winds which drifted the soil in the fields and in places uncovered newly sown grains."[24] The broad area affected by wind erosion suggests the severity of the drought and reminds us that severe wind erosion occurred in the humid corn belt as well as on the semiarid Great Plains.

In the dust bowl, 1934 was the year of fewest dust storms recorded for the period between January 1933 and October 1937. The records at Panhandle A & M College as listed in Table 4.1, show the number of dust storms.[25]

With no major floods or tornadoes, the twenty-two dust storms seemed reasonable to the dust bowl residents. If it had not been so terribly dry and hot, the year 1934 would have been considered good. But despite the relatively mild weather, many of the area's weather stations rain gauges recorded the lowest level during the entire drought. At Clayton, New Mexico, the drought was devastating; there were only 7.21 inches of precipitation for the year. For comparison, Perryton, Texas, received 14.23 inches of precipitation while Goodwell, Oklahoma, recorded 14.27 inches of rain.[26]

TABLE 4.1
Dust Storms, 1933–37

Month	1933	1934	1935	1936	1937
January	4	2	2	0	9
February	4	0	7	9	14
March	14	6	11	18	18
April	17	6	20	16	21
May	12	2	6	14	23
June	7	2	1	1	17
July	3	0	1	2	15
August	3	1	1	1	10
September	3	0	0	0	7
October	0	1	2	1	—
November	2	2	1	7	—
December	1	0	1	4	—
Total	70	22	53	73	134

The *Texhoma Times* reported on April 12 that "Crop Prospects Here Are Good."[27] But between Dalhart, Texas, and Boise City, Oklahoma, only 15 percent of the acreage would be harvested. At harvest time the Texhoma elevators handled over 200,000 bushels of wheat. That was far short of the two to three million bushels handled in 1931, but well ahead of the 200 bushels sold at the elevators in 1933. In Hansford County, Texas, the fourteen elevators handled nearly two million bushels of wheat, one of the best crops of the drought years. In Morton County, Kansas, "a greater acreage [was] cut than was anticipated."[28] Although the crop was better than in 1933, it was scattered. The harvest in Beaver County, Oklahoma, was nearly a total failure.

The continued drought, which forced the sale of herds of livestock, and the rabbits blotted the prospects for the future. In August, black widow spiders took the life of a little boy at Rolla, Kansas, and several people in Stevens and Morton counties were extremely sick after being bitten. In spite of the difficulties, the farmers who raised some wheat were able to sell it for 75 cents per bushel at harvest time, and in August wheat was worth 94 cents per bushel at local markets. This was a considerable improvement over the 25 cents received in 1931. Business conditions were improving, and the oil and gas industry was beginning to revive. There were no serious floods or tornadoes. Although the Kansas Public Health Reports show that nearly 300 people died from excessive heat that year, apparently no one in the heartland of the dust bowl expired from the heat. All in all, America's Next Year People could look to 1935 with renewed hope.[29]

The prospects for the new year dimmed quickly. A severe dust storm swept the heartland of the dust bowl on January 1, 1935. In late February storms began to follow each other in quick succession. By March conditions were extremely harsh. Throughout the county, buildings and windmills were damaged or destroyed by the flying dirt and hurricane winds. Twelve miles north of Goodwell at the W. M. Moore farm, hail accompanying the dust and wind did considerable damage to the farmstead.[30]

In late March the *Texhoma Times* reported that "Dirt Barrage Is Undiminished."[31] On March 21, the *Boise City News* told its readers, "Worst Storm in History of County Lasts Four Days Here." On the night of March 15 a dirt barrage that made travel impossible and life difficult hit the town. "One business man attempted to pilot his car home from his store and drove a block, only to abandon it and spend the night in a hotel."[32] Part of the movie patrons were unable to get home, even though they lived only a few blocks from the theater.

In Baca County, Colorado, on March 23, "a small caravan of farmers was leaving the dust area."[33] Roads in the county were being closed by drifting soil. Stockmen in Bent, Prowers, and Baca counties, Colorado, were attempting to move their stock to range land in South Park and the San Luis Valley. During the dirt barrage, the First State Bank of Pritchett (Colorado) closed its doors to business.[34]

In late March the dust storms began receiving national attention. The report of six deaths from dust pneumonia in Baca County received front page coverage in the metropolitan papers. "Baca County Makes Page 1 In The Dailies," reported the Springfield *Democrat-Herald* on March 28. "Last week the big press associations broke with a big yarn about the dust pneumonia with which many of our citizens have been afflicted and by the time the stories reached New York and Los Angeles it ap-

pears that most of us were dead or dying." The article went on
to discuss candidly the situation in the area. After recounting
some of the events the paper commented: "To the folks from out
of the county we can truthfully say that it has been plenty bad
here but not as terrible as the eastern and far western headline
writers would have you believe."[35]

The remaining headlines and stories in the paper suggest how
life and normal activities continued during those trying days.
There were stories informing the readers that "Soil Erosion Plan
Is Given," and "No Relief If You Can Get By Without: Local
Administrator Wants Names Of Those Fudging Upon Relief."
Stories on a proposed meeting of the educators appeared along
with the local news and the story of a hit-and-run accident.
Readers were also told that Miss Eunice Seeley and George William Ream of Campo were married and that the Junior Class
play, "You're Telling Me!" was to be presented on March 29 and
30 at the High School Auditorium. During the siege of dirt
storms, one Baca County farmer revealed his eternal optimism
when asked what he thought about the dust storms. "If we can
just get some moisture we'll make it."[36] But by mid April the
dust was still blowing and little moisture came.

The editor of the *Morton County Farmer* sat in his dust-filled
office and penned:

DUST

DUSt

DUst

Dust

dust

Is my face red—or is it black—Darn this dirt. Do I see
red or do—Yes! Folks it is either Tuesday or Wednesday
afternoon—who knows for sure? We had a train once—
some hours ago—don't?? whether it was today's, tomorrow's,
or yesterday's.

We can see nothing out our windows but dirt, every time
our teeth (or the dentists, or maybe you have your store
teeth paid for) come together, you feel dirt and taste it;
haven't heard a thing for hours, my ears are full, can't
smell, my nose is full, can't walk, my shoes are full but not
of feet.

Yes, my friend (if he is present or not too far away) we are and have been having a dirt storm. It hasn't been real light for two days. Everything is covered with a little of ole Mexico or Texas or Colorado or what have you.

The earth looks hard and barren—everybody has a dirty face—even your creditors hardly know you. But there is no way out—Not even out of our front door.

We live in a dugout and slide down the steps now. Diving out the window is fun after you get used to it—you can't slide up hill, you know, or have you ever tried it?

But such is Kansas, the poets rave about it in rainy seasons and everyone raves about it all of the rest of the time, that is, all who have lived here.

But, by heck, we are here to stay! We've seen it in all of its beauty and we like it—we are here to stay—we like the people, the food, and what shelter we can find. We know that this can't last forever and take heart with each lung full of dirt.

Adieu, my Children, I leave you to crawl under my water soaked umbrella for another breath of something or other.

Yours—until we can no longer see red.[37]

In southwestern Kansas and southeastern Colorado people were seeing more than red. They were suffering and dying from dust pneumonia. During the dirt barrage the region was stricken with an epidemic of measles, strep throat, and other bronchial diseases (that turned into pneumonia) and respiratory illnesses (generally called dust pneumonia). Children and adults alike suffered and died. In some families two or more members were killed by dust pneumonia. Nearly everyone suffered some form of illness during those hectic days. At Springfield, Colorado, and Elkhart and Hugoton, Kansas, emergency hospitals were set up to treat the sick and dying. The combination of constant dirt storms, depression, drought, and the epidemic of fatal illness caused immeasurable amounts of fear and anxiety among the folks. Oddly enough, south of the Colorado and Kansas lines in the Oklahoma Panhandle and the northern Texas Panhandle, there was only one reported death from dust pneumonia.[38]

The strain of those trying days was too much for some residents. In February and March, Morton County was shocked by unusual acts of violence. One woman who had cared for her father for years suddenly turned on him and took his life. Later she committed suicide. A father lost control of himself and beat his adopted son to death. Later the father took his own life. A drunk man attempted to shoot his former wife as she sat in a cafe. All that saved the woman's life was the drink, which had made the gunman unsteady. Although the entire region had always had an undercurrent of violence dating back to the days of Robbers Roost and the Wild Horse Lake Massacre, and continuing through the bootlegging and bank robbing of the 1920s, the violence in Morton County during the 1935 dust barrage was unparalleled for concentration of area, time, and emotions.[39]

The spring day of April 14 sharply contrasted the best and the worst weather of the dust bowl. Everyone who lived through the roller of that day vividly recalled the experience forty years later. April 14 was a day to relax and forget the previous hard weeks. About 3 o'clock in the afternoon nearly 300 people were fishing and picnicing at Two Buttes Lake when they saw a long, black cloud rolling in from the north. Some hurried for their cars and tried to make it to safety before the onrushing storm caught them. But the roller soon covered the area with total darkness.[40]

At their family home in Liberal, Kansas, Lila Lee King and a friend were alone when the roller approached. The two terrified girls raced frantically to a neighbor's house. "I was sure I was going to die," recalled Lee King, "and I can vividly recall the dust storm although I was only eleven at the time. We lit matches and held them before our face and we couldn't see the light unless it was quite near."[41]

The funeral procession for Mrs. James Lucas was traveling under a peaceful sky from Boise City to Texhoma, when suddenly the earth rolled in from the north and turned the procession into a night of horror and confusion. Even the dead could not be laid to rest with dignity and respect on that day.[42]

The roller caught Arthur N. Howe while he was feeding cattle on Barbie's Ranch in Beaver County. During the storm, Howe huddled against the sides of the wagon. After the storm lifted a little he started the team for home. Blindly, but unerringly, the faithful team found their way to safety. After reaching home and resting, Howe went to Beaver, Oklahoma, to see his sweetheart, Letha Kachel.[43]

Cleo Rainey was only four years old when she and her parents were stranded on the road between Goodwell and Guymon by the roller. Although she was very young, the rolling of the cloud, the total darkness once the storm struck, and her fright were indelibly printed in her memory.[44]

On her farm near Texhoma, Mrs. Vesta Tuna went into a wheat field to gather her cows when she saw the storm approaching. Before she regained the shelter of the farmstead, the roller overtook her. She lay flat on the ground and covered her face with her apron so she could breathe until the worst of the storm had passed. Then she rose and followed a row of wheat to safety.[45]

The storms of the spring were violent and the crop was poor, but there was enough wheat to lead Mrs. Tuna and many others in similar situations to safety. Times were hard and nature was ugly, but the hard-pressed land and its sparse crop never completely defeated America's Next Year People.

By May, it seemed an eternity had passed since it had rained and the wind and dirt not blown. The members of the Prairie Center Sunday School south of Pritchett, Colorado, asked the nation to join them in a day of prayer for rain. On May 5, hundreds of thousands of people across the nation knelt and prayed for rain for the stricken dust bowl. On May 8, the rains came and Bear Creek, Butte Creek, Plum Creek, Cat Creek, and Clay Creek were filled with water. Baca County had more water than the residents had seen in years. With the rain came new hope. Many farmers decided to stick it out rather than sell their land for "peanuts" to the Resettlement Administration.[46]

Towards the end of May a devastating hail storm lashed southern Cimarron County. Along a wide strip from Felt to Midwell, Oklahoma, "cue-ball-size" hail broke out windows and killed livestock. A soil conservation crew near Midwell took refuge from the storm in a car. Soon the men were cowering under the dash and behind the seats while the hail broke out the windshield and head lights. The car roof was destroyed and the fenders and radiator badly bent. After the storm passed, the soil conservation crew limped back to Boise City.

At the Cap Williams farm near Felt, Oklahoma, the school bus was forced to stop. Into the terrible hail Cap rushed with a blanket. He threw the blanket over a child. Cap then made a shield with his body and dashed to the house. The process was repeated several times until all the children were safe. In a dazed condition, Cap made one more trip to save what he believed to be the final child. He hurried to the bus, threw the blanket over the body, and returned to safety. When he revealed the precious contents of his blanket, the school children broke into laughter. The final rescue had brought in a greyhound.

The Williams home was badly damaged but the children were safe. The hail was so thick the following morning that it was necessary for parents to use tractors to get their children from the Williams home. And the dust that settled on top of the hail formed an insulation that preserved the hail for nearly a week.[47]

By the end of May the drought was temporarily broken by drenching rains, and a new terror began. Along a 600-mile stretch from northeastern Colorado to eastern Missouri, rivers went on the rampage. In Kansas, the Solomon, Republican, Blue, Kansas, Marias des Cygnes, Neosho, and Kaw rivers took at least 140 lives. Those were the first of the season's killer floods.[48]

In Baca and Prowers counties, Colorado, on the night of July 11, a cloudburst sent raging water down Granada and Wolfe creeks. The racing water assaulted the home of Antone Elder and caught the family by surprise. Mr. and Mrs. Elder and five of their seven children lost their lives in the flash flood. Mrs. Algada Karn and her son Leo sought refuge from the rain in the unoccupied home of L. C. Lally. When the Lally home was swept away by the torrent, the occupants who had sought shelter under its roof were drowned. The flood rushed on to Granada, Colorado, where it did extensive damage before subsiding.[49]

Next, on August 21, hard rains on Horse Creek sent the stream rushing into Holly, Colorado. The rains weakened the new Horse Creek Dam and it gave way, sending a wall of water towards the town. The watchman at the dam, Ted Harper, was able to warn the residents of Holly, who retreated to safe ground, and prevent a tragic event.[50]

Then, in September 1935, the year of extremes took another turn. "Best Rain of Year Fell Here Sunday," reported the *Texhoma Times*.[51] The rain was general across the dust bowl, and hope for a better tomorrow was revived. Some farmers began planting wheat while others waited for more moisture. Rains continued until most of the wheat land was planted by late November. Those who planted very late hoped to raise enough wheat to furnish a cover crop when the spring winds blew in 1936. By December the *Texhoma Times* reported that "Cimarron County's wheat prospect is now better than any it has had since 1931."[52]

The wheat harvest of 1935 was spotted. It was "wonderful what even a small harvest can do in the way of reviving business and all lines of industry," reported the *Texhoma Times*.[53] Implement dealers sold several tractors. Most of the crop in the Texhoma area was south and east of town on the Texas side. "The hum of the combine continues to be heard throughout the Hooker wheat area, but the yields are not coming up to expectations," reported the *Hooker Advance*.[54] To the east of Hooker, towards Adams, there were several good fields, and the Hooker Equity and Wheat Pool Elevator was handling as much as sixty-five loads of wheat per day. Wheat brought from 79 cents to 93 cents per bushel at local markets in July and in August reached $1.03. In September the price stood at $1.21 per bushel at local markets. The price had not been that good since 1929. The farms that harvested a little wheat in 1935 were not the same ones that had a crop in 1934. Thus everyone was getting a little nibble. Data collected by Fred Floyd shows that Beaver County produced 148,100 bushels of wheat, Cimarron County produced none, and Texas County produced 451,300 bushels of wheat. Floyd does not have pre-1935 figures; therefore, it is hazardous to compare data to early years. The figures suggest, however, that the 1935 crop was much larger than a year earlier. It is clear that although the crops were very small, the area did not experience a complete failure. And even a small crop worked miracles in renewing hope.[55]

Finally the long hard year of 1935 came to an end. In January 1936, Spearman, Texas, had above-normal precipitation. Out in Union County, the *Clayton News* reported, "Dust Bowl Turns to Snow Bowl When Storm Blankets County."[56] At Texhoma the editor of the *Texhoma Times* reminded his readers that "In 1926, from January 1st until harvest time, less than six inches of moisture fell, yet we had one of the best wheat crops in the history of the panhandle."[57] The brighter prospects for the coming year soon faded as the region slid into one of its worst drought years. Although the region received some hard punches, it was not as severe a year as 1935.[58]

In April several dust bowl residents took a measure of comfort in knowing they were not the only area suffering from the whims of nature. High winds did extensive damage to oil derricks at Long Beach, California, and tornadoes ravaged the south, taking 300 lives in Georgia and another 100 lives elsewhere. Federal authorities were urging people to evacuate threatened flood areas along the Ohio River. And earthquakes were reported in Montana.[59]

At this point it should be noted that some precipitation was recorded at each of the five Oklahoma Panhandle recording stations every month except five, during the entire decade of the 1930s. None of the five rainless months were consecutive. Springfield, Colorado, reported precipitation every month except three and none of those were consecutive. Table 4.2 suggests the different years that the drought of the 1930s reached its worst in different areas and where the drought was most severe.[60]

In the heartland of the dust bowl during 1936, the wind and dirt blew, and in June hard rains sent Butte Creek out of its banks where it took the lives of five people and flooded Holly, Colorado. Other floods occurred at Granada and Wiley, Colorado. In September, hard rains sent the streams in Ochiltree County, Texas, on the rampage. But dust storms and floods were becoming part of the normal life by 1936. The biggest surprise to the residents was the earthquake that shook the Oklahoma Panhandle and Ochiltree County, Texas.[61]

At harvest time the crop was small, as it had been for several years. In May, however, the Hooker area received 3.21 inches of slow, steady rain. "Moisture of this type," reported the local newspaper, "has not visited this section of the state since 1928."[62] At harvest time the *Hooker Advance* told its readers: "While Hooker's acreage will not produce anything like a crop, there are many farmers who were contending they will harvest a fair yield." The paper went on to state, "at least some of the Hooker farmers will get acquainted with the 'hum' of their combines and the 'purring' of their tractors and will harvest a crop that was given up as a total failure less than six weeks ago. . . . What a country!"[63]

TABLE 4.2
Precipitation (in inches), 1930–39

Year	Beaver	Boise City	Goodwell	Hooker	Springfield	Clayton	Perryton	Richfield
1930	15.19	21.09	18.53	23.65	20.42	17.05	16.45	21.65
1931	18.46	14.64	15.24	21.72	13.51	10.79	17.35	12.52
1932	20.37	12.27	15.31	15.51	17.85	10.10	19.31	13.06
1933	10.03	15.57	12.62	17.47	12.24	7.13	16.00	15.12
1934	15.40	8.62	14.27	10.82	11.45	7.21	14.23	7.65
1935	14.49	9.62	11.69	12.16	10.42	9.30	13.40	7.09
1936		10.05	9.69	13.75	10.48	5.54	16.37	4.96
1937	12.61	11.82	11.56	12.18	13.73	12.56	15.88	8.58
1938	17.55	18.50	14.86	14.07	16.10	12.19		15.47
1939	14.39	14.03	13.64	13.82	11.68			9.15

In Hansford County, Texas, where the wheat crop was expected to be better than in most counties in the dust bowl, a severe hail storm swept across approximately 170 sections and destroyed an estimated 85 percent of the wheat in less than two hours. In spite of the hardships, across the entire eighteen counties the wheat harvest was about the same as that of 1935. No one raised a real crop, but enough people came close enough that farmers still believed in the land. Offsetting the crop failure was the oil and gas boom at Sunray, Texas, and the increased leasing of gas and oil lands across the entire area. Accompanying the petroleum activity was the renewal of railroad construction and improvement.[64]

The citizens were enduring the drought and the economy was improving when nature produced a new threat to the realm. Waves upon waves of grasshoppers descended on the five-state area. During the summer months, the grasshoppers did extensive damage to range land. "When it is possible to locate the exact home address of the pesky creatures," wrote the *Spearman Reporter*, "we are suggesting that that section of the nation be referred to as the grasshopper bowl, as the people have dubbed this country the 'dust bowl.' "[65]

The new year, 1937, marked a definite change in the dust bowl. Briefly Ochiltree County, Texas, was dropped from the official list of dust bowl counties. The extreme hardships remained, but hope for the future was much stronger. To be sure, dust storms lashed the region with a fury not previously experienced. In the spring an epidemic of dust pneumonia brought renewed fears of death and anguish. The dirt storms and the accompanying static electricity caused extensive excitement. Some people panicked under the pressure of the constant bombardment of the fierce dirt storms. They wanted the federal government to place the area under martial law and bring in the army to lister the whole region in an attempt to stop the blowing dirt. Despite the excitement, most people were resolved to stick it out.[66]

The tragic flood along the Ohio River stirred the dust bowl residents to new heights of compassion and resolve. To aid the Red Cross drive for funds for the relief of the flood victims, residents dug deeply and gave freely of their wealth. While attempting to help others, residents of the dust bowl were becoming deeply aware of the fact that every climate had its drawbacks and they became more resolved to stick it out.[67]

Even though the numerous dirt storms took their toll, wheat prospects looked good in most areas of the dust bowl until March. During that month much of the wheat blew out or died from the static electricity. But even March was different than it had been. In Texas County, one of the worst hit areas, the editor of the *Texhoma Times* reported: "March came in like a lamb, went out like a lamb, but it sure played hell along about the middle of everything. We had more rain and snow, and more wind and dirt than any of the other months of the year, and besides that there were several mighty fine days."[68]

The wheat harvest in many areas promised to be the best in years. In the Hooker area nearly 100,000 bushels were harvested. Southeast of Texhoma nearly 60,000 bushels of wheat were harvested. Texas County produced 831,000 bushels, compared to 419,100 the previous year. Although hail again took an extensive toll of wheat in Hansford and Ochiltree counties, Texas, the harvest was better than in 1936. This was accomplished with fewer acres being planted to wheat. The crop in Beaver County doubled its production from a year earlier.[69] As Table 4.3 indicates, the crop in southwest Kansas varied extensively.[70]

Nationally the 1937 wheat crop was better than it had been in years. Increased production drove the price down from $1.09 per bushel at local markets at harvest time to 88 cents in August. Even the drop in price was acceptable, accompanied as it was with larger harvests.[71]

The year 1937 also differed from all the other drought years (except 1933) in tornado activity. The edge of a terrific tornado struck Stratford, Texas, and did extensive damage. The storm stayed on the ground for several miles as it passed just west of Texhoma. Along the path of the storm several farm homes and buildings were destroyed and many head of livestock killed. The families, luckily, were in town doing their Saturday marketing and the storm did not directly hit any of the towns.[72]

Another tornado struck near Moscow, Kansas, and there took the lives of several people. With the tornadoes came cloud bursts. In Union County, New Mexico, there was a flash flood, not as destructive as floods of previous years.[73]

TABLE 4.3
Wheat Yield in Bushels, 1933–39

County	1933	1934	1935	1936	1937	1938	1939
Hamilton	7,567	47,132	2,362	50,744	11,700	16,330	60,000
Grant	9,490	77,289	16,271	30,181	30,900	35,150	68,000
Morton	6,855	53,847	7,297	16,325	none	none	66,000
Seward	7,957	69,737	36,709	49,596	60,300	70,070	101,000
Stanton	28,486	81,644	4,310	41,778	9,600	27,040	75,000
Stevens	9,490	77,289	16,271	30,181	24,500	45,600	59,000

The primary threat to the dust bowl in 1937 was the invasion of grasshoppers. The range-land counties were severely hit by the insects. In Beaver County, over 175 tons of grasshopper poison were spread. After counting the dead hoppers found under five watermelons, R. I. Allen estimated that the insect population, if evenly distributed over the county, would equal 23,400 grasshoppers per acre. "He also estimated that if 30 percent of the total land in the county had been poisoned and an equally good kill had resulted there would have been a total of 93.3 carloads of hoppers killed in that county."[74]

Governor Clyde Tingley of New Mexico used part of the national guard to assist highway department employees, relief workers, and private citizens to spread poison in Union County. Poison mixing plants were set up at Amistad, Sedan, Clapham, Pennington, Sofia, and Clayton. In the fight against the grasshoppers, the "arsnite used amounted to 19,555 gallon drums . . ."[75] The arsnite was added to 176 boxcarloads of sawdust and mixed with molasses and banana oil. In Baca County, Colorado, poison was shipped in the boxcarload. The county had five mixing plants. Seventy-eight trucks from the highway department and numerous private trucks hauled poison around the clock to stop the grasshoppers. In the remaining dust bowl counties, poisoning the insects was conducted at a rapid pace. In spite of the vigorous activity, "in every direction from Texhoma," remarked the *Texhoma Times* on September 23, "grasshoppers are thick and are reported as eating the wheat almost as fast as it comes through the ground."[76]

During the 1938 winter months some fair snows visited the region, and dust storms were fewer than the previous year. Then the snuster struck. On April 7 and 8 sixty-mile-per-hour winds whipped the dirt high in the air while driving heavy snow before it. All the roads were blocked with deep drifts of dirt and snow. School buses and travelers were stranded at many locations across the five-state area. The *Panhandle Herald* compared the blizzard to the one of April 7, 1919. During the storm hundreds of head of livestock were lost. For some residents the snuster of April 7–8, 1938, was much worse than the famous roller of April 14, 1935.[77] Snuster or not, America's Next Year People continued to look for an end to the hard times.

For some farmers, the 1938 crop was another failure and disappointment, but most farmers found the year to be a marked improvement over previous years. In Beaver County over three million bushels of wheat were raised. In Texas County the harvest was over 1.5 million bushels. Although hail again took a large share of the crop in Hansford and Ochiltree counties, Texas, the harvest was good. The increased production brought low prices at local elevators. At 56 to 58 cents per bushel, the market was near its 1933 level.[78]

The grasshoppers undermined the federal government's land-use plan of establishing a stable agricultural economy in the region. The plan suggested returning the land to native grass and encouraging livestock raising. In the fall of 1937, hundreds of thousands of acres of grasshopper eggs were located and mapped. In the summer months of 1938, grasshoppers attacked with a greater fury than they had during the previous year. In Sherman County, Texas, the national guard united with other groups and individual farmers to spread poison. During the first week of June the crews "averaged between 50,000 and 60,000 pounds a day" of mixing and spreading poison.[79] In Union County the war was renewed. The work of the men was discouraging since five separate flights of grasshoppers flew over Clayton as the insects migrated from Colorado and Oklahoma. Vernon Hopson recalled traveling the highway across Baca County where long stretches of the highway were extremely slick from the dead insects.[80]

In August the army worms invaded the grasslands of Sherman County, Texas. Near Kerrick, Texas, the invasion was especially heavy. "The worms were so numerous," stated Woodson Wadley, "that when a door at home was opened, the worms which cover the screens fall inside, and must be swept from the house with a broom."[81] What was worse, no one seemed to know how to fight the army worms.

Thoughts of grasshoppers, army worms, and drought were set aside in the fall. The rains were the best in years and the ground moisture was high. Reading the 1939 local newspapers, one senses the optimism in the dust bowl. To be sure, there were dust storms and grasshoppers. But, let some of the headlines tell the story: *Ochiltree County Herald*, January 12: "Slow Downpour Lets Every Drop Soak Into Ground; Is Followed By Spring Weather—Moisture During 1938 Was Above Normal; . . . Best

Crop Prospect In Many Years."[82] On March 31, the *Elkhart Tri-State News* wrote: "Wettest Season In Years: . . . A soaking spring rain falling all night Tuesday put the final touches on the old time dust bowl, . . ."[83] The headlines for the *Stratford Star* for April 6 were: "Heavy Rains Insure Harvest of Large Yield of Wheat."[84]

After the harvest the headlines in the *Texhoma Times* of August 8 were followed by this article:

> Dust Bowl Stages Greatest Come-Back Of All Time In 1939
> Seven years of choking dust, whipped over the Southwest by restless winds, vainly tried to lick the faith and hope of the people. Many became discouraged when things looked blackest, but kept on hoping and trusting in themselves and in this country. Some left for various reasons, . . . Then came 1939. There were comparatively few dust storms. Rains came and green covered the land. Wheat looked excellent, although hail took some of it. A million bushels came to Texhoma and all this has instilled new hope and courage in the citizens of the high plains. "Dust bowl" is a term to be discarded and forgotten. The new term should be "the land of beautiful sunsets—where the sun rises and sets on the most courageous and friendly folks in America."[85]

5

Depression in the Dust Bowl

It was Christmas, 1933. Bill Kraft, who had been away from home for several years, drove through the night, preoccupied with his thoughts. He did not notice the windswept wasteland. He arrived home at Wild Horse Lake near Hooker, Oklahoma, tired, and quietly ascended the stairs to the familiar room of his youth. Not wanting to wake his parents, the weary traveler went to bed, where he slept peacefully until the sun streaming through three different windows overcame his slumber. Sitting up on the bed, Bill looked out the windows to the west, the north, and the south. Quickly he rose and walked to each window in turn and looked out. Everything was a sickly white. The fields and the pastures were covered with a white sand. Not a blade of green wheat or yellow maize stock was visible. Bill had come home to the dust bowl[1]

Hard times were not new to the old-timers. Caroline A. Henderson noted: "Our children still have pioneering work to do."[2] In the pioneering spirit, the residents of the dust bowl prepared to meet the crisis which struck after the 1931 wheat harvest. Relief organizations collected food and clothing for the destitute. Churches raised funds for the needy and schools staged benefits for assisting the poor. The Guymon Equity Exchange hauled wheat to the flour mill at Elkhart, Kansas, for its members. A seventy-five-bushel load of wheat was worth $18.75 before milling; it was valued at $61.00 after milling. After the Guymon

87

Equity Exchange piloted the milling project, several town folks and others began a community effort to purchase wheat at a very low price at the elevators and haul it to the flour mill. To aid the needy, L. C. French, J. O. French, and R. J. French of Boise City, Oklahoma, in January 1932 made a deal with the Ralston Brothers to reopen the flour mill at Boise City. Any needy person in Cimarron County could have a free sack of wheat from the French brothers, and the flour mill would process the wheat for the shorts and bran.[3]

In the spring of 1932, state and federal assistance was increased for the drought area. In April, Governor William "Alfalfa Bill" Murray of Oklahoma began distribution of funds raised by a special tax on gasoline, and federal monies for the construction of highways were sharply increased. But in May, the *Texhoma Times* reported: "Relief Fund is Exhausted."[4] Although badly needed highways were being surveyed and constructed, the road work was inadequate to stave off the onrushing depression.

New Year's Day 1933 ushered in the worst year of the dust bowl era. Wind and dirt storms were terrific. At the Panhandle A & M College Experiment Station, seventy dust days were recorded. Ten miles to the southwest, at Texhoma, L. E. Job reported 139 dusty days and 195 nice days during the first eleven months. The blowing dirt and drought killed the crops. The harvest of wheat and row crops was the poorest of the entire decade.[5]

While the dirt blew and the crops failed, the depression tightened its grip. In July, 587 Baca County, Colorado, families were receiving limited federal relief, and 50 families per month were being added to the relief rolls. The deposits at the Springfield, Colorado, bank dropped from a high in 1929 of $650,000 to $150,000. In the newspapers, want ads and local advertisements were scarce, and the papers contained only half as many pages as a year earlier. Schoolteachers, who had already taken a major decrease in wages, were being paid with warrants. A few children were not attending school because their parents could not afford to purchase needed books and supplies. At Texhoma the city fathers turned off most of the street lights because the electric bill could not be paid.[6]

To help people weather the depression, H. H. Finnell began experimenting with dishes made primarily with wheat. He published a series of recipes for hot and cold cereals, macaronis, cookies, and breads. One Baca County farmer recalled how his family ate wheat three times a day for several months. Another farmer remembered eating water gravy and wheat for most of the meals. Since jackrabbits were plentiful, a common diet consisted of rabbit meat and bread made from locally ground wheat. Families like the Krafts lived off their larder, accumulated through years of canning and preserving.[7]

Although times were difficult in the heartland of the dust bowl, they were no worse, and in many ways better, than in other parts of the nation. The depression struck the area much later than many eastern cities. In May 1932, Caroline A. Henderson movingly expressed her concern for children in Chicago, who had only oatmeal to eat and adult clothing to wear to school. And the people who lived in "Starvation Gulch" (a local name) near Pine Cliff, Colorado, ate cornmeal mush three times a day. The headlines of the *Morton County Farmer* on February 5, 1932, reminded the readers: "Farmers Here Are Not So Pessimistic: Can Stand The Gaff As Long As Eastern Friends." The story that followed compared conditions in Morton County to eastern areas. It was not until September 1932, that Rolla, Kansas, made an application for any federal drought relief funds.[8]

President Franklin D. Roosevelt declared a bank holiday in March 1933, in order to allow inspectors to determine which banks were sound. Every bank in the heartland of the dust bowl was allowed to reopen, and only the bank at Ulysses, Kansas, had any restriction on withdrawals. In November, however, the Texhoma Farmers National Bank merged with the First National Bank of Texhoma, with no loss to investors or depositors. Through the 1930s, only four banks completely closed their doors—a bank at Ulysses, Kansas, closed in 1930 before the drought and depression hit; the bank at Goodwell, was closed by state inspectors in 1932; the bank at Pritchett, Colorado, closed in 1935; and the First National Bank at Spearman, Texas, liquidated in 1936. The bank at Goodwell was too small and did not have sufficient trade area to justify its operations. The bank at Pritchett closed because of a loss of business resulting from the continued drought and depression.[9]

During the decade several banks consolidated. When the First

State Bank of Texline, Texas, consolidated with the Farmers and
Stockmens Bank of Clayton, New Mexico, in June 1936, the
Clayton News commented: "The mode of transportation and the
oiled and paved highways no longer required the small bank
in every town."[10] Based on the published reports of banks
throughout the heartland of the dust bowl, and on other data,
there is no reason to doubt that the consolidation was the result
of improved transportation rather than the depression and the
drought. When the owners of the First State Bank of Rolla, Kansas, purchased the First National Bank of Elkhart, Kansas, in
December 1939, a much smaller bank with a much smaller trade
area took over the larger operation.[11]

Texhoma lost a tremendous amount of ground as a major regional trade center during the depression and one of its banks
closed its doors. The assets of the banks reported in the
Texhoma Times (Table 5.1) suggest the banking trends in the
heartland of the dust bowl for the years 1930 through 1939.[12]

TABLE 5.1
Dust Bowl Bank Assets, 1930–39

June	1st National Bank Assets	Farmers National Bank Assets
1930	$415,187.77	$139,352.60
1931	325,008.51	119,843.10
1932	281,085.35	81,616.36
1933	251,067.98	80,893.69
1934	405,416.04	—
1935	494,505.66	—
1936	430,457.95	—
1937	490,717.30	—
1938	401,357.33	—
1939	417,614.48	—

By the end of the decade, The 1st National Bank had not regained the vigor the two banks had in 1930, but after 1933 the
bank was stable and its assets remained near or above its 1930
record. It is worth noting that the Farmers National Bank had
floundered during the early 1920s, but a change in management,
the very prosperous years (with substantial growth in communities, railroads, oil and gas, and advanced farming methods)
saved the bank until 1933. The 1920s also saw a strong growth in
regional banking throughout the heartland of the dust bowl. In

fact, the bank at Pritchett, Colorado, resulted from the starting of a new town when the railroad arrived in the mid 1920s.

A check of thirty-seven newspapers, with an emphasis on the two western Oklahoma Panhandle counties, the two counties in southeastern Colorado, and the six southwestern Kansas counties where the dust bowl was most severe, provides some interesting data on the impact of the drought, depression, and governmental programs. The only newspaper in Cimarron County, the *Boise City News*, in 1933 lost most of its advertisements and reduced its number of pages by one-half. The paper's advertisements increased in 1934, and the paper returned to normal size. The five newspapers in Texas County, Oklahoma, reduced their size in 1933 but returned to normal in 1934. And the *Guymon News* became the *Guymon Daily News* in 1934. Thus the two western Oklahoma Panhandle counties showed a net gain of one daily during the depression.

In Prowers County, Colorado, seven newspapers were published in 1930. Anticipating a boom, the *Wiley Leader* began publication in 1927; by 1930 the hoped-for boom was gone and the paper stopped publication. At Lamar, Colorado, there were a daily and two weeklies publishing when the *Lamar Daily Times* began publication in 1930. The competition was too keen and the *Lamar Daily Times* folded in 1932. Thus one newspaper closed before the depression and drought struck the region and the other probably would have failed even if hard times had not occurred. Throughout the depression, the county was served by four weekly papers and one daily.

In Baca County, Colorado, the residents were served by five weekly newspapers in 1930. Of the five newspapers, one began publication in 1928 and two started publication in 1930. The *Two Buttes Sentinel*, one of the older papers, folded in 1933 as a direct result of the depression. The *Pritchett News* stopped publication in 1938 and the Springfield *Democrat-Herald*, the Springfield *Plainsman*, and the *Walsh Tab* merged in 1939. By 1938 prosperity, resulting from an increase in farm production, improved rainfall, and better business conditions, was returning to the region; however, in the late 1930s the federal government was attempting to depopulate the region in order to turn it back to grass. And Baca County was one of the prime targets for the government's depopulation efforts. The closing of the *Pritchett*

News and the merger of the other newspapers was the result of governmental activities rather than of drought or depression conditions.

In the six dust bowl counties of Kansas, twelve newspapers were examined for publication dates. Two papers, the Elkhart *Messenger* and the Grant County *New Era*, closed in 1932 and 1933 as a result of the depression. In Seward County the Kismet *Klipper* moved to Liberal in 1931 and became the *Southwest Tribune*, which continued publication through the dust bowl period. The weekly Liberal *News* became the *Southwest Daily Times* in 1935. At Hugoton in Stevens County, the *Ad-Viser* began publication on June 1, 1934, but failed to establish itself and stopped publication on May 17, 1935. In Morton County the *Elkhart Tri-State News* and the *Morton County Farmer* merged in 1937. In one of the last publications of the *Morton County Farmer*, the editor bemoaned the fact that the federal government had ended relief programs and forced several residents to abandon their homes and the region. In Grant County, the *Grant County Republican* and the *Ulysses News* merged in 1937.[13]

The leading newspapers in Beaver County, Oklahoma, and Ochiltree, Hansford, Sherman, Dallam, and Hartley counties, Texas, and Union County, New Mexico, all showed a sharp decrease in size and advertisements in 1933 but recovered in 1934. Only one of the papers, the *Dalhart Texan*, was a daily.

The overall view of the papers demonstrates some interesting patterns. The closing of newspapers occurred during two time periods: 1932–33, when all the publications were hard-pressed, and 1937–39, when economic and drought conditions were improving but the federal government was establishing its land-use program. Between these two periods of closing papers, two newspapers became dailies, which gave the eighteen-county area four dailies in addition to the daily city papers from Amarillo, Texas, and Pueblo, Colorado. The *Guymon Daily News* increased its publications in the community that was popularly identified as the very center of the dust bowl, and that carried the connotations of poverty and mass migration.

The financial conditions in the dust bowl were further reflected in the receipts of the postal service (Table 5.2).

Money order receipts for 1936 were $46,612.98. A year later

the receipts were \$47,996.69.[14] And at Perryton, postal "receipts for 1937 were \$12,667.60 against \$11,983.67 in 1936. This figure does not include money order fees."[15]

TABLE 5.2
Annual Postal Receipts at Spearman, Texas, 1929–38

Year	Price	Year	Price
1929	\$7,487.00	1934	\$5,685.19
1930	6,744.50	1935	5,227.82
1931	5,269.62	1936	6,280.63
1932	4,900.53	1937	6,330.49
1933	4,332.11	1938	6,609.57

If economic conditions in the heartland of the dust bowl were as severe as generally indicated by the national news media and the federal government during the years 1935, 1936, and 1937, and as is commonly accepted by scholars, the postal receipts, newspapers, and banks should reflect the poverty and mass migration. But that is not the case.

Let us explore the extent of the depression and drought in terms of mass migration. A check of farming community post offices in the Oklahoma Panhandle shows that in Beaver County five post offices closed in the 1920s, none in the 1930s, and two in the 1940s; in Cimarron County four post offices closed in the 1920s, three in the 1930s, and one in the 1940s; in Texas County one post office closed in the 1920s, four in the 1930s, and none in the 1940s. Of the seven post offices closed during the 1930s, three were discontinued or moved to other communities in 1930 and 1931 as a result of the construction of the Liberal-Amarillo branch of the Rock Island Railroad. The post office at Wilkins in Cimarron County was discontinued in 1930 as a result of railroad construction, which shifted the community center. Of the twenty post offices discontinued between 1920 and 1940, only three closed during the years of depression and dust storms. These three may have been closed as a result of improved transportation (which, as noted above, was the reason for the consolidation of the First State Bank of Texline, Texas, and the Farmers and Stockmens Bank of Clayton, New Mexico) and farming technology rather than of drought and depression.[16]

In the six southwestern Kansas counties, sixteen post offices closed between 1920 and 1950. Of the total number, twelve closed in the 1920s. Feterita, in Stevens County, had a turbulent history. It was closed in 1920, reopened in 1922, and closed again in 1937. The only other post office to close during the 1930s was Irene in Hamilton County. One post office closed in the 1940s. The pattern of post office closings resulted from changes in technology, i.e., railroad construction and automobiles, rather than from drought and depression.[17]

Extensive research of the Oklahoma Panhandle newspapers and other sources failed to reveal a single farming community school that closed during the drought and depression. Knowledgeable teachers and residents of Texas County recall the closing of rural schools during the consolidation period from 1928 to 1931 and more schools were consolidated during the 1940s, but, to their recollection, there were no rural schools closed during the depression. Surely, if there was a mass migration from the dust bowl, as has generally been believed, several of the one-room schools would have gone out of business. But this does not appear to be the case.

In fact, the available school records suggest that enrollment was stable or growing. The sizes of the graduating classes at the Hardesty School were surprisingly uniform: in the years 1932, 1933, and 1934, twelve students graduated annually. During the years 1935, 1936, and 1937, the senior classes had eight students, sixteen students, and eleven students, respectively. In 1938 the senior class had twelve students and in 1939 ten scholars completed high school. The research of Kathryn A. Sexton on Panhandle A & M College reveals that enrollment increased at the college, although the high-school portion of the institution was discontinued in the spring of 1935. By the end of the dirty thirties, 835 students were enrolled at Panhandle A & M College—a figure competitive with enrollment after thirty-six years of general prosperity.[18]

Let us turn our attention to agri-business to see if this segment of dust bowl life displayed symptoms of mass migration from the region. In the major commercial communities, three or more large elevators were found and numerous smaller elevators were located in the smaller towns and at railroad sidings; all the elevators survived the drought and depression. A new elevator was built at Campo, Colorado, in 1937, and another was built at Texhoma in 1939. Other elevators were enlarged and improved in 1939.[19]

Although the cattle industry suffered during the 1930s, the decade was marked more by a shift in emphasis rather than by a decrease in livestock raising. G. W. Cafky opened the Beaver Livestock Sale in 1933. Although the first years were difficult, by 1938 the Sale was firmly established and doing a profitable business under the same ownership and auctioneer. The sales rings at Dalhart, Texas, and Clayton, New Mexico, became more important to the economy of the five-state area during this same period.[20]

The success of the sale barns reflects the shift from a heavy reliance on cow-calf operations to a greater emphasis on yearlings. Calves were safely fed on winter wheat. But the chemical composition and plant activities often caused cows to abort their calves. Weaners were purchased in the fall and were run on winter wheat until spring, when they were sold, if the market was right. If the market was not good, or if the wheat did not appear to be making for a good harvest, the farmer would continue to graze the fields until the cattle could be moved to grass pasture or sold on an improved market. This gave the farmers and stockmen more diversification than they had if they raised only wheat or tried to raise stock and wheat as two different operations. Because livestock changed owners more often in the yearling business, the demand for sales rings increased. The new livestock trucking industry became more important.

Even in severe drought years, several thousand yearlings were run on wheat. In 1936, over 20,000 yearlings were on wheat in Hartley and Dallam counties. There were several thousand more yearlings and sheep on wheat in Sherman, Hansford, and Ochiltree counties, Texas, as well as in Beaver and Texas counties, Oklahoma. The importance of the yearling business increased as the drought ran its course and markets improved.[21]

The farm implement industry was an important aspect of agri-business that can be examined to determine the depth of the depression and amount of permanent abandonment during the dust bowl. It was noted in an earlier chapter that the number of tractors and combines increased in Kansas during the 1930s. In the *Ochiltree County Herald* of March 18, 1937, the Perryton Implement Company named 85 farmers who had purchased 105 John Deere tractors in the past thirty months. Those thirty months spanned the worst harvest years experienced during the dust bowl. Yet, obviously, some farmers could afford tractors. The Perryton Implement Company was only one of three implement dealers in the city.

The headlines of the *Ochiltree County Herald* for March 11 read: "Building Construction Activity Now At Highest Peak Since Slump Hit Perryton."[22] The list of firms carrying on building included food stores, gas stations, and implement companies. The North Plains Implement Company built a new warehouse and office building, the Ellis Grain Company expanded its warehouse for J. I. Case implements, and Perryton Implement Company constructed a new storage building. The growth of the implement business was not peculiar to Ochiltree County; it occurred across the entire dust bowl. It was slower, however, in Baca County, Colorado, and Morton County, Kansas.[23]

The myth of absolute poverty and mass emigration in the dust bowl is further deflated by checking the sales of new cars and the legitimate vacations that were taken by the people who lived in the stricken region. Two months before the dust bowl became a prime area for news stories in 1935, the *Guymon Daily News* reported that the three local car dealers had sold thirty-seven late model cars and twenty-five prospective buyers were awaiting the arrival of the new cars before completing their purchase. In 1935 Nash Brothers at Guymon opened a Pontiac dealership. A year later the firm added GMC pickups to the business. There were also new car dealers at Texhoma and Hooker, Oklahoma, in 1935, which gave the county at least five dealerships for a population of ten to twelve thousand. Every leading community in the eighteen counties had at least one car dealer, and the larger trade centers of Liberal, Guymon, Dalhart, Spearman, Perryton, and Lamar had two or more dealers. Someone had to be buying new cars in order for them all to stay in business. At Elkhart, Kansas, the Chevrolet dealership closed between 1934 and 1938; when it was reopened it gave the town of approximately twelve hundred people three new car agencies. A further indication of new car sales was the record for 1937 in the Oklahoma Panhandle. In that year Beaver County residents purchased 212 new cars; Cimarron County citizens bought 146; and Texas County buyers purchased 311.[24]

To cover items of local interest, the Beaver *Herald-Democrat* reported extensive vacations taken by residents of the community. Under the heading, "Beaver People Are Restless," the paper provided a lengthy list of names and destinations of people who had traveled extensively during the months between school terms.[25] Since these trips were taken during the months of few dust storms and the sojourners returned for the new school term, they cannot be considered refugees fleeing to safety, nor can they be classified as people at the absolute subsistence level.

Another indication of the financial conditions in the dust bowl is land values. The Kansas State University bulletin, *Trends in Land Values in Kansas*, points out: "Land values declined more in eastern Kansas than in western Kansas from the high in 1920 to 1940, . . ."[26] And the recovery in land values after the depression was much better in western Kansas than the other two sections of the state.

To understand the history of the dust bowl, it is necessary to keep in mind that the region had two frontier settlement and development patterns occurring simultaneously. One frontier was based on farming, the other on oil and gas development. The early years of the depression were extremely hard on the petroleum industry, which had, of all things, a vast surplus of production. During these years many oil companies went broke and failed to pay their leases. In February 1932, Argus Production Company began dropping several leases in Morton County, Kansas. As the *Morton County Farmer* observed, "Farmers Are Alarmed At Prospect Of Having To Do Without Rental Revenue."[27] The leases that were dropped were not in proven areas of production. The same process was followed by other companies throughout the eighteen counties.

Although the depression sharply restricted gas and oil development, such development never entirely stopped. In 1932 Shamrock Oil and Gas Corporation purchased the Apache Refinery at Sunray, Texas, and in 1933 a gasoline plant was built in Moore County. In Kansas on February 9, 1934, the *Morton County Farmer* reported that, "Leases For Gas And Oil Again Being Written Here." Later that summer the Chenault well near Guymon began producing ten million cubic feet of natural gas per day, and Phillips and Skelly oil companies built two gasoline plants in Moore County, Texas. The drilling and leasing activities increased in 1935. The completion of a gas well in Grant County, Kansas, by the Kuhn Brothers, and the starting of construction of a $10,000 transmission line by McNab Oil Company, ushered in a new era of oil and gas development.[28]

The gas and oil business boomed in 1936. On a 40,000-acre lease south of Springfield, Colorado, a test well was drilled, and another test was completed in Stanton County, Kansas. In southern Union County, New Mexico, the Olsen Drilling Company made the Zurich test on a large lease, while the Gypsy Oil Company assembled two leases in the northern part of the county and began drilling a test well near Guy. In northern Hansford County, Texas, and southern Texas County, Oklahoma, Charles Hitch and James P. Pierson assembled two blocks of land and began test drilling. To the northwest of the Pierson test, Cities Service Company assembled 122 sections (square miles) in a leased block and began thirty-five test wells. Out in Cimarron County, Oklahoma, Joe Williams assembled a 150,-000-acre tract for testing. Large tracts of Sherman County, Texas, were leased. Although all the leasing and tests stirred up a lot of excitement and provided many farmers with needed cash, the big play was at Sunray, Texas, in Moore County.[29]

"Development In Sunray Oil Field Hits New Boom Record," said the January 18, 1936, headlines of the *Dalhart Texan*. "Two Carbon Black Plants Bring 600 Families to Area." Phillips Petroleum Company was starting work on thirty wells, Anderson & Kerr were completing fourteen wells, and Shamrock Oil and Gas Company and Sunray Oil Company were drilling one well each. By early spring Continental Carbon Company began construction on a large carbon black plant located between Sunray and Dumas, Texas. The plant was completed and began operation in 1937. Apparently the second carbon black plant was not constructed at this time. In June 1936, the Illinois Zinc Company began construction of a smelter between Dumas and Sunray that employed over 100 men. The plant operated only a short time, however, before it was closed by a strike, and it remained closed until 1940 when the American Zinc Company of Illinois began operating the facility.[30]

The Panhandle Natural Gas Field joined the Hugoton Natural Gas Field in northern Moore and Hutchinson counties, Texas. Combined, the two fields began north of the Arkansas River in Kansas and ended south of the South Canadian River in Texas. The Panhandle Field stretched roughly east and west through large portions of Hartley, Moore, Potter, Hutchinson, Carson, Gary, and Wheeler counties, Texas; smaller parts of the field were in Oldham and Collingsworth counties. In 1936, in the Panhandle Field some 475 oil wells, 159 gas wells, and 31 dry wells (for a total of 665 wells) were drilled. With all the excitement in the north central Texas Panhandle, many families from surrounding counties began to move in.[31]

At Sunray a critical housing shortage developed. At Texhoma, Oklahoma, there was an exodus of many businesses; most relocated thirty-eight miles south at Sunray. A critical housing shortage also occurred at Dumas, Texas, where people were living in chicken houses and anything else they could find. The population of Dumas took a tremendous jump.[32] There was a general increase of business and employment at Dumas, Stinnett, Borger, Pampa, and other leading communities of the Panhandle Field.

While the oil and gas industry was breathing new life into the economy of the southern High Plains, the Rock Island and the Santa Fe railroads began extensive improvements and construction. In 1936, the Santa Fe started construction of 111 miles of line from Boise City, Oklahoma, through Springfield to Las Animas, Colorado. During the two years of construction, hundreds of men and teams were employed to build the bridges and roadbed. While the Santa Fe was building a new line, the Rock Island started an improvement program that included extensive work on the line between Dalhart, Texas, and Liberal, Kansas. And, north of Liberal, the railroad spent $1,500,000 on the construction of a steel bridge over the Cimarron River Valley. When the bridge was completed in the summer of 1939, it was over 1,320 feet long and stood more than 110 feet above the river. Long cuts over sixty feet deep were carved through the hills along the valley to provide approaches to the bridge. Hundreds of men and machines were steadily employed in this construction.[33]

The gas and oil play continued in the Panhandle Field through 1937, and developments in other fields and pools sharply increased. On January 14, the *Texhoma Times* reported extensive leasing of land in the Oklahoma counties just east of the Panhandle. To the west, new test wells were being made at Conlen, Texas, and on the C. Hurley-Crawford well near Dalhart. The biggest news came in April, when it was confirmed that Panhan-

dle Eastern Pipeline Company was definitely going to build a
$35,000,000 pipeline from the dust bowl to Detroit. To supply
the needed natural gas, numerous new wells were necessary.
Several sections were leased to provide access to the needed
gas. On July 29, the *Texhoma Times* reported that "Oil and Gas
Leases Will Pay Texas County Land Owners Over $400,000 Per
Year."

As part of their development, Panhandle Eastern built a large
gasoline plant at Kismet, Kansas. The new plant was designed to
process approximately five railroad tankcars of gasoline per day. The
new plant nearly doubled the new taxable property in Seward
County and employed a permanent force of forty-seven men.[34]

Panhandle Eastern was not alone in expanding its operations.
Among the major companies, Republic Natural Gas, which had
been organized two years earlier, began expanding its operations
and so did Northern Natural Gas and Cities Service. Among the
lesser companies that became more active were Central Gas
Utilities, Argus Pipe Line Company, Liberal Gas Company,
Peerless Carbon Black Company, and Tri-County Gas Company.
Tri-County Gas Company put in a small gas line to Scott City,
Kansas, where a refinery was built. South of Ulysses, Kansas, a
small carbon blank plant was constructed. The American Association of Petroleum Geologists reported that during 1937 some 307
wells in Finney, Grant, Haskell, Kearney, Morton, Seward, and
Stevens counties, Kansas, Texas County, Oklahoma, and Hansford County, Texas, were producing 2,277,071,000 cubic feet of
natural gas. Republic Natural Gas, which had 91 wells when it
was organized, and had added more by 1937, was not included
in the report. Neither were the natural gas wells in Sherman
County, Texas, which, if included, would bring the total to over
400 wells.[35]

Oil and gas exploration was not limited to the Panhandle and
Hugoton fields. In 1937, deep tests were made in Cimarron and
Beaver counties, Oklahoma, Ochiltree County, Texas, and Hamilton County, Kansas. The only successful deep test was in
Ochiltree County. The Norris No. 1 had a strong flow of gas, but
was capped in April 1938. Each of these counties had to wait
until after World War II, and especially until the 1950s, before
profitable amounts of gas and oil were discovered; however,
much of the land received lease rents from the 1930s.[36]

With the increase in development in natural gas, several petroleum firms increased existing divisional or regional headquarters, or established new offices. These offices, primarily located at Liberal, Kansas, had large staffs of clerical, administrative, and scientific personnel. As a result of the headquartering of firms, Liberal became more cosmopolitan, as well as more prosperous.

An interesting side story to the development of oil and gas occurred in Union County, New Mexico. The test wells in 1936 and 1937 were dry holes. But in the Bueyeros Valley, five carbon dioxide wells were drilled and a plant built near the wells with the necessary railroad spur. By June 1937, the region had become a leading producer of dry ice. Near the dry ice plant, miners began working the potash deposit in the hills.[37]

The general reversal of the national economy in 1937 and 1938 slowed the pace of gas and oil development in the heartland of the dust bowl. Nonetheless, development continued at a steady rate. A controversy in 1938 between Republic Natural Gas and the Kansas Corporation Commission resulted in the company moving most of its drilling operations to the Oklahoma Panhandle, where several wells and feeder pipelines were drilled and built. Meanwhile, Texaco and other companies completed extensive drilling and leasing operations in Sherman County, Texas. During 1939 drilling and development of natural gas and oil continued in the dust bowl.[38]

Several years after the Hugoton Field opened, Malcolm A. Furbush attempted to recount the history of the field for the Kansas Geological Society. His record showed 277 producing wells in southwestern Kansas at the end of 1939—an increase of 137 wells between 1934 and 1940. Among the chief purchasers of gas at the well head were "Cities Service Gas Company, Northern Natural Gas Company, Panhandle Eastern Pipe Line Company, Colorado Interstate Gas Company, Kansas-Nebraska Natural Gas Company, Hugoton Production Company, and United Carbon Company."[39] The figures in Furbush's report on gas development for 1937 were well below those in Clenon C. Hemsell's report in the *Bulletin of the American Association of Petroleum Geologists*. Neither man includes Republic's production in his report. None of the reports include the entire spectrum of the field. But, it is clear that substantial petroleum development did occur and its development in the heartland of the dust bowl was of major importance to regional economic activities.

The general economy of the dust bowl was far better than portrayed in government reports and news articles of the 1930s; however, at the individual and community level the impact of the depression varied sharply. While describing how people survived the dust bowl days, M. D. Minor commented: "They were fortunate in many cases to have royalties from gas and oil which had made its appearance in 1926. Others hired out to the oil and pipeline companies in various capacities to sweat out the coming of better farming years."[40]

A good example of those who survived thanks to gas and oil royalties was Alex Kraft. He arrived in Texas County during the early years of the century and worked, suffered, and saved until, by 1928, he could afford a large home on his five quarters farm. But by the Christmas of 1933, his farm was in a desperate condition. During those trying years Alex, who refused to give up his draft horses for advanced farming methods, went into debt and would probably have lost the farm if the development of the gas industry had not saved him. In the natural gas industry only one well is drilled on each section of land, and all the mineral right owners in the section receive royalties from the well. In 1937, two natural gas wells were drilled on sections of land and from these Alex received royalties. With this money Alex paid his debts and made several needed improvements on the farm before he and his wife, who were getting on in years, retired comfortably at Hooker. Here their last years were spent in leisure without the worries of making ends meet.[41]

Cecil Grable, who farmed with his father near Eva, Oklahoma, recalls how the lease money of a dollar per acre made it possible for them to pay their taxes and purchase a few necessary items for the house and the farm. Although no wells were drilled on their property during the 1930s, the lease money helped the family through the lean years.[42]

Not everyone was as fortunate as the Krafts and Grables. Croatian immigrant Bartol Modrick brought his family to a farm near Elmwood in Beaver County, Oklahoma, to build a new life and pursue a new dream. Mr. Bartol died in the flu epidemic of 1919. And during the dirty thirties the family lost their home and farm. But the Modrick family was made of tough material, and they banded together to build another future on the high plains.[43]

James Rueben "Tom" Grice moved his family to the new land during the early years of settlement. He wanted to escape the poverty of the poor whites in the mountains of Georgia. On a farm near Guymon he worked and built for the future. Grice failed to grasp the importance of the new technology and did not get a tractor until 1929. The tractor soon broke down and he was caught holding the bag when the bottom fell out of the wheat market. His place was too small and his mules no match for the onslaught of the drought and depression. Just when the depression and the drought years were near their end and a brighter future was in sight, James Grice lost his farm. But the Grice family were also of hardy pioneering stock. During the 1940s, and even during the very severe drought years of the 1950s, the family worked to improve their lot. Neither the Modrick nor the Grice families had the benefit of oil and gas leases to help cushion the shock of the dust bowl, nor did they have the fortune to have a royalty check to provide for the old folk's retirement.[44]

The weather during the drought was fickle, and spread its rewards and punishment unequally across the dust bowl. The only year that all the counties of the dust bowl came close to having an absolute failure of all their crops was in 1933. In the Texhoma area, farmers brought only 200 bushels of wheat to the elevators. In 1934, they brought more than 200,000 bushels in. That same year the farmers near Hooker failed to have a crop. In 1935, the Hooker area farmers raised nearly 500,000 bushels of wheat and the Texhoma farmers had a very short crop. The difference in areas of crop and market value of wheat often determined the severity of the depression on individual farmers.

Within a community's trade area there were sharp variances in crops. The *Texhoma Times* often commented that the railroad tracks were the dividing line between wheat and no wheat. Farmers south of the tracks had much better crops than those to the north. One old-timer near Forgan, Oklahoma, recalled how his fields completely failed one year because they did not receive moisture from a couple of showers, but his neighbor across the fence had a small crop because the rains fell on his land. Another farmer near Felt, Oklahoma, watched his crop destroyed by hail, while his neighbor's field was spared.[45]

Nature was not the only force that shaped the destiny of residents of the dust bowl. The revolution in farming, resulting from tractors, combines, trucks, and one-way plows and other technological improvements, meant that many hired men were no longer needed. It also made the small farm uneconomical to operate. The adjustment of the region to these changes was in full swing when the depression and the drought struck. For those farmers who had adjusted to the new technology, the throes of the hard years were not as difficult as for those who were still in the process of coming to terms with the future.

Technology was ringing another major change in the heartland of the dust bowl. When discussing the consolidation of the Texline bank with a bank in Clayton, the editor of the *Clayton News* wrote: "The mode of transportation and the oiled and paved highways no longer required the small bank in every town."[46] With cars and good roads, people were driving to the larger towns to do their business. People who had cast their lot with the smaller communities were losing trade during a period when they could ill afford the loss.

This was well-illustrated in 1937 when the Oklahoma Supreme Court ruled in favor of constructing a large carbon black plant in Texas County. Members of the Guymon Chamber of Commerce had invited the construction of the plant on a tract of land three miles northeast of town. Before the year was out, construction of the plant was underway and local merchants were preparing to serve the permanent employees of the plant.

Just before construction of the carbon black plant began at Guymon, the editor of the *Texhoma Times* wrote:

> The drilling of two wells west of Goodwell is not going to fill up what few houses there are in Texhoma, or the empty business houses. . . . People usually go where they are invited. That is true the world over, and right now when oil companies, or other companies might be seeking a location, would be a good time to invite them to cast their lot in Texhoma.[47]

Texhoma failed to attract new business and suffered a great deal more than Guymon.

The general impression of the dust bowl is that the area was rampant with poverty and misery, far above the national average. The generalization of complete poverty, misery, and mass migration, however, does not apply to the eighteen counties in the heartland of the dust bowl. The region did not plunge into the depression until nearly two years after it struck the East. In fact, much of its prosperity and development occurred after the depression had struck the eastern cities. By exploring the many aspects of dust bowl business life, it becomes obvious that economic activities in the heartland were no worse, and in many respects better, than in other areas of the nation.

When the nation's economy suffered severe set backs in 1937–38, *Nation's Business* map on the nation's business conditions showed southwestern Kansas suffering the largest reverses of the eighteen dust bowl counties. Nevertheless, during the twenty-four-month period, southwestern Kansas had only six months when business conditions were below the national average. The maps of business also show that the Oklahoma Panhandle had thirty-four months of average and above-average business activities during the four year period between 1934 and 1938. Of the fourteen months that were below average, ten occurred between the harvest of 1934 and the harvest of 1935. The maps suggest that the worst of the depression was over by the time the nation discovered the dust bowl.[48]

The dust bowl had its advantages and shortcomings, but in the main, the region's economic life fits into the general trends of the national depression. Times were "hard" everywhere.

6

Countercurrents

From the settlers' point of view the Great Plains offered new hope. On the windswept, dust-blown land, pioneers developed a new farming science to bring man and climate into harmony. Pioneers of the urban industrial frontier extracted gas and oil from under the earth's surface. Advancements in technology made it possible to abandon the subsistence standard of living that had historically been the lot of settlers of new lands. The new commercial farming elevated the living standards, and created a strong desire for further improvement. The boom years that resulted from technological advancements, improved transportation systems, new sources of wealth, and profitable wheat crops gave the residents of the dust bowl a sense of pride and security. The fact that the depression did not hit the five-state area of Kansas, Colorado, New Mexico, Texas, and Oklahoma until two years after the stock market crash had paralyzed other regions, reinforced the plainsmen's conviction that the country was a great place to live.

Although the years from 1932 to 1939 were hard, there was always a ray of hope. After the wheat harvest of 1935, economic conditions in the heartland of the dust bowl greatly improved. Residents were very much aware of the tough conditions outside the region. The majority of America's Next Year People wanted to remain in the area they called home, a region they were sure was as good as any found in the United States. "They were in no

106

mood to abandon their land," commented the Great Plains Committee. "They were willing to do all that was humanly possible to save it."[1]

Among drought veterans there was a keen awareness of danger, but a confidence of a "good outcome." Those farmers without long years of experience were inclined to panic and give up hope. Farmers and stockmen, veterans or novices were fully aware of the arduous struggle necessary to achieve success, and in the end it was the weather that determined success or failure.[2]

With an acute awareness of man's frailties and dependence on conforming to the whims of nature, settlers of the Great Plains developed their culture—a culture in which, Walter Prescott Webb believed, "the dominant truth which emerges is expressed in the word *contrast*."[3] The contrast was between eastern, humid, tree-covered, small-farm agricultural society, and western, semiarid, treeless, large-farm agricultural society. It was further differentiated by large industrial cities and small agricultural cities. The contrast between the ideas of the people living in the heartland of the dust bowl and the impressions of eastern policy makers collided, and made history turbulent during the dust bowl era. To understand the forces causing the turbulence, it is necessary to define the eastern thinking that was developing simultaneously with western settlement.

At the time of the Louisiana Purchase in 1803, Thomas Jefferson began developing a land-use policy, which included reorganization of society and resettlement. Land was to be purchased from the Indians and opened to white settlers. The natives were to be encouraged to give up their hunting culture and become farmers, resulting in more intensive use of the soil and reducing the amount of acreage they needed. In order to gain control of the Indians' economy, federal traders were to drive out competitive traders, who might excite the natives or distract them from the government design. In the area west of the Mississippi, Indians were to be resettled under government protection and supervision. "In leading them to agriculture, to manufactures, and civilization; in bringing together their and our settlements, and in preparing them ultimately to participate in the benefits of our governments," wrote Jefferson, "I trust and believe we are acting for their greatest good."[4] Thus for the humanitarian reasons of improving a marginal culture and meeting the necessities of the greatest number for the greatest good, the Indians' use of land was to be reorganized, their culture remolded, and their place of residence changed. The end result was to be a happy integration of conflicting ways of life.[5]

By the mid 1820s, the backers of Indian Removal constituted a powerful force in the United States. The resettlement of the Indians was far from humane; however, proponents defended the process by arguing the necessity for proper land utilization and the superiority of a selected culture. When the Cherokee Nation opposed removal by appealing in court their property rights, recognized by treaty, the Supreme Court in the Cherokee Nation v. Georgia acknowledged that the United States had indeed treated with the Indians. But the court ruled that the Cherokee Nation was not independent. It was a domestic dependent nation. The Indians were in "a state of pupilage; their relation to the United States resembles that of a ward to his guardian. They look to our government for protection; rely upon its kindness and its power; appeal to it for relief to their wants; and address the president as their great father."[6] Thus the courts transferred land title, while establishing a condition of dependency on the federal government.

In 1834, the Indian Intercourse Act set aside land to which the Cherokee, Creek, Seminole, Choctaw, and Chickasaw tribes were removed. Once the Indians were resettled in Indian territory (the eastern part of present-day Oklahoma north of the Red River), the concept of agricultural zones was advanced. East of the Indian Territory was a broad zone where pioneers could develop farms. Along the eastern edge of Indian Territory were the "civilized" Indians, who worked the soil. To the west on the Great Plains were the "savage, wild" Indians who followed the grazing buffalo. Thus, the regions were defined not only geographically, but also according to cultural superiority and inferiority.

The approach of the frontier to the Choctaw Nation in the 1850s prompted Elias Rector, superintendent of Indian Affairs for the Southern Superintendency, candidly to explain:

> But necessity is the supreme law of nations. All along the Indian border the country is now populous, and the railroad will soon reach their frontier. Necessity will soon compel

the incorporation of their country into the Union, and before its stern requisitions every other consideration will give way, and even wrong find, as it ever does, in necessity its apology.[7]

The Dawes Severalty Act of 1887 formalized another system of land allocation and supervision of occupants. The Dawes Act was joined with the Cherokee Tobacco Case 1870 to deny the Indians their land title and force the opening of Oklahoma for settlement. The end result of the land use, resettlement, and social reorganization was a tragic period in the decline of Indian sovereignty.

These tragic events opened the way for advancement of the federal policy of developmental agriculture, i.e., increasing the number of farms and food production in order that the haunting fear of famine would be laid to rest. With the success of developmental agriculture came new problems, problems of overproduction, revolutionary advancements in technology, and shifting farm size. In 1936 the *Report of the Great Plains Drought Area Committee* recognized that "mistaken public policies have been largely responsible for the situation now existing." The committee believed "the federal government must do its full share in remedying the damage caused by a mistaken homesteading policy, by the stimulation of war-time demands which led to over-cropping and over-grazing and by encouragement of a system of agriculture which could not be both permanent and prosperous."[8]

The westward march of the frontier spawned a precedent that allowed the federal government to reorganize or remove a society, as well as two concepts that would play a major role in the formation of subsequent land-use policies. First, as already noted, the High Plains was viewed as a rich agricultural area by the settlers who resided there during the 1920s and 1930s. Second, traditionally, it was viewed as a grazing land fit only for a pastoral society. The connotations of the "Great American Desert," reported by Zebulon M. Pike, and repeated by Stephen H. Long and other travelers from well-watered regions, gave the Great Plains the reputation of being a sterile land. Although the desert concept was modified somewhat during the late nineteenth century, it never died. In the last quarter of the past century, cattle kingdoms ruled the Great Plains and fostered the romantic legend of the cowboy. The cowboy and rough rider had a special place in the folklore of the Roosevelt families, for without the Rough Riders, Theodore Roosevelt would probably not have become president of the United States. And Franklin D. Roosevelt was part heir to the legacy.

The western movement also spawned the myth of the "yeoman" farmer: a farmer who faithfully worked his homestead, while giving moral fiber to the nation and backbone to democracy, a farmer who lived in harmony with nature and had all his needs for food and shelter met. He was seen in myth as a contented person, not plagued by the adversities of the complex society.

The reality of the frontier farm life was one of want and poverty. Socially the farmer was often viewed as an ill-mannered, crude, uncultured backswoodsman. He was often treated as a second-class citizen, derogatorily called "white trash." He was a man who was often afflicted by hunger, disease, and hardship. Even the homesteads of 160 acres were intended to provide only a subsistence standard of living.[9]

With the engrained complexities of history, policy makers attempted to develop a new land-use system after World War I. During the war, the United States experienced a rare revolution: a food surplus. How many untold generations had wished to face the awesome problems of what to do with more food production than could be consumed by the nation? While the boom in agriculture continued during the 1920s, spurred on by a revolution in farming technology, agricultural leaders were concerned with the perplexing problems of this revolution. The per capita consumption of wheat and other cereal grains was decreasing. Census trends suggested that the nation's population was approaching its apex and the future demand for expanding agriculture seemed limited. The United States and other nations were flooding the world grain market. Unless something was done to control production, the rate of increase would soon place the surplus of agriculture beyond hope of any control.

As a result, the decade of the 1920s saw several farm programs put forward. The plans ranged from flooding the world market, to storing grain during good years and selling during bad years, to eliminating the middle men in the agri-business fields, to subsidies based on parity. One of the most extensive programs was the comprehensive land-use plan presented by Lewis C. Gray. "Its policy implications," Albert Z. Guttenberg claims, "were broad and far-ranging, ultimately involving every facet of American society."[10]

From the time Gray presented his plan in the *Yearbook of Agriculture 1923*, the Department of Agriculture took the lead in promoting and refining the program. Basically the program favored eastern, established farming over western, frontier farming. The plan called for the zoning of the agricultural districts according to soil, climate, population centers, historical development, cultural conditions, and recent changes in agricultural methods. Farming was to become more intensified around small, industrial communities. Societies were to be classified in terms of supermarginal, marginal, and submarginal.

In regions where submarginal societies and, of course, submarginal farms, were found, the people were to be resettled on subsistence homesteads. Surplus land would be returned to timber and grass for recreation, wild-life reserves, and livestock pasture. The frontiersman of the future was the farmer-laborer. The farmer-laborer was a person who worked on the farm part time and in a factory part time. The blight of the large city was to be solved by moving people to smaller industrial centers. Thus the city population would be decentralized into many suburbs. Acting as guardian of the people, the government would develop the scientific plan and enforce adherence.

The heartland of the dust bowl would cease being a farming region since it did not have the historical background, industrial possibilities, or long-standing population centers necessary to meet the requirements of a marginal society. The recent change from livestock raising to farming was viewed with disapproval by the scientific land-use planners of the 1920s and 1930s. The Christgau Bill, which never got beyond committee, was an effort to pass into law the rational land-utilization plan. Guttenberg believes, "At the heart of the bill was the amiable notion that flourished on both sides of the urban-rural border in the 1920s—that scientific land use planning, informed by progressive economic and ethical ideals, could be a cure-all for the nation's social, cultural, and economic ills."[11]

During the 1920s and early 1930s, several experiments were made to test various forms of Gray's rational land-utilization theory. And with the floor dropping from under farm prices, in 1930 the Department of Agriculture extended its efforts to establish a planned agriculture based on land use and social margin. The Department of Agriculture was convinced that

> much of the economic hardship suffered by farmers has been caused by too rapid expansion of the area devoted to farming. The eagerness of land-owning interests and selling agencies to induce farmers to occupy undeveloped areas, public encouragement to land settlement, and other influences have contributed to overrapid agricultural expansion in the country.[12]

While Secretary of Agriculture Arthur M. Hyde was questioning the wisdom of farm expansion and endorsing Gray's land-use plan, the farmers in the newly expanded area were sure they had found the right combination of climate, farming method, and crop to assure the success of their enterprise. In Baca County, Colorado, Tom Hopkin boasted: "We can produce wheat here cheaper than any other section of the United States, . . ." Hopkin enthusiastically endorsed the Great Plains and "since somebody has to raise wheat in the United States, we will be staying in the game."[13] Thus the proposed plan to stabilize agriculture by restricting land use, and promoting cultivated cropping near established communities where small industrial towns could flourish, was in direct conflict with the thinking of the farmers in the five-state area.

Franklin D. Roosevelt was a strong supporter of the land-utilization plan. His long-range agricultural plan included "allocating lands to their best use, moving farmers off of poor, submarginal acres onto better soil, and through decentralization of industry, to encourage millions of people to return from cities to villages and the countryside."[14] Roosevelt was enchanted with the myth of the abundant and wholesome life of the subsistence farmer.

> Country life to Roosevelt was a way out of the depression and a guarantee of permanent comfort. His persistent dream was of a wholesome existence for quantities of previously deprived city people, moved to healthful country surroundings, raising their own food, and earning some income

from employment in a nearby small factory. It would have been a return to the way of life in hamlets of their grand-parents' days."[15]

Apparently the promoters of the farmer-industrial laborer system were not aware of its shortcomings. In the heartland of the dust bowl, numerous small farmers had combined farming with nonfarm employment. Winter wheat, which did not need cultivating for weeds, was ideally suited for part-time farmers. The depression in agriculture and industry was especially harsh for the farmer who was on a farm too small to earn a decent living and who had no nonfarm employment available.

The plight of the farmer-industrial worker was not limited to the Great Plains. In Colorado's mountains, Routt County coal miners combined farming with mining. At the time Roosevelt took office, over one-third of the county's land had been sold for taxes. And the bulk of the farmer-industrial workers were out of a job and out of a farm.

Frank Freidel tells us: "Roosevelt as an imaginative idealist liked to think in terms of great national plans. Yet he was also a political realist who at each given point usually decided to opt for the possible, the enactable. Hence the immediate measures he came to propose were often no more than a segment or shadow of his grand schemes."[16] The Agricultural Adjustment Act of 1933 was a shadow of Roosevelt's grand scheme for agriculture.

After the AAA had wended its way through the legislative process, Roosevelt was prepared to take the next step in developing a land-use plan. He appointed the National Planning Board under the Public Works Administration in the Department of Interior. The chairman of the Land Planning Committee was M. L. Wilson, who had spent several years experimenting with resettlement while promoting the land-use plan. Director of the Land Section was Lewis C. Gray, the father of the land-use plan. Thus the committee had a built in bias at the outset. The Land Planning Committee of the National Planning Board published its report on December 1, 1934. The report claimed, "extensive areas of the Great Plains . . . must be classed as unsuited to sustained cultivated crops, and should therefore never have been plowed, but retained in grass for stock raising."[17]

Several months before the National Resources Board published its report, government buyers were purchasing land to return to grass. In February 1934, the Agricultural Adjustment Administration instituted a submarginal land purchase program under authority provided in the National Industrial Recovery Act. The purchase of land continued under the Emergency Relief Appropriations Act of 1935 and other programs.[18]

The passage of the Taylor Grazing Act in June 1934, was an important victory for the supporters of land-utilization planning. "More significantly," wrote Mary W. M. Hargreaves, the Taylor Grazing Act was "an expression of land-use planning, it marked acceptance of the view that livestock rather than agriculture utilization was to be the focus for future expansion of the Great Plains."[19] Professor Hargreaves is correct so far as the upper levels of government are concerned. But the folks in the heartland of the dust bowl entertained a difference of opinion.

The highly respected Great Plains soil scientist H. H. Finnell in 1934 took sharp issue with the supporters of turning the High Plains back to grass. "Recent agitation," wrote Finnell, "for the abandonment of the plains on the grounds the land is submarginal or even marginal are not founded on any knowledge of the actual potentialities of our resources nor of the technic of utilizing them." Finnell went on to say: "Putting the plains land under cultivation cannot be justly blamed for wind erosion. It should be in cultivation." The question as Finnell saw it was not one of cultivation or noncultivation, but rather of *how* the farmers cultivated what they did. "The blame, if any, rests on the unwitted neglect of certain factors necessary to the most profitable use of cultivated lands as such."[20]

A year earlier the residents of the heartland of the dust bowl had expressed their opposition to abandoning the region. The occasion was a statement by Secretary of Interior Harold Ickes. From Hooker, Oklahoma, the *Hooker Advance* told its readers: "Secretary Ickes' [suggestion] that citizens of the drouth-stricken area of the Oklahoma Panhandle be removed 'to more arable lands' brought a storm of protest over this *productive* plains country Sunday."[21] (Italics added) In southwestern Kansas, the *Morton County Farmer* angrily reported "that Secretary of Interior Ickes had announced that no federal relief projects would be allotted to the Panhandle of Oklahoma, and that he advised the people to get up and move out to more productive lands." The news report sarcastically concluded: "Relief projects of the Panhandle are to be again reviewed by the Department of Interior, and the chances are that even Ickes will take a different slant at the subject than he did before he found out that Oklahoma was one of the states."[22]

Clearly the federal government was moving in the direction of comprehensive land-use planning, which would return vast acreages to grass, change the region's economy to stock raising, and reorganize the society of the dust bowl. These changes were viewed as necessary to correct serious national problems. What were the problems to be corrected? What caused the difficulty? Federal spokesmen for the National Resources Board and the Great Plains Committee believed that dramatic measures were necessary to rebalance agriculture, stop the loss of topsoil to wind erosion, and provide a marginal standard of living.

These spokesmen saw several causes for overproduction and soil waste. As a result of the Homestead Act and its later amendments, they said, farm size was too small. Interestingly, the impact of technology in shifting requirements in farm size received only casual consideration. The Homestead Act was also faulted for failing to restrict and rationalize land settlement along the lines of a preconceived plan. Since wheat was in great surplus, the planners saw wheat production as a primary cause of the disaster facing Great Plains farmers. They also argued that Great Plains farmers used methods of farming adapted to humid areas, that farming practices were deeply ingrained in the peoples' mind, and that they could not adjust to change without drastic measures being applied. The system of private land ownership was viewed as another cause of the disaster that stalked the Great Plains, as was unstable tenure on farms, especially with tenant farmers.

Having satisfied themselves as to the nature and the cause of the problems confronting the dust bowl farmers, spokesmen for comprehensive land-use planning put forward several proposals for solving the crisis. They believed that the federal government should purchase several million acres of land—from submarginal farms, tax delinquent lands, and sparsely settled areas. The acquired lands were to be added to federal and state public domain. Direct federal control over further acreages was to be expanded by lease, contract, formation of grazing associations with private individuals, and expansion of grazing land under the Taylor Grazing Act.

Farm size was to be increased through "extension of credit under suitable restrictions."[23] The minimum size for a family farm was to be determined and demonstration farms established to instruct the farmers in proper farming methods. Because of the "suitable restrictions" clause, and other aspects of the land-use plan, little credit was extended to farmers in the heartland of the dust bowl to expand their farm holdings.

To handle the excess farm population, and to prevent further settlement in sparsely settled areas, federal planners proposed several programs. The surplus population was to be resettled on subsistence farms. States were to restrict funds for roads and other governmental services in frontier regions. Private real estate dealers were to be licensed and regulated. Zoning laws, which would restrict settlement patterns and cropping practices, were to be passed. The zoning laws were seen as a primary means of controlling many aspects of agriculture and they revealed the desire to establish soil conservation districts, which would control the farming and grazing practices of the individual farmers. The regulatory capstone was the removal of English Common Law rights for private ownership. Land was to be owned by the public at large, with the federal government becoming the primary administrator and watchdog of the public interest. The entire program was to be directed through a closely coordinated series of local, state, and federal agencies, and the farmers were to be placed in a condition of pupilage.

Although the *Report of the National Resources Board* did have a brief section on the importance of mechanical progress in agriculture (which recognized that technology had made it possible to farm new lands and that technology had drastically affected the size of the family farm), the Board did not attempt to control the impact of new implements on agriculture. The role that tractors, combines, trucks, and one-way plows had in causing the disaster in agriculture was not recognized by the land-use planners. One reason for this oversight was that the planners wanted to "be free to shape our agricultural policy in the direction of affecting a maximum economy of human labor in order to spare as much labor as possible for nonagricultural employment.

This would mean the adoption of all available mechanical and scientific methods in farming and the development of the most efficient types of farm organization." Maximum economic efficiency meant "elimination from farming of the numerous farm families now engaged in crude, self-sufficing systems of farming. It would probably make possible reducing the proportion of the population engaged in agriculture by perhaps one-third to one-half."[24] Thus the government planned to aid the small farmer by driving him from his land in the name of economic efficiency. Implied in the statements on technology was the recognition that mechanization of farming was making the small family farm submarginal. By accelerating technological development, more farms would become submarginal, and would compound the plight of the farmer.

There was another aspect to technology with which the comprehensive land-use planners did not come to grips. Webb points out: "What science and its servant, technology, did was speed up the rate at which resources already in existence could be utilized. In short, it speeded up the rate of destruction of the forests, the minerals, and the soils without creating any of these things."[25] Technology was the key to dry land farming, and so far as H. H. Finnell was concerned, technology was the key to reducing destruction by the wind to a more normal level.

Technology was a primary cause of the dilemma faced by dust bowl farmers. But federal administrators chose to look elsewhere for solutions. "Although crop failure, speculative expansion, absentee ownership, and depressed price levels were among the factors that precipitated the relief situation," wrote Assistant Federal Emergency Relief Administrator Corrington Gill, "the roots of the trouble obviously lay deep. . . . The frontier philosophy which assumed that the individual, if given complete freedom will pursue an economic course that was to the best interests of society, led to the present dilemma of stranded communities, bankrupt farmers, and widespread unemployment."[26]

The federal leaders had come up with a far-reaching program that would drastically change the lives of Americans. The residents of the heartland of the dust bowl were key figures in the plan. How was the scheme to be carried out in light of the dust bowl farmers' desire to remain on the land and maintain their culture?

Shortly after meeting with Roosevelt and getting the go ahead on developing a comprehensive agricultural program, Rexford G. Tugwell compared notes with Secretary of Agriculture Henry A. Wallace. "Tugwell reported, 'We both feel that the greatest need we have is for more trees and more legumes and he is going to try to find a feasible way for holding out a bait to farmers for this long-run improvement.' "[27]

The program for turning the heartland of the dust bowl back to grass was to be achieved by holding out bait to the farmers. Roosevelt's removal of George Peek as head of the Agricultural Adjustment Administration in December 1933, and the institution of the Jerome Frank-Rexford Tugwell faction of the Department of Agriculture to control the AAA, gave supporters of a strictly planned agriculture control of the crucial policy-making posts. They were ready to start fishing in the troubled waters of the dust bowl. Like the Indians before them, dust bowl farmers were tempted with removal, improvement in civilization, and a shift in land ownership.

7

Uncle Sam's Relief

A young Morton County, Kansas, farmer set out to follow in his father's footsteps as an honest tiller of the soil. To get started, Bud leased a small place east of Elkhart, Kansas, and borrowed some money from the Federal Land Bank to purchase a team of horses, a few milk cows, and some chickens. He and his family struggled through the early years of the depression by marketing broomcorn, cream, and eggs. Although they could provide for their immediate needs, the debt could not be paid. When the Resettlement Administration was making its first large land purchases in Morton County in 1935, the Federal Land Bank foreclosed on Bud. Although he was able to market a ton of broomcorn, the federal government took all but twenty dollars of the gross receipts, as well as his team of horses, cows, and chickens. After one quasi-governmental agency removed the tenant from the land, another federal agency purchased the property for its experiment in improving the quality of life and the ecology on the High Plains.[1]

Left with twenty dollars, Bud moved his family to Tulsa, Oklahoma, where he lived with a brother for a year without finding steady employment. In 1936 he moved the family back to Elkhart, where he worked at various jobs and on relief projects. For Bud the depression and the government foreclosure and land purchase left a bitter memory. His dream for a better tomorrow died in 1935 and there was nothing to replace it except despair.

The relief work did, however, play a major role in Bud's ability to care for his family after his return from Tulsa. The story of the young farmer represents the mixed blessing of government relief and land-use planning experienced by many people in the dust bowl.

Numerous farmers like Bud hoped to get a start in farming by leasing a small tract of land. Most of these moved often in their effort to get the right combination of soil, crop, and price that would provide the stepping stones to ownership of their own farm. Although the tenants moved often, the vast majority were concerned with preserving the soil. "Tenancy in its present form," explained the McMillan Report on Baca County 1936, "is neither a cause nor effect of land misuse, . . ."[2] In addition to the tenant farmers who were wanting their own land, there were the small landowners. Many had only recently made the shift from tenant to landowner: with the construction of the railroads in Kansas, Colorado, Oklahoma, and Texas during the 1920s, farmers purchased small farms with prospects of providing a good life. Usually these farmers raised milk cows, pigs, and chickens. Often the cash crop came from a small field of wheat, sorghum, or broomcorn. Family income was supplemented by nonfarm employment. Too few small farmers were able to take advantage of tractors, combines, one-way plows, and trucks. Simultaneously, the forces of technology were making the small farm obsolete. During the depression the small farmers were reduced to a low level of poverty with nowhere to go to find a better life.

By the time the Agricultural Adjustment Act of 1933 became law, farm conditions were desperate. The act marked a new direction in American farm policy; however, the bill in its final form was an omnibus bill, which provided the secretary of agriculture with the power to employ "production control, allotment, export dumping, stabilization holding, co-operative control, differential prices—in fact, practically any or all of the devices included in the principal [farm] relief bills and acts which had preceded it."[3] After the bill was passed, its meaning was uncertain. To satisfy the various competing agricultural factions, the preamble was a "declaration of emergency" followed by a section "to establish and maintain such balance between the production and consumption of agricultural commodities, and such marketing conditions. . . ."[4] It seemed, thus, to be only an emergency bill, which would end after the crisis has ended, while paradoxically continuing to maintain a balance.

Although the AAA contained many paradoxes, federal agricultural leaders soon interpreted the law to include extensive land-utilization planning. They believed that "land settlement remained chaotic; public agencies did not try to coordinate the farm uses with the nonfarm uses of land and did not check wrong land uses. It was impossible to leave matters in that stage after the passage of the Agricultural Adjustment Act." The federal men argued: "New uses had to be discovered for land withdrawn from production for export, submarginal farming had to be discouraged, and crop adjustment had to be coordinated with land utilization in general. . . . Land planning became an integral part of agricultural planning and, for the first time in our history, inspired vigorous action."[5] With the passage of the bill, Secretary of Agriculture Henry A. Wallace began developing a farm policy for wheat.

By the summer of 1933, farmers across the nation were asked to join the program. Soon, county committees were recording the individual farmer's previous three years of wheat production to determine each person's allotment. The new program received strong support from the dust bowl farmers, although there was a tremendous amount of confusion over the size of payment for domestic allotment (as prorated by the number of participants in the program), over the prorated domestic consumption, and over methods of measuring a field. The question of who would receive payment, the tenant or the property owner, threatened the program. It was soon decided that payment for allotments was made on previous lease contracts. If the renter paid a cash rent and was entitled to the full crop, he received the full allotment payment. By autumn, most of the administrative snags were worked out and the farmers began signing wheat contracts.[6]

The largest wheat producing county in the dust bowl, Texas County, Oklahoma, had a thee-year average production of 5,352,126 bushels of wheat. From this was derived an allotment of 2,889,184 bushels, or 54 percent of the average production. "The compensation payments," stated a government news release, "[were] based upon these individual allotments. The amount of payments which [was] made depend[ed] upon the number of wheat growers who [took] advantage of the opportunity to participate in the wheat program." After all the administrative formulas were completed, the average national wheat acreage reduction was 15 percent. The majority of the farmers, especially the larger farmers, signed contracts; however, farmers who had only a small patch of wheat did not believe it would pay them to sign a contract.[7]

The story of the Agricultural Adjustment Act of 1933 and its replacements, the Soil Conservation and Domestic Allotment Act 1936 and the Agricultural Adjustment Act of 1938, is a turbulent piece of history. In time, the three acts did provide vast amounts of money, which aided the dust bowl economy. Many farmers who otherwise would have gone broke were able to survive as a result of allotment assistance. While giving due credit to the program's success, it is necessary to recognize the shortcomings.

One of the most serious weaknesses in the three different agricultural allotment acts was the failure to assist the smaller farmers, who were often in the deepest economic distress, adequately. At a national level, "the sign-up of wheat-production-adjustment contracts cover[ed] approximately 80 percent of the total wheat acreage of the United States. The proportion of the total acreage which was signed up by the comparatively large producers was greater than first thought would be the case." The *Yearbook of Agriculture 1934* further reported: "There was a tendency for the smaller producers who had been growing wheat for only local and home consumption and livestock feed to remain outside of the program."[8]

Of the farmers who signed contracts, 46.8 percent of them, who produced only 17.2 percent of the wheat, received $100 or less. These were the smaller wheat farmers. A much smaller percentage of the total number, 16.7 percent, produced 27.7 percent of the wheat and received allotment checks ranging from $200 to $399. These were larger farmers although not the giant wheat kings who received allotment checks of $10,000 or more. Comparing the distribution of allotment payments of farmers who received $400 to $599 to the smaller farmers further illustrates the point. The larger farmers represented only 16.7 percent of the wheat farmers, but they received $1,207,400. The smaller farmers represented 46.8 percent of those signing contracts. They received $1,542,300. Of the total $96,807,000 paid by the AAA to farmers during 1933, only $1,542,300 went to 46.8 percent of the farmers.[9]

The neglect of the small farmers was not entirely accidental. It fit into the overall plan of the federal government to be "free to shape our agricultural policy in the direction of affecting a maximum economy of human labor in order to spare as much labor as possible for nonagricultural employment. . . . This would imply . . . the elimination from farming of the numerous farm families now engaged in crude, self-sufficing systems of farming."[10]

To stimulate the removal of numerous farm families, the National Industrial Recovery Act of June 16, 1933, empowered the Agricultural Adjustment Administration to further the land-use plan through the purchase of land. By February 1934, the Agricultural Adjustment Administration, the agency with primary responsibility for farm relief, was purchasing land from farmers who most needed relief.[11]

Ranking high among the failure of the AAA was its inexcusable oversight of the climatic conditions that existed on the High Plains. In 1933 dust storms were crisscrossing the High Plains for the second consecutive year. Ignorance on the part of the government was no excuse, since federal agencies and affiliates were recording the storms. Yet the provisions of the AAA were not geared toward placing a cover crop on the acreage of government leased lands (allotment acres). Since the land was left unprotected, it was a primary source of wind erosion. A large share of the soil that settled on Washington, D.C., during the historic storm of May 12, 1934, was government "tenant soil" dropping in to visit the "absentee proprietor." Although the storm stimulated some activity and verbosity in Washington, it was several months before Uncle Sam made a clear-cut effort to assure that the land he leased from the farmers did not waste natural resources or cause undue suffering and hardship to residents of the dust bowl.[12]

Contrary to the view expressed in government reports during the 1930s, that the heartland of the dust bowl was a one-crop system based on wheat, livestock raising was a major agricultural industry. Cattle were not listed as a basic commodity under the

AAA because stockmen feared that the processing tax would increase the price of beef and drive consumers to purchase substitute products of pork, fish, and poultry. A second factor was that the increase in the supply of cattle was not apparent. "Between January 1, 1928, and January 1, 1933, the number of cattle on farms had increased by 8 million head or 15 percent, but cattle marketings had declined steadily for six years and in 1932 federally inspected cattle slaughter was 15 percent less than in 1926, the post-war peak."[13] With the low rate of slaughter, the price of cattle was near parity. But in 1933 the bottom fell out of the cattle market. Shortly after the creation of the AAA, stockmen reversed their position and began calling for federal assistance for the cattle industry. Efforts at developing an equitable program dragged on for months as representatives for the cattlemen and the AAA attempted to hammer out a program. The negotiations bogged down over questions of markets, planned production, and relief programs. The protracted talks were further delayed by the question of who had the decision-making powers of running the business. While the debates were continuing, the Federal Surplus Relief Corporation did purchase some canner and cutter cattle, which were used for the relief of needy people.

Nature interrupted the lively discussions by sending a drought in 1934 that was more severe than the earlier record national drought of 1930. Beginning in 1933, and continuing into 1934, precipitation was well below normal across the midwestern and Plains states. With the drought conditions, feed supplies were being consumed at an alarming rate. Finally, in April 1934, the Jones-Connally Relief Bill provided some help to hard-pressed stockmen and starving cattle. On May 9 the government began its first phase of drought cattle purchases. Secretary Wallace told the government buyers that "no expense should be spared."[14] They spared none. The result was chaos in administrative ranks, but cattle were being removed from the range and stockmen were receiving much needed relief. During the months of May and June, the bulk of the purchases were in the northern plains and midwestern states, but by the first of July, the drought had spread across a larger area. The government began purchasing cattle on the southern plains.[15]

A look at a few headlines from the *Boise City News* suggests how the Drought Cattle Purchase program operated and what it meant to the heartland of the dust bowl. July 19: "County Cattle Selling—Applications For Appraisal On 173 Herds Have Been Received Here—2,608 Head Sold—High Percentage of Animals Bought in County have Been Condemned." The article said that 22.8 percent of the cattle purchased were condemned.[16] July 26: "Cattle Sales Bring Cash into Cimarron: . . . With the drouth situation in the panhandle growing more acute with the passing of each day, government cattle appraisers and buyers are kept at a high tension."[17] August 2: "Quota Of Cattle Is Lowered."[18] August 9: "Cattle Shipments Show Good Increase: . . . With the drouth unabated in Cimarron County, the government purchases of cattle continue."[19] August 16: "Cattle Buyers Change—Quota is Raised—Rains are Helpful."[20] August 30: "Increase In Cattle Purchase—Federal Buying Speeds Up As Rains On Pastures— Cow Shortage Is Probable—Hold Good Cows—County Agent Urges Best of Herd Be Retained—Feed Value of Thistles Rated."[21] By mid September rains had improved the pastures and winter wheat prospects for feed during the cold months looked bright. The government had purchased several thousand head of cattle and herds were further decreased by shipments to market through the normal process.

Not all the heartland of the dust bowl was eligible for cattle purchase at the same time. In the Oklahoma counties of Texas and Beaver, cattle purchases did not begin until the first week of August. Cattle buying was stopped in late September but renewed in early October. By the end of the cattle purchase program, thousands of cattle were removed from the disaster area. Texas County received $93,440 for 9,187 head of cattle. Nationally, the Drought Cattle Purchase program bought approximately 8.3 million cattle (this approximates the increase that occurred between 1928 and 1933). Nearly 18 percent of the cattle were condemned under the program. The remaining 82 percent of the purchases appears to represent a substantial reduction in the basic herd. As a result, the drought cattle purchase was, as the stockmen wanted, a federal relief program that definitely helped the stricken areas.[22]

Of all the government programs in the dust bowl, the drought cattle purchase program was the most successful in terms of providing immediate relief and placing the recipients on the road to recovery. It was a shame that the federal government marred its record by using questionable methods to gain power over the people. During the negotiation to entitle stockmen to subsidies, the Department of Agriculture attempted to further its land-use scheme.

The hard-pressed stockmen, during the early period of the purchase program, were required to sign a contract, which gave the government extensive powers over production and marketing. "Although cattlemen were not physically forced to sell their cattle," writes C. Roger Lambert, "many felt the drought and price conditions created an atmosphere of compulsion." Numerous citizens believed that "Both Congress and the rancher were being victimized by the bureaucrats." And "Hoard's Dairyman denounced the agreement: 'Hailed as a humanitarian act to aid drought stricken farmers, the government's contract for the purchase of cattle ties the farmer hand and foot to the chariot wheel of a dictator.' "[23] In the dust bowl the vast majority of the stockmen refused to sell their cattle until the offensive contracts were dropped. Thus, badly overgrazed ranges were further depleted. Eventually the contracts were not enforced, but they were an effort to "bait the farmers" into adopting the far-ranging plans of Guy Tugwell and Henry C. Wallace.

The counter points of view of government plans and citizens' desires are demonstrated by the need and use of farm credit. From the wheat harvest of 1932, until 1935, the depression was at its worst in the five-state area. It was during these years that the farm markets and the oil and gas business were at their low ebb. Making conditions harder were the drought and dirt storms. It was a time when the farmers needed the largest amount of assistance. Emergency farm credit was desperately wanting. The federal government attempted to meet the challenge of the credit requirements of agriculture by providing sources for lending money.

The Federal Land Bank, established in 1916, and the Land Bank Commissioner Loans, established by the Emergency Farm Mortgage Act of 1933, were major sources of credit for the economically depressed farmers. From May 1, 1933, to December 31, 1935, the Land Bank loaned $1,004,100 to 320 Texas County farmers. At the same time, 444 Texas County farmers borrowed $774,400 from the Land Bank Commissioners. The

Land Bank loaned up to 50 percent of the insurable value on improvements and implements and up to 75 percent of the appraised value of farm property. Because of the loan policy, many of the high-risk farmers, who most desperately needed assistance, were unable to borrow from the Land Bank. Thus the system did not help those who needed the help most.[24]

Some farmers found the Land Bank loans a road to disaster. One Morton County farmer borrowed a little over $600 from the Federal Land Bank Commissioners. Because of the hard years he was not able to pay the note when it fell due in 1935. He hoped that he could refinance the mortgage since his indebtedness did not exceed the limits of the Land Bank. But land buyers for the Resettlement Administration convinced the old farmer that the loan would not be renewed and he would lose everything unless he sold out to them. Convinced that the federal men knew what the federal government was planning to do, the pioneer sold his hard won and beloved land. Since many farmers who borrowed money under the Emergency Farm Mortgage Act had notes falling due during the autumn of 1935, the Federal Land Bank and the Land Bank Commissioners did refinance most of the loans. But the intentions of the Land Bank were not announced until the last minute; in the meantime, the Resettlement buyers were using the uncertainity to their advantage. Thus, the federal government was giving with one hand while taking with the other.[25]

Although the Great Plains Committee "recommended that assistance in the enlargement of undersized operating units be provided: (1) through extension of credit under suitable restrictions. . . ," obtainable credit for most of the undersized farms was rarely available.[26] The most economical land for a small farmer to purchase was tax-delinquent lands. Usually the soil on tax-delinquent land was rich, but the farming unit had been so small that the farmer was starved out. By combining into one operating unit a small farm with some tax-delinquent land, an economically sufficient farm could be organized. But, "it is desirable," argued federal spokesmen, "that the states should avoid the resale of such lands to private individuals, . . ."[27] The second recommendation of the Great Plains Committee for providing assistance to undersized farms was "(2) . . . through Federal purchase of selected land and its subsequent lease or sale under covenants protecting its use."[28] The National Resources Board "recommended that so-called commissioner loans . . . be authorized for employment in facilitating the purchase of small agricultural holdings when these constitute an essential part of a Federal or State small-holdings program."[29] In the heartland of the dust bowl the program was for large holdings and regrassing. Thus credit for small farmers to expand was extremely limited.

Under the conditions of extremes it was necessary for farmers to have a system of credit to meet emergencies. Although the financial conditions of the eighteen counties were no worse than those of the nation, which were bad enough, local banks were too small to handle emergencies. To fill the void, the federal government provided emergency feed and seed loans to drought areas. The feed and seed loans became a vital part of the short-term credit for the heartland of the dust bowl. Often, emergency feed and seed loans were only available after a crisis was in full swing and equally often, funding was limited.

After several drought months, loans were available in the Oklahoma Panhandle only in the middle of July 1934; thus, it was too late in the season to raise a cash crop to pay the debt incurred. A crop could not be "made"; nevertheless, the government wanted its money back, plus 5½ percent interest, by November 1935. The farmers who borrowed money and planted a cover crop, but who were unable to meet the November deadline, suffered a loss in credit rating and faced possible foreclosure.[30]

Since feed and seed loans were the primary source of emergency credit, many farmers came to rely on the credit source to get through the lean years. But in 1936 President Roosevelt vetoed the feed and seed loan bill and cut off the vital credit line. At the time Roosevelt vetoed the bill, the Department of Agriculture was beginning a concentrated effort to establish its land-utilization program. In the *Yearbook of Agriculture 1934* it was noted: "In the long run, it would be cheaper for the Government to purchase farms than to lease them." (That is, pay allotments.)[31] A year later the *Yearbook* considered the future of agriculture after the drought. After a description of previous land policies, the nature of the Agricultural Adjustment Act of 1933 was considered. "This is the stage of comprehensive agricultural planning. . . . land settlement remained chaotic; . . . It was impossible to leave matters in that stage after the passage of the

Agricultural Adjustment Act. . . . submarginal farming had to be discouraged, and crop adjustment had to be coordinated with land utilization in general."[32] And President Roosevelt, by his veto of the feed and seed loans, had "sure enough" found a way to discourage farming on what the Agriculture Department defined as submarginal land. After receiving a tremendous amount of pressure from several quarters, including Congressman Marvin Jones, who was from Amarillo, Texas, and chairman of the House Agriculture Committee, Roosevelt did provide limited crop and feed loans.[33]

Perhaps it would be advantageous to recall what was generally meant by submarginal farms. A submarginal farm could and often did have rich soil; however, the farm unit was too small to provide an adequate income or the farm manager failed to perform his responsibilities properly. The usual problem was a farm unit that was too small.

In 1937 Congress passed, and the president signed, a feed and seed bill which provided a revolving fund and was intended to be ready when an emergency started (not after it was well advanced). In spite of the provisions of the feed and seed loans, in late April 1938, it was necessary for farmers in the five-state area to address a petition to high government officials.

> Whereas, our farmers have made application for these loans in good faith, and have had cause to believe that these loans would be available to them for the purpose of producing a crop; and that these loans have been rejected by the Regional Emergency Crop and Feed loan office, without regard to the moral standing of the applicant and without regard to the recommendations of the local committees;
> . . .[34]

In May delegates from the Southwest Agricultural Association met with Roy I. Kimmel, Resettlement Administrator and Federal Coordinator for Region Twelve, to inquire about the continued delay in proving emergency credit as provided by law. "He [Kimmel] flatly refused their request on the grounds that the refusal of dust ridden counties to organize soil conservacy districts did not entitle them to assistance and prevented him from securing funds for their dust abatement."[35] Thus loans were being restricted because the farmers refused to take the bait.

The organizational structure of the soil conservation districts, if accepted, would have been a major victory for the land-use planners, who were at the summit of the decision-making process. But the soil conservation districts were defeated at the polls by the farmers "because of the dim and obscure promises and the red tape and technicalities insisted upon by the government, which might pass land control from the hands of the individual farmer to a distant committee or supervising body."[36] To put it more bluntly, the voters did not want to become tenant farmers for an obscure and distant absentee landlord.

After the meeting with Kimmel, the Southwest Agricultural Association drew up a second set of resolutions and began a campaign to encourage residents of the dust bowl to write their congressmen. Of course, having the Chairman of the House Agriculture Committee, and one of the sponsors of the bill establishing the feed and seed loans, depending on the Texas votes in Region Twelve helped the protesters. After a fashion, emergency credit monies were made available by the federal government. Another form of "baiting the farmers" was making emergency loans available where they were least needed. The drought of 1936 was less severe in the Texas Panhandle section of the Resettlement Administration Region Twelve than in the remainder of Region Twelve. "The Texas Panhandle . . . received a more liberal allotment [for feed loans] than other portions of this district," stated Kimmel. "The Oklahoma Panhandle, which has suffered from a feed shortage, was allotted $15,000."[37] The Texas Panhandle, which needed the feed loans the least, received a $45,000 allotment. The difference in the size of individual feed loans suggest the importance of the loans to separate areas. Loans in Texas averaged only $25, while loans in "other sections of the R. A. region average[d] as much as $100."[38] Clearly it was a case of the area that needed emergency credit the most receiving the least.

An article in the 1937 *Land Policy Circular*, published by the Resettlement Administration and entitled "The Coordinated Program for the Southern High Plains," candidly states the objective and methods of the policy makers: "Basically the permanent rehabilitation program for the Southern Plains which is now going forward is directed towards a shift in the type of farming from wheat cultivation to a combination of crop and livestock production. In this manner, considerable areas of land now in crops will be restored to grass, . . . " The report went on to say:

> For many farmers in the area this will mean a considerable change in methods of operation. For many it will also require additional land resources, for one of the outstanding problems to be overcome is the prevalence of numerous farms of 640 acres or less which cannot be adapted to a sound plan of use without additional acreage. It is generally considered that a minimum of 1,500 acres should be included in a successful farm for the southern plains area. A large part of this acreage would be used for range, and varying percentages devoted to feed crops and cash crop production.[39]

The federal government meant to return the region primarily to grass, and landholdings were to be doubled in size. But the government provided no meaningful alternative for the people who were to be displaced from the soil. The small farmers forced from the land would simply have to migrate somewhere else. And the government provided very little credit for farmers to use to double or even triple the size of their farms. Thus, one farmer would be forced from the land, but another farmer could not purchase it. The only large land buyer in the heartland of the dust bowl was the federal government.[40]

While discussing government efforts to shift the dust bowl from farming to ranching, the *Land Policy Circular* explained the methods used:

> Guidance of the rehabilitation loan program and the Agricultural Adjustment activities to encourage this shift in type of farming will be one of the outstanding features of the co-ordinated program of the Department. Already, for example, the Resettlement Administration is making certain changes in its rehabilitation loan policy in order to promote a change towards less wheat farming in the drier areas.[41]

This points to the fact that the policy was coordinated throughout the Department of Agriculture. The Department of Interior was also cooperating in the plan to remove the wheat farmers. The method used was denying rehabilitation loans to wheat farmers while loaning money to stockraisers.

A person who borrowed from the federal government signed an agreement that gave the government far-ranging powers. In a news release, the Home Management Supervisor for Hansford County, Texas, Gertrude Brent, lists some of the areas in which the Resettlement Administration played a major role: "Many people do not realize the relationship between the Resettlement Administration and the farm families who borrow money. In so doing they become business partners with the federal government."[42] The Resettlement Administration played an active role to:

> plan gardens which will meet the family's needs; determine what quantity and kinds of foods are needed to supply the family's dietary needs; determine what foods may be utilized during the growing season and what foods may be processed for use during the winter months; plan the family's clothing budget, including an analysis of old clothing that may be utilized for wear or to make rugs, etc.[43]

The list went on to include household furniture and fuel. The Resettlement Administration farm management plan included planning of the divisions of labor for the farm family, i.e., who would do the dishes, work in the gardens, feed the chickens, tend the stock, and so forth. Thus the partnership allowed the government a decisive voice over most aspects of the borrower's life. The federal efforts of agricultural relief were contradictions; they helped and harmed the citizens.

Now let us investigate the make work relief program. The New Deal came in with a flurry of activity in March 1933, but it was not until after Christmas that relief activities increased in the dust bowl. The first New Deal relief was payment to farmers for allotments as provided under the Agricultural Adjustment Act of 1933, and most of the dust bowl farmers did not receive any money until January 1934.

As noted earlier, in the fall of 1933, Secretary of Interior Ickes advised "that citizens of the drouth-stricken area of the Oklahoma Panhandle be removed 'to more arable lands.' "[44] And during 1933 there were no relief programs in the dust bowl except those started under the Hoover Administration. By mid December, the Civil Works Administration in Cimarron County, Oklahoma, completed registration and classification of 832 eligible relief workers. By December 28, the number had increased to 960, of which 162 were to be employed on CWA projects and 226 on reemployment road construction jobs. During the first week in January 1934, the CWA began work, while increasing the number of projects and employees. Things were looking up for the residents of the dust bowl. Two weeks later Harry L. Hopkins, National Director of the CWA, cut relief workers from 30 hours to 15 hours per week, which resulted in a cut in wages from $12 per week to $6 per week. Hopkins's policy allowed for the employment of twice as many men with the same budget and in turn provided some income for more relief workers; but no one was able to save enough to pay past debts at the grocery store or delinquent rent or taxes.[45]

In Texhoma, residents had difficulty raising the matching funds necessary for the CWA curb and gutter project. It cost each property owner $12.50 to have a curb and gutter run along the street side of his lot. During the winter of 1934, the fee was more money than many residents could lay their hands on. The result was many delays and much confusion.[46]

By March 15, Texas County, Oklahoma, had nearly 2,600 people enrolled for relief work, but only 500 men were working. The following day the force was cut to 393 men, and by the end of the month the CWA had come to an end in the dust bowl.[47]

Relief workers were led to believe that the Federal Emergency Relief Administration, FERA, would quickly replace the defunct CWA. But there were major breakdowns in re-registrations, transferring organization records, and providing adequate funds. Although the FERA allotted Cimarron County 300 men on relief work, only 97 men were working by the end of April. In Texas County no FERA projects were under way by the third week in April, and only two NRWR road projects were active. Both of the road projects were near Guymon and did not provide any assistance to men from other locations in the county. The *Hooker Advance* on May 3 spoke of the situation to its readers. Hooker relief workers had "nine continuous weeks— without an hour's work, to citizens who have large and dependent families, and who are justly entitled to relief . . . conditions are intolerable."[48] In Kansas the editor of the *Grant County Republican* sarcastically remarked, "CWA leaves monument in the form of a snow fence . . . left in the middle of the Highway K25

one mile north of town. . . . Road [was] once under construction."[49] The fact was, residents of the dust bowl had little relief
in 1933, and just when the future began to look brighter, relief
efforts broke down.

During the transfer of agencies, the *Hooker Advance* claimed
that work was only done on "projects favored by county seat
politicians."[50] The editor remarked that the roads from Guymon
to Hardesty and from Guymon to Hugoton were being worked,
while the work on roads from Hooker to Hardesty and Hugoton
was cancelled. In July, after the FERA began working several
men, the *Hooker Advance* attacked the FERA for not having a
more equitable distribution of relief projects in order that towns
other than Guymon could keep their people and have them
earning an income. "There are certified to work . . . at the present time 850 men," replied Ruth Philippe, Texas County Relief
Administrator, to the *Hooker Advance*. "Of these, 391 were on
the payroll for the week ending July 19, 1934. This leaves 450
men available for work. It is not necessary to go outside the
FERA to hunt laborers when that many certified men are
idle."[51] Since the majority of the certified men were in or near
Guymon, and the FERA was not going to look outside its organization, men needing relief work soon got the message. They
moved to the county seat where they could be certified and find
work. This was a hard blow to other county communities. The
loss in population and potential customers forced local merchants
to reduce their inventory and lay off help. The result was the
reorganization of communities.

Funding of FERA projects fluctuated immensely from month to
month. The program finally got off the ground in early June 1934.
By the last week in August, 506 of the 1,200 eligible Texas County
relief workers shared in $5,211.09 pay. Then during the first week
of September, FERA work stopped for several days. By October
FERA projects were reopening but at a reduced rate. On
November 1, the editor of the *Texhoma Times* wrote, "Pay Roll Up
Again."[52] FERA employees were allotted $2,026.20 per week for
November. Of the approximately 1,200 eligible relief workers, 183
men received $11 apiece for a week's work. Relief workers were
allowed to work only one week per month.

The breakdown in transferring relief work from the CWA to
the FERA, and the inadequate funding of relief work, resulted

in violence in Morton County, Kansas. The county administrators, E. C. Dean and Mrs. Gertrude Goddard, were attempting to distribute the limited funds equitably throughout the
county. In Elkhart, with the largest number of unemployed,
men became restless and threats were made. One night in mid
October, someone shot up the relief office. This resulted in a
series of investigations, and in the middle of November, Morton
County FERA relief work was stopped for a short time. When
work resumed Elkhart residents were the primary recipients of
relief work.[53]

In Morton County during 1934, the federal government spent
$189,207 on forty-seven projects. If nothing was allowed for
material or administrative costs, the county's 960 relief workers
received approximately $17 per month for the year. During
these months, residents in the heartland of the dust bowl began
referring to relief work as $10 a month employment.

The erratic nature of FERA continued into 1935. In Baca
County, Colorado, relief funds for January were small, but in
February they increased significantly. Accompanying the increase for February was a word of caution from Robert W.
Kelso, the state director: "Every person on relief is urged to
spend his February money as wisely as possible and use all care
to provide for his family for the month of March."[54] March allotments were to be lower.

In March and April the dust bowl drew a tremendous amount
of public attention because of the reports of sickness and dirt
storms. As a result, relief spending was increased; but in July,
while newsmen were busy elsewhere, FERA lists of eligible recipients were cut 60 percent. The Rural Rehabilitation Corporation admitted part of the men cut from the FERA rolls and the
CCC inducted a few men. When FERA cut its forces, the
county had 1,336 men on its rolls; of those dropped, most of
them were simply set adrift. In a few weeks FERA closed up
shop and the Resettlement men moved in to provide relief.[55]

The grimmest years of the depression lasted from July 1932 to
July 1935. For approximately eighteen months during that period the area received very little relief. The programs of the
CWA and FERA were characterized by great confusion and long
lapses of virtual idleness. Generally, only one-fourth of the eligible workers were employed in a given week. Thus, the programs

became a policy, which maintained the status quo (at a very low level), but did little to improve the area's economy.

The relief value of the Works Progress Administration (WPA) was sharply limited. The WPA activities on the Texhoma school was an example. Voters in Texhoma, who realized that the area needed immediate relief projects, approved the bonds for the construction of a new high school in April 1934. In August, the school board reported that everything had been given approval by state and local officials. But it was not until February 1935 that the WPA approved the projects, and Cowan Construction Company received a contract for construction in May. It was more than a year between the time the voters gave their approval and any work actually began. It took two years from the time local approval was given for the building of two dormatories at Panhandle A & M College for the WPA to begin work on the structures. These delays were standard.[56]

In January 1936, the WPA began to reduce its list of eligible employees. In an open letter saluting the WPA workers in the Oklahoma Panhandle and paving the way for the cut in forces, W. S. Key, Oklahoma WPA administrator, briefly recounted the history of the program. He noted that the three panhandle counties had provided $491,253 of the total $835,357 spent on projects. Key also reported that the panhandle had paid 50 percent of the cost, while the remainder of Oklahoma paid an average of only 20 percent of the total cost. Why the dust bowl paid a much higher percentage of the matching funds was not explained by Key. The difference in percent of revenue sharing suggests that either the heartland of the dust bowl was better off financially than the humid areas of the state or else the government was deliberately bleeding the Great Plains.[57]

In 1936, farmers were prohibited from working on WPA projects except on a limited basis. For example, Texas County farmers could work on the Pony Creek project until their "rehab" loans were approved. To work at Pony Creek required many farmers move off their farms to be near the work. Union County, New Mexico, farmers were required to move 140 miles to receive WPA jobs at the Conchas Dam. Many of the farmers and local businessmen protested the policy of moving men to distant places. It would be impossible to maintain their farms and communities if the people were moved out, and many local projects were discontinued because of a labor shortage. For example, the bridge over the Beaver River, north of Texhoma, was only half completed when it was discontinued, and work on the State Line Road was far from finished when it was stopped.[58]

The "rehab" loans the farmers had to take out if they could not find another source of income were controlled by the Resettlement Administration. The Resettlement Administration wanted to implement the government plan of moving the people off their land and away from their homes, but the farmers did not want to go. Nonetheless, Uncle Sam was going to find a way to encourage the farmers to agree with him. To further government plans, relief, farm, and conservation programs were consolidated under the direction of the Region Twelve Administrator, Roy I. Kimmel.

By controlling and directing relief activities, the federal government was able to offer some strong bait to the farmers. The *Morton County Farmer* for August 20, 1937, reported:

> In the past two weeks many families have left Morton County. Some of them have gone to California, some to Colorado, and some to east Kansas, and others to various points in all parts of the country.
>
> With the cessation of relief work and the prospects of crops there seems to be little alternative for families which hope to regain a foothold here.[59]

Soon the federal government accelerated the acquisition of land near Rolla. The AAA, Drought Cattle Purchase program, Federal Land Bank loans, Feed and Seed Loans, and the CWA, Fera, WPA, and other programs did provide much needed relief, and many useful projects were completed. But the vacillation and delay involved in the programs undermined much that was accomplished. It was a shame that high government officials failed to spend as much time developing and promoting a rational relief program as they spent developing and promoting a far-ranging land-utilization program. All too often relief programs were used as bait to further a semisecret (and profitable) scheme rather than to meet the challenge of the depression.

8

Federal Policies:
Land Use and Conservation

Federal policies associated with comprehensive land-use planning and soil conservation were often characterized by hazards and misunderstanding, and their goals were never reached. The overriding goal of the federal government was comprehensive land-use planning, which was closely associated with fully planned agricultural production and marketing. The policy had many facets, including land acquisition, resettlement, and soil conservation. In an effort to reach the preconceived goal, federal planners failed to recognize many important factors concerning residents and soil in the dust bowl.

A brief chronology of agencies primarily responsible for directing federal efforts in the dust bowl suggests the primary direction and the route taken by national leaders. The Comprehensive Land Use Plan, introduced in 1922, grew in acceptance in the Department of Agriculture and the Executive Branch of the federal government. Under the Agricultural Marketing Act of 1929, the Federal Farm Board was authorized to investigate and report on land utilization for agricultural purposes. This work was followed by the National Conference on Land Utilization in 1931. "In 1933 the National Land Use Planning Committee prepared a report primarily directed to the concept of public acquisition, retention, and management of submarginal lands."[1]

Control of farm surplus and land acquisition assumed an active role in land-utilization policy in February 1934, when the government began purchases of submarginal land through the Agricultural Adjustment Administration. Later that year the National Resources Board published its report, which favored the purchase of 75,000,-000 submarginal acres. Land Utilization Project (L U Project) purchases were accelerated in 1935, with funding under the Emergency Relief Appropriations Act. By Executive Order 7028, dated April 30, 1935, the Resettlement Administration became responsible for the purchase of lands. The Resettlement Administration, first as an independent organization and then under the Department of Agriculture, maintained control over land utilization programs and played an important role in relief, credit, and conservation until September 1, 1937. Then the Farm Security Administration (FSA), quite similar to the Resettlement Administration, took charge. Under Title III of the Bankhead-Jones Act July 22, 1937, land purchases were accelerated.

Finally, on October 16, 1938, by Secretary of Agriculture Memorandum 785, L U Projects came under the auspices of the Soil Conservation Service. Thus the Soil Conservation Service became the last on the long list of New Deal agencies that experimented with and attempted to implement comprehensive land-use planning and to handle associated problems, such as wind erosion, which were of extreme interest to Great Plains residents.[2]

One feature was common to all the agencies dealing with land utilization—management of "submarginal land." As noted earlier, the report of the Great Plains Drought Committee referred to submarginal lands and commented, "The soils are among the richest on the continent."[3] Thus the term "submarginal farm" or "submarginal land" often did not refer to the soil itself, but had an entirely different meaning when used in government reports.

The *National Resources Board Report* acknowledged this different concept of submarginal land when discussing the Federal Emergency Relief Act. The *Report* stated: "An important feature of the program [FERA] is the rehabilitation of the present occupants of the purchase areas now living a socially degraded existence as a result of their inadequate income, poor schools, and roads, and infrequent contacts with an outside civilization."[4] While making no comment on the soil itself, the policy makers

Figure 21. Thriving seven- and eight-year-old elm trees in Texas County, Oklahoma. Photo taken June 29, 1937. Courtesy of the Texas County Soil Conservation District Office, Guymon, Oklahoma.

who prepared the *Report* believed the folks on the land to be socially degraded and needing contact with higher civilization. This attitude on the part of all land-utilization policy makers toward residents of the dust bowl was remarkably similar to the thinking of Thomas Jefferson concerning the Indians.

Let us now consider the federal implementation of the land utilization program through the various acts, agencies, and reports as well as through actions by the government.

For the heartland of the dust bowl, the National Resources Board *Report* mapped the "Areas in which it Appears Desirable to Encourage Permanent Retirement of Substantial Parts of the Arable Farming and Develop Constructive Use of the Land Not to be in Farms." Included in the land to be retired was the bulk of Baca, Prowers, and Bent counties, Colorado. In southwestern Kansas the land south of the Cimarron River in Morton, Stevens, and Seward counties was included in the area where a "substantial part" was to be permanently retired. The area included the population centers of Elkhart, Hugoton, and Liberal, as well as numerous smaller towns. The report stated. "Further investigation will make possible a refinement of this map."[5]

Figure 22. Trees planted along road for shelter belt in Texas County, Oklahoma. Few of the trees survived. Photo taken October 27, 1936. Courtesy of the Texas County Soil Conservation District Office, Guymon, Oklahoma.

Figure 23. Native grass and planted trees killed by wind erosion and drought. Photo taken October 5, 1937, near Guymon, Oklahoma. Courtesy of the Texas County Soil Conservation District Office, Guymon, Oklahoma.

Figures 24, 25. In figure 24 the cane is over six feet high. The two photos were taken on government project land, within a short distance of each other, on the same day, September 28, 1938. Both farms were farmed by the same method and planted to the same crop (cane). One crop had a good rain; the other did not. Courtesy of Texas County Soil Conservation District Office, Guymon, Oklahoma.

Figure 26. Severe wind erosion and a crop failure are illustrated in this photo taken in Texas County, Oklahoma, on October 5, 1937. Courtesy of the Texas County Soil Conservation District Office, Guymon, Oklahoma.

Figure 27. A fine stand of kafir appears in this Texas County, Oklahoma, photo taken on November 4, 1937. Courtesy of the Texas County Soil Conservation District Office, Guymon, Oklahoma.

Figure 28. Pasture land which was contour listed to store water. Courtesy of the Texas County Soil Conservation District Office, Guymon, Oklahoma.

Figure 29. The topsoil had been blown down to the plow pan. Photo taken November 12, 1934. Courtesy of the Texas County Soil Conservation District Office, Guymon, Oklahoma.

Figure 30. Typical terraces built in Texas County, Oklahoma. Note blow dirt which fills the lister rows on the terraces. Photo taken May 25, 1938. Courtesy of the Texas County Soil Conservation District Office, Guymon, Oklahoma.

Figure 31. Land being prepared to return to native grass. Courtesy of the Texas County Soil Conservation District Office, Guymon, Oklahoma.

Figure 32. Land which had been chiseled to prevent wind erosion. Note the large solid clods which helped break the force of the wind. Photo taken August 24, 1938. Courtesy of the Texas County Soil Conservation District Office, Guymon, Oklahoma.

Figure 33. Grain sorghum cover was raised on a badly blown pasture. This view is especially interesting since farming methods and crops were used to control wind erosion on grassland. This is a contradiction of many of the traditional theories blaming the plow for causing the dust bowl and of arguments that native grasslands did not suffer from wind erosion. Photo taken August 26, 1938. Courtesy of the Texas County Soil Conservation District Office, Guymon, Oklahoma.

Figures 34, 35. During the dust bowl years numerous farms were barren and bleak. The soil was blown down to the hard pan. But in 1939 the wheat was thick and green and prosperous. It was a land of promise. Courtesy of the Texas County Soil Conservation District Office, Guymon, Oklahoma.

Without any extensive investigation, the Resettlement Administration activated plans to purchase 300,000 acres in Meade, Seward, and Stevens counties, Kansas, in 1935. During the dirt storms, dust pneumonia epidemic, and excited national publicity of 1935, the Resettlement Administration began appraising land in southwestern Kansas. In March plans were announced to purchase 50,000 acres of Stevens County as part of a much larger purchase. But the farmers were not enthusiastic about selling at $2.75 per acre. In May the appraisers finished their work and the Resettlement Administration attempted to purchase land at a bargain price. Before the purchases could start, it rained and the hysteria of the spring subsided. Farmers in the three counties decided to stick it out a while longer. Then in July the *Hugoton Hermes* announced that the McNab Oil Company was going to start a $10,000,000 natural gasline construction project and that gas-leasing activities were increasing. The local interest in gas development further intensified in August when the Cabot well came in with a roar north of Guymon, Oklahoma. The new well produced 55 million cubic feet of gas. With the new hope for success, farmers in the three counties took heart and did not sell to the Resettlement Administration.[6]

The federal government might have purchased large acreages in the target counties if it had not insisted on receiving the mineral rights and had offered a fair price. The *United States Census of Agriculture: 1935* shows that the average value per acre of Stevens County land was $22.20, not the $2.75 the federal government wanted to pay. And the farmers were not ready to sell their land at a ridiculously low price. In Morton County, however, where the financial distress was greater and the gas development was slower, the federal government did purchase land at bargain prices—after convincing the residents through various means that they must sell. At this time federal land buyers were telling the farmers that the Federal Land Bank would not renew loans. The loans were renewed after some farmers had already sold out. The Resettlement Administration paid from $3 to $5 per acre; the *Census of Agriculture* reported the land was worth $13.66 per acre.[7]

Although the Resettlement Administration did purchase some L U land in Morton County in 1935, the majority of the farmers resisted the pressure of the federal government. When the federal land buyers informed one old-timer that they were going to purchase all the land around his farm and close all access roads to the property, the old-timer replied, "I've a pair of wire plirers." The old-timer kept the place and his neighbors did not sell their land.[8]

But what happened to those who sold to the Resettlement Administration? The recent federal publication, *The National Grasslands Story*, states: "the Resettlement Administration purchased thousands of uneconomic farms, retired them from intensive cultivation, and helped farm families find opportunity in other areas."[9] Will that statement stand the test of close investigation? To attract business, the Resettlement Administration mailed several advertisement brochures to farmers in areas where land purchases were planned. One of the advertisements entitled *Better Land for Better Living* noted that "They [the farmers] do not want to live in poverty on poor soil." The brochure asked the question, "What does resettlement mean?" The answer was "Resettlement is the relocation of farm families from land where they cannot make a decent living to land where they have a better opportunity to succeed." The farmers were to be placed on farms, from 25 to 100 acres in size, with good buildings and other excellent preparations for farming. The brochure was designed to appeal to young married couples, tenant farmers, and poverty ridden families.[10]

The advertisement was couched in terms designed to make farmers believe they had an opportunity to trade their poor farms, where they could not make a living, for good farms. But as the National Resources Board pointed out, "Such people [would] be aided in developing small subsistence homesteads, the returns from which may be supplemented by part-time work in nearby forests, parks, or grazing districts, on farms operated by more capable individuals, or in nearby industries which may be introduced."[11] Thus, if the resettled farmer improved his lot, he would have to do it some place other than on the farm.

The small plots of land on which the farmers were resettled were aptly labeled "subsistence homesteads." The tract of land was too small to raise the poverty ridden farmer above the bare subsistence level. And many of the farmers and tenants who sold were not resettled. They were simply left to fend for themselves.

A check of one of the settlements suggests the real estate development aspects of resettlement. Farmers near Mills, New Mexico, in 1935 agreed to sell their drought-stricken and depression-ridden farms and be resettled on good farm land chosen by the Resettlement Administration. Forty families from the Mills area were to be settled with forty families from the Taos area on 2,400 acres near Los Lunas, New Mexico. The land was to be irrigated from water impounded at the El Vado Dam. Apparently the farmers' land at Taos and Mills was acquired before a resettlement tract was purchased or improved to the standards promised by the government.

In time, the government purchased land on which to settle the Mills and Taos families. Immediately the settlers began to move in because "they had encountered so many delays in getting themselves re-established it was not considered advisable to exclude them from the resettlement area until everything was made ready for them." Part of the land was in cottonwoods, which had to be cleared, and none of the new irrigation ditches were built. The families were housed in barns and abandoned adobe shacks. Soon the families were "becoming restless and discontented over interminable delays."[12]

The families had sold their land in good faith to the federal government. But the government was planning on the resettled families doing the development work and paying for the costs. In the project's budget, "No items of subsistence for the resettlers are included since it is planned that they shall be self-supporting until permanently established on their farms by reason of the labor for which they will be paid in connection with the development of the resettlement area." The total labor costs were to be charged to the entire project and included in the price of the land paid by the resettlers.[13]

The Resettlement Administration did not even have a general plan for development of the resettlement project at the time the farmers at Mills were promised land. A broad general plan for development was not completed until after the families arrived at their new homes.

Apparently the resettled families did not know how much land they were to receive at the time they agreed to move to the Resettlement Project. The "Final Plan" for the project submitted by the Project Manager D. R. W. Wager-Smith suggested that the maximum size of an individual tract might be forty acres; however, the average size of an individual tract was to be thirty acres or less. But Wager-Smith was not certain what size farms higher authorities had in mind.

"The Budget for Mills Resettlement On Basis Of Average Of 30 Acres Per Family" was Land, $900; Improving Land, $300; Buildings, etc., $1,500; Stock, Equipment, Miscellenous, $1,000; for a total of $3,700. The average equity from purchase to be applied on resettlement was $700 per family, which left a net cost of $3,000 plus interest and taxes to be paid to the government. The all important water right for irrigation was not included in the purchasing budget. Apparently the federal government kept the water right and charged the resettlement families a fee for the water. The one who controls the water right on irrigated farms also controls the land, the crop, and the farmer's income.[14]

The Mills resettlement families traded an improved homestead of at least 160 acres, and often much more, for 30 acres of unimproved land, paid an additional $3,000, and did not get the water right. After the settlers were permanently established, they were on subsistence homesteads. If the family wanted to rise above the poverty level, the members had to go to Albuquerque or Los Lunas to find a job. This fit in nicely with the Land Use Plan of factory farmers and restriction of production without great cost to the government. The resettlement families paid the costs.

The Mills Project in New Mexico was representative of all actual and proposed resettlement projects in that any new opportunity the resettlement families found, or any improvement they made above the poverty level, was the result of their own labor, endurance, suffering, and ability. The Resettlement Administration was simply a real estate developer who operated at advantage and kept control of vital aspects of the farm operation.

To further the federal policy, in 1936 the government moved towards coordination of all federal programs under one administration. The Resettlement Administration already controlled loans and had a powerful voice in relief projects. That year all aspects of farm relief came under the control of the Resettlement Administration. The consolidation of agencies boded ill for farmers on the Great Plains. On July 8, the *Clayton News* reported:

Plans are being made in Washington today by Relief Administrator Harry Hopkins and six other government agencies, to move 100,000 or more farm families out of the drouth stricken "dust bowl" of the plains states.

The program will involve the greatest single transplanting of population since the depression began.[15]

The report caused a stir of excitement in the heartland of the dust bowl. When President Roosevelt was asked about Hopkins's plans, "the President said there is work for the people to do in all this area and a reason for their living in it." A few lines later Roosevelt tactfully admitted the planned removal and described it as a long-range policy.[16] After the Amarillo, Texas, meeting of the Great Plains Drought Area Committee in August 1936, Rexford G. Tugwell was asked if the government planned to turn the dust bowl back into a "pastoral economy." "Suggestions that the entire area be returned to grazing land," replied Tugwell, "are foolishness."[17] Yet, he was a primary supporter of the depopulation of the Great Plains. Despite statements to the contrary, the federal government was involved in removal and steps were being taken to force people out. It was planned to return the vast majority of the land to grazing under government control. The federal authorities were deliberately deceiving the people directly involved in the plan.

The soil conservation programs, farm production control programs, and the federal land-use plan came together in 1937 in one gigantic effort to develop the ideal economy and society. Before exploring those days in the dust bowl, it is advantageous to consider early conservation programs, problems of controlling wind erosion, and policies of the Soil Conservation Service.

Early in March 1934, a group of farmers and interested people in Dallam, Hartley, Sherman, and Moore counties, Texas, organized the Four County Wind Erosion Control Association, with A. M. James of Dalhart as chairman. The association began surveying the counties to determine how much damage wind erosion had done, and the committee called on the farmers to cooperate by beginning early control work. The Wind Erosion Control Association contacted government officials and asked for assistance to purchase seed to plant a cover crop. In July, the federal government did provide some seed. Meanwhile, in Morton County, Kansas, a group of farmers and citizens were pressuring the county commissioners to pass a county ordinance requiring the farmers to list or plow their fields to check wind erosion. In Stanton County, Kansas, farmers were moving to finance control of soil drifting on abandoned land.[18]

The majority of the farmers were making genuine efforts to meet the crisis caused by wind and drought. Attempting to meet the challenge and actually meeting it were often different, however. Perhaps the greatest difficulty in the farmers' efforts was that there was no agreement on what should be done. Once the land had blown away to the hardpan, some farmers were inclined to think it was best to leave the land alone. It took a tremendous amount of persuasion to change the practice. Another problem that faced the dust bowl farmers was the abandoned farms. Tax lands and land owned by absentee landowners went unattended and blew severely. These lands were a prime source of damage to neighboring farms, where crops were destroyed and conservation efforts defeated by wild, drifting soil. A third problem for conservation was overtillage. Before the dust bowl, farmers were inclined to overtill, which stoked the natural burning of organic material, changed the soil structure, and pulverized the soil. The depression was the primary force in reducing overtillage. Yet a fourth problem was the practice of stubble burning. Stubble burning killed the weeds and reduced the cost of farming the land, but the practice reduced the organic material above as well as in the soil. Soil-building life was killed by the fires and land lost much of its absorption ability. Although during the dust bowl stubble burning was sharply reduced, a relatively small percentage of farmers continued the practice.

The farmers were not prepared to meet the dust bowl crisis when it began in 1932, but by 1934 regional farmers were coming to grips with the problem. The federal government was far behind the farmers in meeting the crisis. Despite the numerous reports of wind erosion between 1930 and 1934 by the Weather Bureau, the Agriculture Department's Experiment Stations, and the *Report of the National Resources Board,* federal policy makers remained oblivious to the dangerous condition. As late as 1934, the *Yearbook of Agriculture*'s report on "Soil-Erosion Studies" ignored wind erosion. There were no programs or

techniques available in the federal arsenal that addressed themselves directly to the problem of wind erosion. After the historic
dust storm of May 12, 1934, which deposited dirt on the nation's
capital, the federal government acted by establishing one experiment station between Dalhart and Conlen, Texas, to discover
ways of preventing wind erosion.[19]

Chairman of the House Agriculture Committee, Representative Marvin Jones from Amarillo, supported the appointment of
H. H. Finnell to direct the wind erosion experiments near
Dalhart. Finnell had spent many years working with agricultural
problems on the southern Great Plains. While director of the
Experiment Station at Panhandle A & M College, he had
studied timber windbreaks, soil evaporation, and terraces, and
had conducted other investigations in tillage and cropping. In
1930 Finnell completed his experiments with terraces. Through
a series of demonstrations he illustrated to the farmers that terraces would conserve moisture by preventing runoff. Few farmers contructed terraces. The failure of the farmers to construct
terraces, Finnell admitted, was because "the best results were
obtained by terracing so close together as not to be practical
from the field standpoint."[20]

Shortly after his appointment, Finnell began his work at the
35,000-acre, wind erosion experiment station. But, "even with
past attention to this problem, the science and practice of soil
conservation have lagged behind other phases of agricultural science," wrote Hugh Bennett. "The effect of soil wastage has been
obscured or nullified for the time by other gains, such as the
development and large-scale use of fertilizers, improved ag-
ronomic practices, and improved varieties and hybrids of
crops."[21] The definite lag in the science of soil conservation cost
the nation and the residents of the dust bowl dearly during the
1930s.

The results of the federal soil conservation programs were
similar to relief projects—a mixed blessing. The Soil Conservation Service insistence on using methods designed to prevent
water erosion to stop wind erosion was costly. The basic concept
of conserving moisture to raise a crop, which in turn would provide cover, was the foundation of Soil Conservation Service
programs. The foundation of scientific dryland farming as practiced before the epoch of the dust bowl was precisely the same

policy. The tillage practices of listing, early plowing, deep tilling, subsoiling, soil mulching, packing, and summer fallowing
were designed to conserve moisture. Conserving moisture was
an excellent practice before the soil began blowing. But, even
the dry surface of moist soil will blow.

It took several weeks, sometimes even months, from the time
the crop was sown until an adequate cover crop was established.
During that period the wind was at work, burning the plants and
eroding the soil. The forces of wind erosion could kill a cover
crop even though the soil had sufficient moisture to maintain
plant life. Therefore, after the dust storms began it was necessary to develop a system of first breaking the force of the wind
on the soil followed by conserving moisture and raising a cover
crop. To accomplish this it was necessary to develop techniques
and technology aimed specifically at wind erosion.[22]

Lister rows were useful in breaking the force of the wind, but
had some major shortcomings. To break the force of the wind,
the rows must be at right angles to the wind. Often rows at right
angles pointed down slope and became ditches, which drained
the land of needed moisture. Lister rows on the contour often
ran with the wind and formed wind tunnels. To avoid these
hazards it was necessary to develop an implement for breaking
the wind while saving the moisture.

Charles T. Peacock began working on such an implement, a
damming machine, in 1927. The principle of the machine was to
form a lister row and place check dams at regular intervals.
Peacock took out his first patent on a damming maching in 1931;
by 1936 his machine or similar ones were being widely used to
restrict wind erosion and conserve moisture.[23]

Another important development in the advancement of technology to control wind erosion was the pitter. A farmer could
make a pitter by shaping the disks on the one-way plow so that
each time a disk completed a revolution it would dig a hole to
store water. By arranging the pitting section of each disk, a
farmer could control all the water that fell on his land. The pitter, however, often pulverized the soil. Athough the lister, the
damming machine, and the pitter were valuable in checking
wind erosion, they were primarily based on the concept of conserving moisture to raise a cover crop, which in turn would stop
wind erosion.

On his farm south of Hooker, Oklahoma, Fred Hoeme addressed himself to the critical problem of reducing wind erosion in the absence of adequate moisture or a cover crop. Hoeme began his work with a cultivator that left large clods across the soil surface. The rock-hard clods broke the power of the wind and became obstructions to moving water. Thus he *first* controlled the wind, and *then* controlled the water. The problem with the cultivator and other farm implements was their inability to go deep enough to reach the hard soil below the dry dusty surface. From the cultivator it was a short step for the inventor to develop the Hoeme Chisel. By 1935, Hoeme had an implement that could work a sixteen-foot width of the field with each crossing, and the chisel could be adjusted at various depths to twelve inches. The chisel had two sizes of heads. The narrow head was used to bring up clods from deep in the soil; the broad head worked at shallower depths and brought up clods, while forming a trench similar to that made by a lister. The chisel, which required more power to pull, spurred the use of bigger, rubber-tired tractors.[24]

By using the chisel, a farmer could reduce wind erosion when it started blowing in late February or early March. The chiseled land helped protect stands of weakened winter wheat or rye until the plants could gain strength and size enough to withstand the wind's onslaught. The chisel was also used between stubble rows to stop the dirt from blowing. In late April and early May, when the rains started, the chisel was used to conserve moisture. Either the broad or narrow chisel head worked to open the soil for the penetration of moisture and to hold the precipitation where it fell. Fred Hoeme's chisel met the problem of stopping wind erosion once it had started while storing water and protecting the cover crop.

The advancements by the farmers in developing new implements and techniques were not emulated by the Soil Conservation Service. Not a single new implement or technique of preventing wind erosion was developed by the SCS. In fact, the Soil Conservation Service made several damaging mistakes. The SCS insisted that lister rows be run on the contour to conserve moisture, even when the rows were in line with the wind. Thus, a system designed for humid-area, water-erosion control was used in a hostile climate. Ironically, the *Report of the Great Plains Drought Area Committee 1936*, in which Bennett played an important role, believed: "The basic cause of the . . . Great Plains situation is an attempt to impose upon the region a system of agriculture to which the Plains are not adapted—to bring into a semi-arid region methods which, on the whole are suitable only for a humid region."[25]

The uncompromising attitude and unwillingness of the federal government to adjust to the requirements of reducing wind erosion was illustrated in the same committee report. A full two years after Finnell began his research at Dalhart, policy makers still argued: "On arable farms such soil conserving practices as re-grassing, contour plowing, listing, terracing, strip cropping and the planting of shelter trees should be followed."[26] As already noted, contour plowing and listing run at right angles to water, but what works for preventing water erosion did not necessarily apply to wind.

Another pet program of the Soil Conservation Service was planting sorghums after tilling with a lister. The only large experiment with lister rows and sorghums took place during the Colby Blowout in 1914. The listing was done at right angles to the wind and sorghums were planted. "For a time it looked as though even these efforts might be unsuccessful. Whether or not the efforts would have been successful of themselves will always remain a question. At about this time nature came to the rescue."[27] The experiment did not assure control of the wind. It should be further noted that on the federal lands purchased in Morton County, Kansas, soil conservation methods prescribed by the Soil Conservation Service were rigidly followed; but wind erosion on federal lands was not controlled until 1940. By that time nature had come to the rescue.

The Soil Conservation Service also insisted on terraces, which restricted run-off and were more applicable in humid regions than in subhumid climates. The work itself required extensive stirring of the soil. And the terrace tops often crusted, which prevented moisture from soaking in. The terrace tops themselves became a source of wind erosion, while controlling little moisture. Placing a terrace on land sloping from 0 to 1 percent, of which there are millions of acres in the heartland of the dust bowl, was not particularly useful, and was often damaging.

Strip cropping was based on the principle of planting crops and legumes in alternating lister rows on the contour. This system was applicable to the corn belt and other humid climates. The same weakness with listing on the contour applied to the system of strip cropping. And in the drought region, the choices of crops for stripping were sharply limited. In essence, the government was promoting the wrong methods for the climate. Contour listing, contour terracing, and contour strip cropping were methods developed through generations of experimentation in humid regions to stop water erosion and these methods were applied by the federal government to a semiarid environment with meager results.

Yet another federal government program designed to check wind and water erosion during the 1930s was shelterbelts. Although relief crews planted thousands of trees in the dust bowl, very few grew (except where they were carefully cared for and watered). The few trees that did grow, except around farmsteads and in towns, were so far apart and so scrawny they could not work as an adequate windbreak. Even in bar ditches, where relief workers placed check dams to hold water for the trees, the crop failed to prosper.

The idea of regrassing land with the know how of the 1930s was extremely problematic. "The time required for buffalo grass to renew its original virgin condition on abandoned farm land . . . ranges from 20 to 50 years."[28] The study of *Drought Survival of Native Grass Species in the Central and Southern Great Plains, 1935* found that "drought injury, as indicated by the surviving cover of native grasses, was much more acute in certain parts of this district [Dalhart, Texas] than in any other locality, with the possible exception of small areas near Garden City and Dodge City [Kansas]." And, "the indications were that heat and drought were the most injurious factors."[29] The grassland studies of J. E. Weaver and F. W. Albertson also clearly show the grasses were suffering. In short, the drought was killing the grass and the range lands were suffering from wind erosion.

Further hampering regrassing was the virtual lack of knowledge on how to cultivate native grass. In fact, simply to get grass seed constituted a major task.

Many inhabitants of the dust bowl found it necessary to plant their crops even though the land was too dry. Regional farmers were severely chastised for "dusting in their crops," as this practice was called. The federal government, however, dusted in its crops. The sorghum plantings in 1935 were dusted in. And on land-utilization acres, crops were planted even when the ground was too dry to assure success. Federal pressures to establish a cover crop encouraged dusting in.

Despite the long delay (it was three years after the dust began blowing before the government took action), and false premises concerning wind erosion, the indirect effects of Soil Conservation Service programs became highly valuable in controlling the worst forces of nature in the dust bowl. In the spring of 1935 the Federal Emergency Relief paid each farmer ten to twenty cents per acre to cover the cost of running contour lister rows. The FER, by providing a means of "selling" the crop to the government, gave financially pressed farmers an alternative to leaving the crop in the ground, while hoping against insurmountable odds that they would raise enough grain to meet the costs of farming. At a minimum the hard-pressed farmer did not have to lose the additional expense of plowing under his crop. By the time the project ended, approximately 2,000,000 acres of the dust bowl were listed. The program did encourage quick response to wind erosion.

In July 1935, the federal government provided sorghum seeds to many farmers to plant on abandoned fields and government acreages. It was hoped the maize, hegari, and kafir would provide a cover crop when the spring winds started. More important than the crop was that something was being done about abandoned land.

The continuation of the drought relief program of reducing freight rates for the shipment of cattle from the stricken area, or for the shipment of feed and fodder into the disaster area, gave stockmen more options in operating their business. The increased demand for feed and fodder steming from the drought could be met by purchasing from outside the area, with the increased cost partially offset by lower freight rates. With other sources of feed available, stockmen did not have to graze their land as heavily or turn stock onto wheat fields before the crop was established. Thus the cover was better protected.

Paradoxically, while stockmen were importing feed into the drought-stricken counties of Oklahoma, the humid counties in the eastern part of the state were also in need of disaster assistance. "In some parts of the state, rains were too generous. . . .

Feed oats from government supplies have been sent into areas where crops were lost through floods earlier this year [1935]."[30] The floods in eastern Oklahoma were a reminder to area residents that the climatic conditions of the nation during the 1930s were highly volatile. Too much water was as disastrous as too little water. The hardships suffered and lives lost by unusually high amounts of precipitation brought as much tragedy to folks as did drought conditions.

It was not always profitable to ship cattle out of the drought area to green pastures. "I think I told you," wrote Caroline A. Henderson, "of shipping our cattle to pasture. It proved to be a disastrous mistake." Although the cattle received plenty of grass, they lost weight and had to be returned to the farm for fattening. The cost of feed and shipping put an additional hardship on the Henderson family. But it added to the family's pride in the region and their determination to remain on their farm.[31]

The Soil Conservation Service and Agricultural Adjustment Administration in 1936 began four programs that promised to meet the challenge of wind erosion. The Emergency Erosion Program, which was available to the farmers in late February, provided "a direct Federal grant of money in an amount equal to 15¢ per acre. . . . Where a land owner finds it necessary to list or chisel his land solid he was allowed the full allotment of 15¢ per acre."[32] On farms where it was necessary to work only every other row (half the field), the farmers were paid seven and a half cents per acre. Here was a program established before the crisis of the windy months reached its full force, and one that recognized the difference between total disaster to a field and only partial disaster. The program provided a farmer who had to meet the cost of operation and provide for his family with an alternative market for his crop. At fifteen cents per acre the farmer did not make any money, but the destructive sting of the crop failure was minimized rather than maximized.

The second major step in the right direction of soil conservation was the use of the allotment programs. "There are two phases to the earning of the [allotment] payments. First, before any land is eligible to receive the $7.00, or diversion payment, or the bonus, it must first be put through a Soil Conserving practice."[33] By requiring that proper conservation practices be instituted before receiving any subsidy, the government had a

powerful tool to enforce conservation. But having the right tools
and using them correctly were two separate propositions.

The third program advanced by the Soil Conservation Service
concerned one of the most damaging practices by farmers, that
of burning off the stubble before plowing. The Soil Conservation
Service strongly opposed this practice. The SCS advocated leaving the stubble on the fields and plowing it only partially under,
which in turn expanded the practice of stubble mulching. And
stubble mulching was as important as chiseling in controlling
wind erosion.

Range management was the fourth area of conservation interest. Federal policies concerning rangelands were a mixture of
good and evil. Government encouragement to plant grasses and
prevent overgrazing were extremely beneficial. The value of contour listing grass lands was arguable. It was not apparent that
the increased grass crop resulting from breaking the sod was
offset by the amount of grass turned under. In grazing districts,
cattle were frequently delayed from moving onto new range because the grass was not sufficient. Often this resulted in over-
grazing the land the cattle were on.

Federal assistance to build stock dams helped provide temporary watering places for stock, but the dams usually went dry.
Although the dams were hailed as conservation practices that
would help stop wind erosion, they did very little to keep the
water where it was useful to plants. Fred O. Case, project manager of the Springfield, Colorado, Soil Conservation Project,
wanted "stock ponds to be fenced [because the] sharp hoofs tear
down fills."[34] Although Case wanted to build stock tanks down
for livestock, area stockmen rejected the policy because that involved intricate engineering and sharply reduced the usefulness
of the stock pond as a watering place. And fencing the water gap
at the head of the pond was not a simple task. Thus soil conservation rangeland policy had its strengths and weaknesses.

By providing a meaningful economic alternative for the
farmer, and by requiring that conservation practices be followed
on farms receiving assistance, the federal government had the
necessary powers to prevent disastrous wind erosion. The problems that remained were primarily of a scientific and technological nature: that is, perfecting methods of conservation best
adapted to the semiarid Plains. Determining the best way to use

stubble mulching and chiseling, developing new farm implements and refining existing ones, and increasing the manufacture
and distribution of equipment were all a part of the challenge.

The system of emergency tillage broke down. The insistence
of the Soil Conservation Service and Agricultural Adjustment officials that lister or chisel rows be run on the contour caused
great delays because the dust bowl did not have enough trained
"transit" people to survey quickly the contour lines. As a result,
land that needed work immediately did not get it for several
weeks. In the interlude, disaster struck many fields.

By 1936, the goal of removal and resodding the heartland of
the dust bowl was deeply entrenched. To achieve their goal, policy makers were willing to go to great lengths, and in the process to ignore or misrepresent many facts. Even Arthur H. Joel's
*Soil Conservation Reconnaissance Survey of the Southern Great
Plains Wind-Erosion Area* suggested that the survey was a preliminary study intended to justify a preconceived plan.

According to Joel, "Grant County, Kans., is the outstanding
exception to the correlation of serious damage with percentage
cultivated and percentage of soils very susceptible to erosion.
Although 83.6 percent of the land is cultivated or idle, only 27.2
percent of the area is rated as seriously damaged by erosion."[35]
A comparison of Grant and the adjacent county of Stanton gives
us an idea of how outstanding Grant County was. Stanton, similar in percent of acres cultivated and erodibility, had 75.1 percent affected by serious erosion. The three Kansas counties of
Morton, Stevens, and Stanton were at the very top of the list of
those seriously affected by erosion. Grant County was third from
the bottom of the list of counties. This discrepancy needs special
consideration. Joel accounted for the drastic "outstanding exception" by explaining:

> The party that surveyed [Grant] county was assigned to the
> project several weeks after the other parties had initiated
> the survey and therefore missed the opportunity which the
> other men had to correlate their interpretations with those
> of the survey group as a whole. It is therefore quite possi-
> ble that Grant County has been somewhat underrated as to
> serious erosion damage and that its position in table 13
> should be higher in the list of counties.[36]

The explanation leaves some intriguing questions. Why would several weeks' difference in the time the surveys were made make the dramatic differences in the findings? Was the overall condition of serious erosion extremely fluid? If the entire survey had been taken at the time that the Grant County survey was conducted, would all the counties have shown a much lower percentage of serious erosion? Had the Grant County farmers used any outstanding method of protecting the soil from erosion? What did Joel mean when he wrote "to correlate their interpretations"? It suggests that the survey parties met at an appointed time and adjusted their findings to fit a preconceived pattern.

In table 13 in *Soil Conservation Reconnaissance Survey,* Joel lists Cimarron County, Oklahoma, among those least affected by wind erosion, while the *National Resources Board Report December 1, 1934* map on General Distribution of Erosion shows the bulk of that county as "Essentially Destroyed by Wind Erosion."[37] Why did the two studies differ sharply on their findings concerning the effects of wind erosion in Cimarron County? Was the heartland of the dust bowl a rapidly changing region or were the investigators doing the changing?

Joel reports that Oldham County, Texas, had the least wind erosion damage. The National Resources Board map shows the county as "Intermixed mesas, valleys, scablands, Bare Mountain Tops, and Canyons."[38] The Canadian River Breaks were vastly different in topography and natural vegetation than were the level plains. The study itself had a built-in prejudice. The mesas themselves made excellent windbreaks for which there was no counterpart on the level plains.

In light of the position taken by the Resettlement Administration and the Report of the Great Plains Committee that farms were too small, Joel had some interesting comments. He wrote:

> Size of farms and nature of land tenure bear a close relation to erosion and to other prevailing problems. As shown by the data given in table 24 there were 16,805 farms in the area with an average acreage of 1,060 acres per farm. This included ranches. The average size of grain farms alone is smaller. The majority are as large as a half section, or 320 acres, and many are much larger than a section, or 640 acres. It is but natural that on such relatively large hold-

ings, under extensive systems of farming and under the
current handicap of economic stress, a large portion of the
land is not effectively controlled against erosion. The mere
physical size of holdings makes it very difficult to place all
the land under emergency tillage measures during critical
periods when speed and timeliness of operation are necessary. Impaired machinery and lack of funds add consider-
ably to the handicap. The situation is another strong
argument for removal of certain lands from cultivation and
the general reorganization of land use under a comprehensive plan of readjustment.[39]

Thus one group of investigators found the land holdings to be
too small, while another group found the land holdings to be too
large. But both groups wanted to remove land from private
ownership and to establish a comprehensive plan of agricultural
readjustment.

Joel's comments on farm size, timing of emergency tillage, and
the impact of the depression also opens the way for exploration
of other solutions to the farm problem. The problem of timing
could be offset by improved technology and technique, i.e.,
larger and faster tractors and bigger, improved implements. The
developments improving rubber tired tractors, which could pull
larger loads, were answering the problem of time. The development of the chisel, which was also advancing at the time of the
Joel reconnaissance, made wind control faster and more effec-
tive. The advancement out of the depression, with increased
grain prices and federal emergency lister payments, pointed the
way to offsetting the effects of lack of funds. As a result, H. H.
Finnell's conclusion that the region should be cultivated with
adjustments in techniques of farming could be arrived at as readily as Joel's position that land should be removed from cultivation.

Another intriguing question appears. If certain lands were removed from cultivation, what would be the condition of the remaining farms? The problem of farm size, delayed tillage, and
depression would still exist on the remaining farms. Also the
problems of isolated communities and high cost for government
services would still exist.

Comparing the findings of Joel and the Report of the Great

Plains Committee reveals some other interesting aspects. As noted above, the two differed dramatically over the issue of farm size. The problem Joel presents could be minimized if not solved by improved technology and technique. The Great Plains Committee played down the idea of solving the problem by advanced technology and technique:

> Therefore rehabilitation of a great region in which it has been discovered that economic activities are not properly adjusted to basic and controlling physical conditions, is not merely a problem of encouraging better farm practices and desirable engineering works, and revision of such institutions as ownership and tenure. It is also one of revision of some of the less obvious deep-seated attitudes of mind.[40]

Thus the committee wanted to plunge into the hazardous occupation of shaping men's minds as well as making changes in technology and techniques.

The Report of the Great Plains Committee reveals that the land-use planners misunderstood the Great Plains and its people. In the chapter entitled "Attitudes of Mind" the committee asks: "Why should there have been destructive tendencies in the use of land and water in the Great Plains?" Answering its own question, it stated:

> Chiefly, of course, because of the settlers' lack of understanding concerning critical differences between the physical conditions of the Great Plains area and those of the area east of the Mississippi whence they had come. Because of his lack of understanding the colonist applied agricultural practices brought from a humid region under conditions for which they eventually proved to be unsuitable.[41]

The report goes on to claim that the settlers, with ideas developed over generations, would not adapt themselves to the climate.

But the whole purpose of dry land farming was developed very early by Great Plains farmers who adapted their methods of farming to the region. The Department of Agriculture Division of Dryland Agriculture, established in 1906, was intended to aid farmers in adapting farming to the new climate. The large number of new implements and tillage methods developed for dry land farming represents the flexibility and adaptability of the Great Plains farmers. It was the vigorous adaption to changing technology during the 1920s agricultural revolution that spurred the great plow up. The primary cause of the maladjustment was too vigorous a shift from older to new farming methods. It is true that the farmers made mistakes, but it is equally true that the farmers were working to correct those errors. For they are the ones who developed new implements, adapted new technology, and perfected new techniques.

The Great Plains Committee virtually rejected any attempt to solve the problem of wind erosion through advancement in farming methods. Under the chapter entitled "Legal Problems" the committee states: "Erosion is so closely related to farm management and land-use practices that the mere construction of terraces and check dams alone is not adequate to control erosion. The legislative program should encourage also modification of those land-use and cropping practices which are undesirable."[42] Since terraces and check dams were designed to stop water erosion, they would not stop wind erosion. So the question was what modifications in land use and cropping practices they had in mind.

Under the title "Land Utilization," the *Yearbook of Agriculture 1935* explains, "the Agricultural Adjustment Act in 1933, brought the essential features of the preceding stages [land use policies] into a higher synthesis, involving the whole adjustment of agriculture to its economic environment. This is the stage of comprehensive agricultural planning."[43] So modifications in land use meant the development of a comprehensive agricultural plan. The comprehensive plan included the establishment of forest and wildlife refuges, the presumed coherent reorganization of land settlement, the checking of wrong uses of land, discovering new use for land withdrawn from production, discouraging farming on submarginal farms, and the coordinating of land use to crop adjustment.

In comprehensive agricultural planning, a key area of concern was retirement of submarginal lands from farming. The National Resources Board located and described submarginal farms. "In general, these areas are found in hilly forested parts, and the dryer portions of the Great Plains, and regions of light, sandy soil and in areas of serious erosion. With a few notable exceptions they are characterized by sparse settlement, necessitating high per capita cost for public services." The Report continued:

> The poor land areas are replete with social and economic maladjustments. In a very vivid way they are literally the slums of the country. Incomes are low . . . , credit is expensive, the people are often poorly housed and ill fed; educational and cultural opportunities are meager, while governmental services are either at a minimum or are provided at high expenses to both the community and the larger public.[44]

The *National Resources Board Report* shows that most of southeastern Colorado and part of southwestern Kansas were areas where the submarginal farms should be removed from production. The soil in the area, however, was very fertile; thus the proposed removal was not caused by lack of soil fertility. The report also shows the farmers' income among the highest in the nation before the depression. Thus, the heartland of the dust bowl was not a poor-soil, low-income slum. The most poverty-ridden farm regions of the nation were in the humid climate south of the Ohio River. When addressing himself to the question from whence came most of the Okies, Walter J. Stein noted: "The actual dust bowl was but a part of the drought region and most of the Okies came neither from the dust bowl nor from the areas of worst distress in the drought region."[45] The Okies came from the humid areas of Oklahoma, Texas, Missouri, and Arkansas. The humid four-state area was part of the poverty area illustrated on the National Resources Board map. The economy of the dust bowl during the depression was no worse than the nation's economy. And the Oklahoma Panhandle paid a much higher portion of revenue sharing than did other parts of the state. Therefore, the justification for removing the farmers because of poverty or soil fertility was weak.

Comprehensive land-use planning objectives cannot be directed primarily at soil conservation requirements. "Wind and water are the agents of accelerated erosion," reported the *Yearbook of Agriculture 1935*. "Erosion by water is the more serious evil . . ."[46] As noted earlier, the Soil Conservation Service did little to develop methods of preventing wind erosion on cultivated land. In fact, the primary program advocated by all the federal agencies to reduce wind erosion was returning the region to grass.

Baca County, Colorado, experienced a boom in population during the 1920s, and the entire dust bowl was in the process of moving from a frontier society to an established area when the depression hit. Because the transition was not completed, housing was inadequate, roads needed construction, and public services needed improvement. The educational and cultural opportunities were deficient. But in each instance, the standard of living was advancing well before the depression occurred, and, even during the depression, the transition from frontier life to a permanent high standard of living was continued. When asked which was the worst, "settling the region or the dust bowl," one old-timer replied, "settling the country because there was nothing here. Even if you had a pocket full of money you couldn't buy anything."[47]

The advancements in technology during the 1920s, and the shift from frontier society to established communities, did cause some serious problems, but adjustments were taking place. The area did have a small population, but removing a large portion of the population would not solve the problem of providing adequate services and social advancement to those who remained. A logical solution lay in assisting the positive improvements already in process. But the federal land-use planners wanted to discourage further development of the dust bowl. The development of the five-state area did not mesh with the goals of the comprehensive agricultural program that Washington had set its heart on. In 1937, the government began to work to fulfill those goals.

9

Wheat and Land Use

"As you know," wrote Caroline A. Henderson, "however wisely or otherwisely, this region has permitted wheat growing to become its main concern."[1] During the 1920s and early 1930s, the heartland of the dust bowl, as part of the Great Plains, had become a highly successful producer of wheat. Through the use of advanced technology, Great Plains farmers were able to compete most successfully with eastern wheat growers.

"Should farmers with fertile crop land," asked the *Yearbook of Agriculture 1935*, "continue to keep a portion of it out of production, or should the adjustment be made by the elimination of production on the submarginal land?" Answering its own question, the *Yearbook* suggested that submarginal land be removed from production.[2]

Under the Soil Conservation and Domestic Allotment Act of 1936, wheat was listed as a soil-depleting crop. Thus, the primary crop of the five-state area was to be strictly controlled. The success of the Agricultural Adjustment Act in reducing the wheat surplus and providing for a sound farming economy was questionable. It appeared that the drought was better than the government program at restricting wheat production. The question was what would happen after the drought years ended and the most economical wheat producing area of the nation again raised large quantities of wheat. And what was to be done with the Great Plains, where few cash crops could be raised? Return it to

grass and raise livestock, cried the advocates of sustained agricultural planning. Thus the source of the problem between the
New Dealers and the residents of the dust bowl becomes apparent. The men in Washington did not want wheat raised in that
portion of the nation, and the folks on the land wished to raise
wheat.[3]

By 1937, M. L. Wilson was under-secretary of agriculture,
with responsibilities for directing government affairs in the dust
bowl. In the 1920s, Wilson had directed the Fairway Farms,
Inc. experiments of land use by resettlement and scientific farming. The Fairway Farms were the antecedent experiment for the
Resettlement Administration and other government programs.
During President Roosevelt's first term, Wilson was appointed
chief of the Public Works Administration Subsistence Homestead
Division. Wilson was also chairman of the Land Planning Committee under the National Resources Board. And the father of
"rational land use plannings," L. C. Gray, was director of the
Land Section. By the time Wilson became under-secretary he
had several years' experience in promoting his program. With
the appointment he was in a position to carry out his concept of
a rational land-use program on a grand scale.[4]

As part of the effort to carry through the long-sought dream,
Roy I. Kimmel was appointed coordinator of the several federal
agencies in Region Twelve, which included the heartland of the
dust bowl. Kimmel was raised in New Mexico before attending
Colorado College and Yale University. After completing his mas-
ters program at Yale, Kimmel became assistant director of the
School of Public Affairs at Princeton. He joined the Resettlement Administration in 1935, and early in 1936 he came to the
dust bowl to organize the Southwest Great Plains region for the
Resettlement Administration. Kimmel was ready in 1937 to put
his organization into operation.[5]

The new federal structure soon made itself felt by restricting
farm loans, especially on wheat; however, loans were available
for livestock raising. The new organization emphasized livestock
raising by encouraging the construction of pit silos and range-
improvement practices. To facilitate the exodus of people from
certain areas, relief work was stopped. In Morton County, Kansas, a target area for land purchases, in a two-week period in
August, after relief work was stopped, many people became re-

fugees. Most of the families who moved hoped to return and reestablish their lives, but instead they became like characters in *The Grapes of Wrath*. With the loss of customers, the *Morton County Farmer* closed its doors—a victim of high level planning.[6]

The farmers in the five-state area were not ready to give up. They dealt a big blow to the scheme of reorganizing their society and drastically changing their land ownership by voting down the proposed Soil Conservation Districts. The shift in the decision-making power to an absentee landlord with extensive authority was more than the farmers would agree to. Many of the farmers had immigrated from nations where the land use was administered by the government, and they wanted no part of it in their new homeland. With Representative Marvin Jones holding the chairmanship of the House Agriculture Committee, the Agriculture Department had to work carefully to depopulate his congressional district.[7]

The advancement of soil conservation took a major step forward with the approval of state laws and county ordinances that required that idle land be properly protected from wind erosion. Most of the absentee landowners had simply left their land untouched, and these farms became severe menaces to neighboring fields and a primary source of wind erosion. With the passage of laws that required attention to the soil, and the subsequent attention given the abandoned fields, the erosive impact of the wind was significantly reduced.[8]

The laws had an important side effect for the region. With the introduction of tractors, combines, one-way plows, and trucks, the most economical size of farm moved sharply upward. When the drought and depression struck the five-state area, the land ratio of farms was radically out of balance. A better balance in farm units occurred after the laws requiring soil maintenance were passed. Absentee landowners who were unable to care for their abandoned land, and still faced the cost of maintaining the soil, began leasing and selling their property to resident farmers. There was an infinite variety of land agreements, but overall, the land ratio to farm units and farmers was significantly improved. Land control adjustment of farm size was accomplished without major depopulation of the region. The adjustments necessary to meet the challenge of the changing technology occurred without extensively reorganizing the society and its culture. During the 1940s, "the boys that stuck it out did alright."[9] The simple but practical solution of increasing the individual farmer's holdings and land control worked miracles in solving the vexing problem of farm size. While local farmers were making their adjustments for raising wheat, federal policy makers were plunging along a different line.

One of the primary reasons for turning the dust bowl back to grass was to find a permanent solution to the surplus production of wheat. By the government plan, eastern areas would raise wheat while western areas raised cattle. The federal men encouraged digging pit silos in order to develop a winter feed supply for livestock. Instead of grazing cattle on wheat during the winter months, the stock would be fed the sort of silage and stocks used by Iowa livestock raisers.

Agricultural experts ran into a snag with the silage program. Sorghums were raised to fill the silos, but in the process the increased supply of sorghums flooded the market and reduced the income of the farmers who had always raised sorghums and broomcorn. Under pressure from sorghum farmers, the Agriculture Department encouraged wheat farmers to raise sorghum but prohibited them from harvesting it for either grain or silage. Farmers did not see any advantage in building silos if they could not be filled, and without stored winter feed it was necessary for farmers to raise wheat for their livestock to graze on.

The Southwest Agricultural Association met in Guymon in July 1937 and approved a set of resolutions presented to Roy I. Kimmel. The resolutions called for the implementation of several conservation practices and the creation of county committees with broad discretionary powers to assure that the conservation measures were practiced by individual farmers. The association agreed that wild lands should be returned to grass either through government purchase or private effort.[10]

The primary difference between the position of the Southwest Agricultural Association resolutions and the position of the federal government was over what type of economy and society should exist in the dust bowl. The agricultural association wanted a community based on cultivation; the government wanted a pastoral system and government-planned agriculture. The two organizations also differed sharply over what constituted submarginal farms. The association based its definition on the soil while the government formed its definition from a host of conditions.

In January 1937, the Resettlement Administration attempted to persuade Cimarron County farmers to resettle in southwest Texas. A family could lease 80 to 120 acres without charge for two years, after which the family could purchase the land for $20 to $35 per acre, and the government would loan them the money to do so. "The land [was] virgin, some of it with heavy mesquite growth."[11] Apparently some Cimarron farmers did resettle; however, the majority of the farmers did not care for spending two years clearing the mesquite, breaking the land out for farming, and then buying it at the price of developed land. It would be like homesteading again, only the homesteaders would have to purchase an established farm.

In March 1937 the leading citizens in Boise City proposed a program whereby 200 families would be resettled on irrigated farms along the Cimarron River. It was pointed out that Julius Kohler had built a dam on the river two years earlier and had been successfully producing 60-bushel corn on the land. The idea of irrigation was not new to the region. Since 1905 two artesian wells had been putting water on the soil south of Richfield, Kansas. In 1937 Liberal, Kansas, completed an artesian well that produced 750 gallons of water per minute. And at Panhandle A & M an irrigation system was successfully installed. But the idea of resettling dust bowl farmers on irrigated farms in the five-state area was not in keeping with the government's plans for scientifically resodding the region. Consequently the irrigation plan was dropped.[12]

With the passage of the Bankhead-Jones Tenant Act in July 1937, the federal government accelerated land acquisitions. The Beaver *Herald-Democrat* reported that "M. L. Wilson, Undersecretary of Agriculture, said 'department officials hope the whole great area will move in the direction of shifting from cultivated land to grazing land.'" The newspaper article continued: "Other department spokesmen said that through these purchases they hoped to control indirectly the land use of as much as 10,000,000 acres."[13] Thus the government hoped to buy a little and control a lot of land, in keeping with Charles Beard's plan for syndicating farming, a plan Rexford Tugwell admired and which was consistent with the long-range goals for a comprehensive agricultural plan.

The whole situation of credit, farm programs, relief stoppages, government reports, and official statements caused the residents of the five-state region to look askance at the land purchase. To quiet the fears, government representatives began a series of local meetings. In Dalhart, Texas, J. C. Foster, Regional Director of the Land Utilization Division of the Bureau of Agricultural Economics explained that the "acreage sought is 'wild land,' not under lease or operation and which is or may be a wind erosion menace to adjacent land."[14]

The request for the purchase of a tract of land for the Kiowa Grasslands in New Mexico by Felix E. Neff and others in 1938 was revealing when compared to Foster's statement. "It is considered to be very important," wrote Neff, "that such lands be purchased as soon as budgetary considerations will permit, in order that they may be brought under a system of management in conformity with the other lands within the project, and further, to forestall their future acquisition by small farmers."[15] So they wanted to rush the purchase of land lest a private individual buy it first. A farmer who did not have a large enough unit to operate economically might decide to expand onto land desired by the government.

Foster stated that "the acreage sought was 'wild land' not under lease or operation . . ."[16] Of the 91,173 acres sought in the Neff request, however, only 4,133 acres were abandoned. In fact, "emigration from this area is not as great as from other areas of this region."[17] Thus Foster's statement and Neff's action are quite different. The Neff request and *The Future of the Great Plains* provide some interesting comparisons. *The Future of the Great Plains* "recommended that assistance in the enlargement of undersized operating units be provided: (1) through extension of credit under suitable restrictions, and (2) experimentally through Federal purchase of selected land and its subsequent lease or sale under covenants protecting its use."[18] On the proposed purchase for the Kiowa Grasslands, "Approximately three-fourths of the operators are on units too small to support a farm family . . ."[19] The agents wanted to rush purchases and obviously did not want credit, even under proper restrictions extended to any of the small farmers so that they could purchase larger tracts. The federal men wanted the land controlled under covenants to the landlord. Clearly, there was a vast difference between words and deeds.

The justification for the purchase of individual tracts suggests the government's true intent. For example, the justification for the purchase of Tract No. 5106 owned by A. G. Ratlief was: "Tract so small as to require the practice of a type of farming which involves serious mis-use of the land, . . ."[20] Ratlief's farm was 460 acres, which may have been too small a farm, but the federal government did not encourage a small farmer to purchase Tract No. 5116. The justification for the purchase of Tract No. 5116, amounting to 1,840 acres owned by the Federal Land Bank, was: "Consists of an operating unit which is uneconomic in its present and prospective use under existing ownership. . . . The acquisition of this tract with 5124 and 5114 will block up a unit which will be economical in its projected use."[21] Under Land Bank ownership the place was uneconomical. Of course, the Land Bank was in the credit business and not in ranching. But 1,840 acres added to a smaller farm, say 460 acres, would make a unit well above the 1,500-acre minimum expressed for farm size in a 1937 publication of the Resettlement Administration's *Land Policy Circular*. But instead of helping small landowners get bigger, the federal government was looking out for its own interests.

Federal land buyers paid Sarah Hoeffner $8.00 per acre for her land, which was well above the price paid for other tracts. The justification was: "Consists of cultivated land unsuited to crop production and land not previously cultivated, and normally unadapted to the production of cultivated crops, but open potentially to crop use in periods of abnormally favorable price and climatic conditions. *Tract has good water supply which is necessary for proper range management of adjacent units*"[22] (italics added). The justification fails to mention wind eroded land and presumably there was none, but the water was important for setting up Uncle Sam's ranch out west.

The tenor of the justifications for the eighteen parcels of land listed under the purchase request suggests that the government was busy establishing a big cow outfit. To gain control over water, the government was willing to pay the highest of prices. Not all the tracts of land suffered from wind erosion and only a few of the tracts could be described as wild. Of the eighteen tracts of land in the purchase, six were owned by the Federal Land

Bank. And the federal purchasers were not above squeezing a farmer off his land. Part of the justification for the purchase of Tract No. 5115 from Claudia Martin was: "This tract should be purchased because it is a part of the operated unit which includes Tract 93. Tract 93 . . . should be taken out of crop production."[23] The purchase request explained that an unidentified man owned Tract 93 and leased Tract 5115. It was strongly implied that by purchasing the farmer's leased land and breaking up the farming unit, the owner of Tract 93 would be forced to sell to the federal government.

The 110 acres of cultivated land on Tract No. 5115 in the Kiowa Grasslands was not seriously damaged by wind erosion. The purchase request claimed: "The soil is light loam and is a *potential menace* if crop cultivation is continued"[24] (italics added). After eight years of continuous drought, with an average precipitation of 10.60 inches, and one year (1933) with only 4.88 inches of precipitation and strong winds, the cultivated lands in Union County that were inclined to blow had already blown. Apparently the term "potential danger" was a catchall phrase used to meet the soil conservation requirement for justifying land acquisitions. In the case of Tract No. 5115, potential danger was used to squeeze a man out of his home on Tract No. 93.

Land was purchased at the lowest dollar possible, regardless of poverty or needs of the seller. The Base Map Tabular Record for Cimarron and Comanche Grasslands shows the tremendous difference in prices for tracts of land. Table 9.1 illustrates the differences in price for land in one township in Morton County, Kansas.[25] When the farmer was the poorest and least capable of resisting pressure, the federal government paid the lowest price.

TABLE 9.1
Land Prices in Morton County, Kansas, 1936–39

Price	Acre Size	Year Purchased	Mineral Rights
$ 625	160	1939	Vendor sold
1,588	160	1936	Vendor sold
640	160	1936	Vendor sold
640	160	1938	Vendor sold
3,040	360	1936	Vendor reserved for 50 years
2,054	160	1937	Vendor reserved for 50 years
1,040	160	1936	Vendor reserved for 50 years
270	160	1939	Vendor sold

These hardcore poor farmers were the submarginal farmers whom the government professed to help.

The purchases of land for the four grasslands in the five-state area were simply real estate deals. The Resettlement Administration and other agencies provided few additional opportunities, resettlement, or retraining for those forced to sell their land. And most of the land was occupied at the time of purchase. The old owners simply moved off and the new absentee landlord took over.

J. C. Foster told the area residents that the government was only interested in purchasing the "wild lands," not under lease or operation, which threatened adjacent land. But the "Tri-State Land Utilization and Land Conservation Project's Land Acquisition Plan," which started the purchase of land in eastern Union County, said something different. The purpose stated: "Changing the use of land from dependence on crop farming to a system of livestock farming and ranching supplemented by the growing of reliable, supplementary feed crops will stabilize agriculture in this area and in the future will provide an adequate living for operators remaining."[26]

The instability of the livestock industry due to blizzards, drought, and drops in market prices was well recorded. Land-use planners had only to look back as far as the Drought Cattle Purchase Program of 1934 and the problems of the livestock business after World War I. Therefore, what did the land-use planners have in mind when referring to reliable supplementary feed crops? In the project area of 91,173 acres, "forage crops production is the major use given for the cultivated land within the operated unit."[27] The purchase proposal shows 14,574 acres in forage crops with only 1,318 acres planted to wheat. Only 4,133 acres were classified as abandoned crop land; approximately two-thirds of the land was in native grass. Clearly the purchase area was primarily a rangeland and farmers were attempting to raise a crop suited to livestock production. Although the vast majority of the landowners were attempting to raise livestock, they were in an unstable economy that did not provide an adequate living. The average annual gross income per operator was: "Owners $293, Tenant $351, and Part-Owner $484."[28] The critical items of forage crops and rangeland directed towards the livestock business was in existence before the government began their purchases. What the residents needed was credit enough to buy out their neighbors so that they could become large enough to be successful economically.

Before going on with land acquisition and regrassing, let us pause to consider the tenant farmer. One of the big items analyzed by land-use planners was farm tenancy. Statements made by the National Resources Board, the Resettlement Administration, and the Great Plains Committee bluntly say or strongly imply that tenant farmers were the worst, poverty-ridden class of farmers. But in the Kiowa Grasslands acquisition, "The owners are the lowest [in income], no doubt due to the overhead expense involved in maintaining title to their land and also because they are on smaller units . . ."[29] The McMillian Report on Baca County noted, "The evils of short tenure are no more serious than the small size of farms to which the tenants gravitate."[30] Thus the farm size was the problem and not the farm ownership. And the small farms were one of the stepping stones from tenancy to large farm ownership. But federal policies destroyed the stepping-stone bridge without providing anything to help the tenants cross the chasm.

As head of Land Utilization Projects, George S. Atwood arrived in Elkhart, Kansas, in February 1938 to begin purchasing additional acres in Morton County. The *Elkhart Tri-State News* reported that:

> the area in which the program will operate includes a good portion of Taloga, Cimarron and Rolla townships and comprises about 100,000 acres. The area in which the government will buy lies south of the river taking in almost the entire southern part of the county, excluding the land already purchased by the government. The northern boundary runs in a parallel fashion with the Cimarron River while the southern boundary is almost parallel with [the] county line.[31]

Since most of the land within the published boundary was on farm land in the rolling terrain formed by untold dust storms blowing out of the Cimarron River, Atwood received support from most of the county residents. To assist Atwood, the *Tri-State News* made it clear to its readers that he did not represent the Resettlement Administration.

For the first year things went smoothly for Atwood. Then in early January 1939 it was discovered that the government was taking options on good land and much of it was north of the river, along a line not parallel with the stream. Immediately residents began contacting their congressmen and demanding an investigation. Representative Clifford Hope informed the Morton County people that he would insist on an investigation to be held in Elkhart. By the end of January, attorneys for both sides were preparing for the hearing.[32]

In late February, the purchase of land near Kerrick, Texas, resulted in the protest spreading to Texas. A. M. James, who helped organize the farmers to fight the menace of wind erosion back in 1934, and Joe Taylor led the opposition. The men checked the Bankhead-Jones Act and claimed "that the bill authorizing the program directed that only submarginal or 'wild land' could be bought." The men understood "wild land to mean land that is a blowing hazard and that apparently cannot be controlled unless the government takes it over, restores it to a permanent vegetative cover, . . ."[33] When Foster explained the goals of the program, he used the same definition of wild land understood by James and Taylor. But the land near Kerrick was not wild land. With the spreading of the opposition, the Department of Agriculture ordered an investigation into the land purchases. The action stopped any congressional investigations; further land purchases were carried on with much more discretion and, for the most part, remained on wild lands. The remaining purchases were primarily closings of options already taken and efforts to block up land for legitimate administrative purposes. The protests in 1939, the improvement in the region's economy, and the return of more normal precipitation brought an end to the expansion of the government scheme to turn the land back to a pastoral economy, to remove the residents, to reorganize the culture, and to establish a system of land ownership whereby the government strictly managed the area's agriculture.

In 1934, H. H. Finnell took a leave of absence from Panhandle A & M College and moved to the wind erosion research project in Dallam County, Texas. The acreages for the project consisted of the first federal purchases and leases of the land, and later became Rita Blanca National Grassland. In 1935, the

Resettlement Administration began buying land near Mills, New Mexico. These purchases were the first for the Kiowa National Grassland. In 1934, by executive order transferring public domain, and also by acquisition, the Resettlement Administration obtained a large tract of land in Otero County, Colorado. This land became the northern part of the Comanche National Grassland. The first acquisitions in Morton County, Kansas (53,590 acres), became part of the Cimarron National Grassland. The publicly expressed purpose for purchasing the land was to assist in the rehabilitation of the people who lived in the dust bowl and to protect a precious national resource from wanton exploitation and permanent loss by returning the land to grass. Government officials believed that the program they offered was a rational land-utilization program that would stabilize the region's agriculture.

Since the government argued that much could be accomplished if their scheme was followed, it is legitimate to ask how well they did manage their land during the dust bowl days. After the buildings and fences were removed:

> The land was then listed with farm listers, which on hummocky land were pulled by crawler tractors. This work progressed the year round except when the ground was frozen. From May through July, the land was listed and planted at the same time for more effective stabilization. A forage sorghum [most commonly Black Amber] and broomcorn were used in these stabilization plantings. . . . In the fall rye was drilled on some land previously listed, but it was not so effective as listed cane or broomcorn.[34]

Resident farmers in the dust bowl were doing precisely the same thing, though substituting winter wheat for winter rye. Winter wheat was a more reliable cover crop, although "tainted" because of its overproduction and being blamed for causing the dust bowl. Farmers worked their land to prevent blowing and even developed new implements to assist them in the fight. Black Amber and other sorghums, as well as broomcorn and sudan grass, were planted to prevent wind erosion and provide a cover crop.

"Not until 1940, 5 years after the first land purchases, did the temporary stabilization program reduce the blow area to less than 1,000 acres."[35] The above statement gives credit to the temporary stabilization program for reducing the blow area. But the return of the rains made the big difference. The change on all the land, both public and private, was rapid and thrilling to the residents. By 1940, the wind erosion of the 1930s was a mere shadow. Even idle land that had not been extensively worked lay comparatively quiet.

The federal land-use planners advocated returning the heartland of the dust bowl to grass. But, "in 1939, when the first permanent plantings were made, little information was available on methods of preparing a seedbed for perennial grasses."[36] The first plantings failed. The first permanent plantings were made four years after the government had started its program of reseeding the dust bowl to grass, but apparently in the interlude very little, if anything, was done to discover what was necessary to plant to grass, and no implements were developed to facilitate the project. The oversight in making proper preparations—of acquiring knowledge and developing techniques and technology for reseeding the land to grass—hardly denotes rational planning.

After the failure of the 1939 grass crop, the Soil Conservation Service, State Experiment Stations, and other scientific organizations began a series of studies to learn how to raise native grass on the Great Plains. Finally in 1945, (that is, eleven years after Finnell began the studies near Dalhart, ten years after the Resettlement Administration purchased its first land, and five years after the dust bowl died a natural death) it was learned how to plant native grass.

Between 1945 and 1950 reseeding the Cimarron National Grassland proceeded at the rate of forty acres per year. Finally in 1950, through the use of advanced technology (one-way plows, airplanes, seed distributing implements, and sand lovegrass), the federal government began a massive reseeding program of the land purchased during the drought of the 1930s. The project was completed just in time; the extremely wet decade of the 1940s was over and the extremely severe drought of the 1950s was just around the corner.[37]

It was fifteen years between the time the government purchased the land and the time it was reseeded. Two of the years were extremely dry; three of the years were times of the rains returning; and ten of the years were part of the wettest decade recorded on the southern Great Plains. In 1947, H. H. Finnell resurveyed 2,347,480 acres of Arthur Joel's original 16,313,377-acre survey. "What commonly happened," reported Finnell, "on abandoned fields during the 1930's was the eventual stabilization of erosion conditions by natural vegetation; this natural stabilization usually was brought about by invasion of annual weeds and later by invasion of perennial grasses and other plants of a more permanent value."[38] Although the natural revegetation was not complete by 1947, apparently nature was well ahead of man.

What type of land did the government purchase? Generally it was argued that the land was plowed to plant wheat. But very little of the four national grasslands in the heartland of the dust bowl were located on wheat land. They were on rangeland and land planted to row crops. In part, the location of the grasslands was due to the insistance of the area residents that federal purchases be restricted to the wild lands. Back in 1930, the Texas County Soil Survey noted that the row crop lands were blowing. Finnell reported: "the percentage of plowed acreage abandoned from all causes at any one time ranged from 8 to 64 on hard lands at different places, but from 58 to 81 percent on the sandy row-crop lands under like conditions."[39] The row crops were forage sorghums and broomcorn. From these lands came the broomcorn which made Elkhart, Kansas, the "Broomcorn Capital of the Nation" and Wilburton and Rolla, Kansas, Texline, Texas, and Walsh, Colorado, large broomcorn shipping centers. The row crop land was loess soil—born of the wind.

On the four grasslands, two-thirds or more of the land was in native grass at the time the government acquired the property, and most of the cultivated land was in row crops where the farmers were engaged in livestock raising. That was the system of agriculture the government planners desired to establish in the dust bowl. Thus they were buying the wrong places to achieve the expressed goal. The justification for the proposed land-utilization system was predicated in part on the premise that the result would stabilize agriculture in the region and bring prosperity to the people. Examples of how "the people" fared follow.

Ernest C. Hemphill came to Union County, New Mexico, with his family in 1908. Before entering the army during World War I, he homesteaded on a section of land. The Veterans Administration encouraged Hemphill to attend college and he graduated with a degree in Livestock Production and Range Management. He then returned to Union County and in 1924 received the deed to his section of land. That same year he became the manager of a large cattle ranch. The ranch went broke in 1932 because of the depression and the drought. After working a Star Mail Route for a couple of years, Hemphill started working for the Biological Survey, controlling rodents and predators. In October 1935, he began working for the Soil Conservation Service. Here he became a leader in reseeding Kiowa Grasslands so that large-scale livestock production would bring stability to the region's agricultural economy. Ironically, the failure of a large-scale cattle operation forced Hemphill into a position whereby he became a leader in working towards establishing large cattle ranches to bring a stable and prosperous economy to the region.[40]

The holdings of Foster Elliot provide yet another guide to the instability of livestock raising on large ranches. In 1928 Elliot operated in Las Animas and Baca counties, Colorado, Cimarron County, Oklahoma, and Morton County, Kansas. At one time he ran nearly 20,000 head of livestock on his Cimarron, Baca, and Morton county holdings. In 1933, Elliot gave up the operation. In 1938, the Kansas portion of Elliot's holdings, the Point of Rock Ranch, united with Wood and Mae Walsh's 81 Ranch to become the basic unit of Cimarron National Grasslands.

The desires of the federal government to establish constructive conservation practices in the region was illuminated by the agencies responsible for establishing grasslands. In the spring of 1935 the Soil Conservation Service was established to promote conservation practices and to preserve our natural soil resources. Logically the Soil Conservation Service would have been held responsible for correcting the land misuse in the dust bowl and providing methods of controlling the erosion. Instead, the Resettlement Administration held primary responsibility for the soil conservation. The titles of the organizations and their position of responsibility suggest the government's goal. The Resettlement Administration was replaced by the Farm Security Administration followed by the Bureau of Agricultural Economics. Finally in November 1938, the grasslands came under the auspices of the Soil Conservation Service. The shift to the Soil Conservation

Service marked a major shift in the federal government's experiment in land use and social reorganization along lines consistant
with the government leaders' missionary spirit and desires to use
the general public as specimens in a great laboratory for social
experimentation. Yet, many of the folks who fell victim to the
experiment carried its marks.

The national grasslands story of changing dustland to grassland
was not a heroic effort by farsighted men who wished to undo
the sins of the past and give the region the blessings of a re-
birth. It was a sad story of men inflicted with a missionary spirit
and little understanding of the problems or their solutions.

10

Living Through It All

The story of the dust bowl was the story of people—folks who had the courage and fortitude to endure the stress and strain of the dirty thirties, and to emerge scarred but victorious. The hardy men, women, and children who lived through the dust bowl had a rich culture to assist them in their struggle to build a better tomorrow.

The vast majority of the residents had come when the land first opened for homesteading. When they arrived there were no shelters, towns, or community activities. Even those settlers who had a little money were forced to withstand a "starving period" until stores were built and stocked, markets were established, and crops were harvested. Every new farm family experienced a difficult time until dugouts were ready for occupancy, wells were dug, and fuel obtained. When one old-timer was asked which was the hardest period, settling the country or the dust bowl days, he quickly responded that settling the region had been more difficult.

The pioneering days on subsistence farms provided the folks with the know-how to survive depressions and droughts. Most families raised small truck gardens and orchards with fresh fruits and vegetables for canning. During the lean dust bowl years one industrious girl, Miss Anna Cronkhite, put an underground irrigation system in her garden plot and pumped water from the windmill. The garden met the family requirements and yielded sufficient surplus for a small income. Several other farmers and townspeople developed ingenious ways of raising a small truck farm.[1]

When cash was very scarce, local merchants did a lively barter business with farmers. The region's wide variation in weather and crops during the pre–dust bowl had taught the farmers to prepare for lean years and had given them a lively sense of trading. Further, to maintain themselves during difficult times it was common for farm families to have a large larder. Thus the pioneering days had made seasoned veterans of "making do" out of the folks who lived through the dust bowl days.

The pioneering spirit of the people was reenforced with a knowledge of the country when times were good. The bumper crops of the 1920s and the phenomenal crop of 1931 helped sustain the people during the hard years The faith in the land was expressed by E. M. Dean and Bertha Carpenter. In 1935 these authors, who lived in Morton County, Kansas, for several years, wrote a brief history of the region. The narrative vividly describes the early settlement and the dust bowl until 1935. "But like the original colonists," conclude Dean and Carpenter, "hope filters the atmosphere with a golden glamour for a number. Some yet have a pure unfounded faith in the benevolence of nature. They know the rains will fall and another boom will again bring new settlers to the country. A regular alternation of boom and droughts is inevitable."[2]

Edna Barnes, who lived at Forgan, Oklahoma, during the long drought never despaired of the region. Although the family was hard pressed and some years her father failed to raise a crop, someone near them raised enough to encourage the rest to stay and try again. W. D. Ross was forced to move from his leased farm north of Goodwell, Oklahoma, when the landowners sold out in 1934. He moved to Portales, New Mexico, for a year. But responding to the love of home, in 1935 he leased a farm northeast of Guymon, Oklahoma. In the midst of the blowing dirt, drought, and depression he returned his large family to the dust bowl. In 1940 he purchased a farm northeast of Texhoma, Oklahoma, where he and his wife still live. Their return to the stricken area was prompted by a belief that conditions would improve. For as all old-timers knew, it rains at the end of a dry spell. It always has.[3]

"In March 1935," John Carsel Dougherty and his wife Nellie, "got tired of the 'dust bowl' weather, and moved to Rocky Ford, Colorado, but left enough household goods in [the] basement to batch with, . . . [They] lived in Colorado for about a year, but," similar to the Ross family, "got homesick for Oklahoma, so they moved back."[4]

"Why not pick up and leave as so many others have done? It is a fair question, but a hard one to answer," wrote Caroline A. Henderson from Eva, Oklahoma. She continued:

> Recently I talked with a young university graduate of very superior attainments. He took the ground that in such a case sentiment could and should be disregarded. He may be right. Yet I cannot act or feel or think as if the experiences of our twenty-seven years of life together had never been. And they are all bound up with the little corner to which we have given our continued and united efforts. To leave voluntarily—to break all these closely knit ties for the sake of a possible greater comfort elsewhere—seems like defaulting on our task.[5]

For many of the farmers who called the five-state area home, the changing complexion of agriculture doomed their chances of remaining on the land they loved. The tractor, combine, truck, and one-way plow demanded that farms become larger. Before these stern requirements all other forces yielded. The out-migration of farmers and the increase in farm size were in full swing when the depression hit the region. One of the most tragic stories of the depression was the hopelessness of the farmer squeezed from his land by technology, but unable to find other employment because of the depression.

"The Okie migration did not begin in earnest until 1935," wrote Walter J. Stein in *California and the Dust Bowl Migration*.[6] Why did the dust bowl Okies leave their homes in 1935? That year business conditions began to improve markedly and the oil and gas industry took on new life in the heartland of the dust bowl. The worst of the hard years were coming to an end. Caroline Henderson puts us on the trail to answering the question. "In our country the FERA force was being cut down. Three case workers and two from the office force have been dismissed during the past week."[7] Soon President Franklin D.

Roosevelt vetoed the feed and seed loan bill, and WPA workers were forced to leave the farm if they were employed on a project. The number of projects was reduced. In 1935 the federal government began its program of turning the dust bowl back to grass. To achieve that end, they had to drive out the people of the stricken area. The often tragic Okie migration from the heartland of the dust bowl to California and elsewhere was largely caused by policies of the federal government. The government talked a great deal about resettlement and improving the lot of the very poor, but accomplished very little of concrete value.

Despite pressure from Washington, the majority of the Okies in the heartland of the dust bowl remained. Most of the Okie migrants came from the deep poverty ridden, non-dust bowl areas of Oklahoma, Arkansas, Missouri, and Texas. In Oklahoma the panhandle was the only area of the state that truly fit the Great Plains definition of a shortgrass, treeless, semiarid tableland. The census of 1930 reported the total population of the panhandle as 30,960. In 1940 the three counties posted a population of 22,198, a decrease of 8,762 people. Since the people went in all directions when they left the region, it is safe to assume that less than 50 percent went to California. Approximately 4,000 people did not reflect a major national migration. To view all Okies as people migrating from the dust bowl misses some important factors in understanding the dust bowl people and the Okie migration to California. The confusion of combining the refugees from both the humid and semi-humid regions apparently results from the extensive news coverage given the dust bowl in 1935.[8]

The difference in percentage of matching money required for WPA projects suggests the difference in the poverty of the two regions. In the semiarid dust bowl region of Oklahoma, local governments paid approximately 50 percent of the cost of a project. In the humid areas the local governments paid approximately 20 percent of the project cost. If the cost sharing was honestly based on an area's ability to pay, the poverty of the humid area was much greater than in the semiarid dust bowl. The National Resources Board's map locating the worst areas of poverty plainly indicates the humid area was much worse than the Great Plains.[9]

Migration from the dust bowl was also restricted by the lack of

a meaningful place to migrate to. The people who left the dust
bowl for California or other areas left behind friends and rela-
tives. Communications were maintained either by mail or visits.
The conditions and the opportunities elsewhere were realized by
dust bowl residents, for they knew times were tough all over.
The scarcity of attractive places to move to, however, was not
the only reason people remained in the heartland of the dust
bowl. At home there were friends, church, community, enter-
tainment, opportunity, and tradition—a friendly culture. At
home was a sense of history.

Vi Kraft recalled the Baptist preacher at Hooker, Oklahoma,
telling the congregation that "the Lord had put them there for a
reason, and it was their obligation to remain."[10] Churches and
Christ were extremely important to most folks. In the late 1920s
the five-state area experienced a revival that lasted through the
1930s. During these years, numerous denominations organized
and built new churches, while other churches expanded. At one
revival meeting at Springfield, Colorado, in April 1930, "nearly
270 came forward for all churches."[11] Just a month before the
revival, the Friends (Quakers) organized a church in the community. The Methodist and Baptist churches were gaining
membership. South of Springfield at Boise City, Oklahoma, the
Methodists began construction on a beautiful church in 1930.
The Mennonite Brethren Church in Beaver County, Oklahoma,
which was one of the earliest churches in the panhandle, bought
a house in 1931, moved it near the church, and started a school.
During the depression and dust bowl, church activity increased,
until 1940 when it was necessary to enlarge the church to serve
the community residents. For during those hard years the Mennonite community increased in numbers.[12]

Even in the depths of the depression, God's children were
willing to step forward on faith. The Methodist Church at Wilburton, Kansas, and the farming community church of Morning
Star United shared a preacher and had bi-weekly services until
1933. Late in 1933, Wilburton asked for a full-time preacher. In
the spring of 1934, Morning Star United reorganized and developed a definite financial system and asked for a full-time
preacher. Shortly after the permanent pastor arrived, church
membership increased by more than 100 percent. The people of
Wilburton and the Morning Star community were committing

themselves to financial obligations to the churches in order to further spiritual needs, even though the region was one of the worst hit by the drought, depression, and dirt storms. If the people had any plans of leaving, they would have used the money to migrate rather than add to their local obligations.

Much of the active church growth took place in the very heart of the dust bowl. If one wished to locate the exact center of the dust bowl where the depression was most severely felt, the drought was the most damaging, dust pneumonia cases were most prominent, and wind erosion was most severe, it would be within a triangle running from Pritchett, Colorado, southeast to Boise City, Oklahoma, then northeast through Keyes, Oklahoma, Elkhart, Wilburton, and Rolla, Kansas, where the third leg of the triangle would turn northwest and return to Pritchett.

As noted above, Wilburton and the Morning Star community took definite steps to expand their churches in 1933 and 1934. At Keyes the Church of Christ was organized in 1935, and by 1937 the church building was ready for service. The Keyes Methodist Church, which had just been completed when the depression hit the area, continued to be active through the days of the dust bowl. While the Church of Christ was being organized at Keyes, the Lutherans at Texhoma, Oklahoma, purchased a real estate office building and began holding local church services. The Apostolic Faith Church at Hardesty, Oklahoma, was organized in 1933 after a revival where over eighty souls were saved. Throughout the depression the churches grew. The story of growth and building of churches in the five-state area is long and includes all the heartland of the dust bowl. It demonstrates that the churches were an active and vital part of the people's lives. In the churches the members found fellowship and support during the trying days of the 1930s. Believers found a peace and purpose beyond understanding and it helped them through the hard years.[13]

The dust bowl days were hard. Of course, the claim of hard times was not peculiar to the dust bowl during the 1930s. It was a national phenomenon. Nonetheless, the people of the region had their story to tell. During the spring months of 1935–37, the local newspapers in southwestern Kansas, southeastern Colorado, and northeastern New Mexico were filled with tragic tales of death from dust.[14]

Those who did not become ill suffered many indignities, hardships, and fears. One farmer near Griggs, Oklahoma, recalled that his wife placed the food under the tablecloth at dinner time during the dust storms. After the family was seated and grace said each member of the family would raise his corner of the cloth, place his head under the cloth, away from the view of the others, and begin eating. During the necessary ceremony, it was extremely difficult to pass the food or train the children in good table manners.

Gordon Grice recalled his mother insisting on the family taking refuge in a well house during dust storms. On one occasion the dust was especially thick in the well house where the family huddled around a lamp for cheer and comfort. Suddenly the lamp went out. Gordon reached in his pocket, retrieved a match, lit it, and watched in amazement as the thickly settling dust buried the flame from the match.

On another occasion Gordon drove a team of mules to the Beaver River to gather wood. While he was working a strong dirt storm blew in, but in the recess of the river valley conditions were not extremely bad. He loaded his wagon and started for home. When he reached the tableland where the storm was at full force, Gordon could not see. He stepped down from the wagon and worked his way to the head of the team where he took hold of the lead rope and started to lead the team home. Standing in front of the mules he could not see them or his feet. With his toe he had to feel the wagon ruts, which were blowing full of dirt. Slowly and painfully Gordon worked his way home.[15]

During one seige of dust storms that lasted sixty days, "when the wind lifted so you could see a block away at Hooker," Vi Kraft claimed, "women hurried and did the laundry and hung it out to dry."[16] At Eva, Oklahoma, Cecil Grable spent several days at his gas station when he could not see the depot across the street.

Even dust storms became a routine part of life for residents of the dust bowl. In the land of blowing soil, life went on and culture continued its growth. Every town had at least one baseball team, which competed with other town teams. The race for the league championship was hotly contested and supported by the loyal fans (nearly everyone in the region). One old-timer played second base during a dirt storm that was so heavy that "pop ups" were lost from sight in the dust. But the game went on, and everyone had fun. School athletics furnished a diversion for the residents. The games were well attended and strongly supported by the partisan fans. As a young boy, Vernon Hopson played outside in dust storms with marbles and other games that kids play. To him and his friends, wind erosion was the normal condition of life and not worthy of undue consideration.[17]

One of the big passtimes of the area residents came after severe dirt storms. Families would take picnic lunches and spend several happy hours gathering arrow heads. Many fine collections were achieved as a result of this family activity. The county agent in Cimarron County, Billy Barker, became a recognized paleontologist of the region and his arrowhead collection was one of the finest in the nation.

People also found other diversions. Each of the leading communities had a drama club. When the organizations could not afford the royalty on a published play, members wrote their own plays. The productions usually expressed the history of settling the region and contained characters whom everyone knew.

Several excellent poets resided in the dust bowl area. Most of the poetry dealt with nature and man's relation to nature. Sarah Sewell Hall caught the terrific force of the dust storm and the humor of the residents in her poem, "The Sandstorm":

> The motor car and airplane
> > The steamboat, ship, and train
> Are each one noted for its speed
> > And do not run in vain.
>
> Bicycles are not bad to view
> > Or motorcycles true
> The race horse lifts his head and neighs
> > For recognition too.
>
> And recognize them all we must
> > It's right and fair and just
> But the sandstorm beats them everyone
> > For kicking up the dust.
>
> An unseen huge and mighty broom
> > Sweeping field and street and yard, and room

It sweeps the dirt all in not out
A gruesome sight with dust perfume.

And while we all detest it so
Its one good point we truly know
It hasn't got a lazy bone
It's all get-up-and-go.[18]

Perhaps the best known of the dust bowl writers was the editor of the *Dalhart Texan*, John L. McCarty. He wrote several articles for national publications on the dust bowl, "A Tribute to Our Sandstorms" being his most famous. Among McCarty's serious historical works, *Maverick Town: The Story of Old Tascosa* was his best-known. Many other talented writers were in the area. Caroline A. Henderson's letters, which appeared in the *Atlantic Monthly*, exhibit a great deal of ability and refinement. The list of lesser known but capable people is quite extensive.

In art the dust bowl had several accomplished individuals. The work of Russel B., John G., and Eunice Duckett with alabaster is among the finest in the nation. Their sculpture ranged from delicate miniature roses to exquisitely turned large urns. This farm family's artistic ability first found its expression when they sought a new diversion during the dust storms of the thirties. Besides doing superb sculpturing with alabaster, members of the family were accomplished musicians.

Music, too, had its place in the life of dust bowl residents. And several local musicians achieved national fame. In 1937, Dorothy Dean Lehaman from Booker, Texas, was described as America's youngest composer by a California publisher, Guadagno-Davis. Her first piece was "You'll Gain the Whole World For Your Own" followed by "Mother's Crooning."[19]

The list of first-rate painters was extensive. Gwenfred Jones Lackey was a mature artist by the thirties. Several years earlier Gwenfred informed her father she wanted to paint. His reply was "then you must work on a big canvas." He purchased a 4' x 6' canvas and Gwenfred spent two years producing a remarkable work on the Adobe Walls Fight. Among other highly respected painters were the soil scientist H. H. Finnell and Editor John L. McCarty. In fact, when McCarty retired from the newspaper he spent several years running an art gallery at Dalhart.

During the dust bowl, Wright H. Langham was a student at Panhandle A & M College. His work on "Fertility Losses From High Plains Soils Due to Wind Erosion" is a primary work on the effects of wind erosion. Langham later became known for his work with biochemistry during and after the Manhattan Project. Among local inventions Charles Angell's one-way plow, first patented in 1923, and Fred Hoeme's chisel, first patented in 1935, have had a profound effect on agriculture. The most famous athlete from the dust bowl was Glenn Cunningham, a gold medal winner at the 1936 Olympic Games.

From a relatively small population scattered across the wind swept dry plains known as the dust bowl came many people skilled in the arts, letters, science, and athletics. These were people who learned to paint on a large canvas and never lost sight of big ideas and dreams. They had a highly developed culture and broad vistas of the world.

The depression, dirt storms, sickness, and plagues were hard, but people of the dust bowl frequently were able to turn adversity to advantage. Lloyd Chance who farmed near Woods, Kansas, claims, "I've seen [rabbits] start at the edge of a wheat field and soon work their way into it, stripping it as they went."[20] To control the rabbits several drives were organized and at Dalhart, Texas, a bounty was placed on rabbits. Although rabbits did immense damage to range and crops, many families found the rabbits to be a fine source of food. One farmer near Guymon traded his work team for a pair of greyhounds and spent most of the hard years hunting rabbits. He was able to provide meat for his family and trade some for other items. The remainder was sold for fur and for pet food.[21]

Hunting rabbits was only one of the infinite methods used by dust bowl residents to survive the depression. Len Cloninger's family was hard hit by the depression when he was laid off by the Rock Island Railroad. Despite his poverty, Cloninger was able to obtain an old truck and began hauling drought cattle to Arkansas, where he traded them for canned blackberries. These were then traded for cash and supplies.

Edna Barnes recalls that her family closed up most of its house to reduce the fuel bill. The school children only had two sets of clothing. The ones showing the least wear were worn to school, and the worn out clothing was worn at home. During the years her father could not raise a crop he was able to find some work running the county maintainer removing the dirt drifts from the roads. Because of the storms and the design and the condition of the equipment, the work was extremely dangerous. But the small wage helped keep the family on the farm.

Although the repeal of prohibition ended the heyday of the dust bowl's production of liquor, many residents continued illegal production during the depression. "At the peak of the depression it was hard to get a conviction on a charge of illegally operating a distillery because most judges were sympathetic with the plight of the working man trying to eke out a living." The operators were just little men, "whiling away their time, and in order to have something to do while they were out of a job indulged in a little sinning." The wives of moonshiners said nothing about their husband's activities because it brought in a little extra cash and "kept hubby from going insane by not having a job and not having anything to occupy time with."[22] And most of the raw material for the liquor was raised at home, which kept expenses to a minimum.

In response to the early 1930s appeal for farmers to feed more of their wheat crop to poultry and livestock, the number of chickens and milk cows increased just before the depression and dust bowl hit the region. Added to the milk cows were hogs, which were fed skimmed milk. The combination of cow-sow-hen operations provided a means to withstand the ordeal. Of course some farmers in the most drought-stricken and wind-blown areas were forced to sell their milk cows, which also ended the hog business.

The cream checks and the egg money helped tide farmers through the lean years.

> When everything looked very blue to the farmers of this locality, . . . the old hen kept producing a little to keep the family going and all of those who had a fair supply of poultry on their farms managed to get along without going into debt further.
>
> And the old milk cow kept producing a little butterfat when it seemed impossible for her to pick up enough to nourish her body. The price of butterfat held up much better than the prices of grains and other farm products.[23]

So many farmers depended upon the sale of cream and eggs that the depots became a popular meeting place when the cream cans came in. From these meetings each farmer achieved a new sense of resolve to carry him through until the next week's meeting. This philosophy of taking things a week at a time held farmers on the land.

During the worst of the drought years the manager of the Anchor D Ranch allowed many small farmers to graze the pasture even though the ranch did not have enough grass to meet its own demands. During the depression the ranch went broke, but farmers along the ranch boundary had found a supporting hand. The ranch manager was a man who gave to his fellow man even when it hurt and hurt badly.[24]

George Devers, who was raised in Ochiltree County, Texas, worked with his father and at various jobs until 1936 when he helped drive 1,000 head of cattle to Buffalo Springs on the XIT land. After moving the cattle he worked on one of the Whittenberg ranches until it was sold in 1938. He then went to work with Willy Walker on a ranch near Kenton, Oklahoma, until the grasshoppers ate the range. Next he moved to a ranch near Boise City; this was followed by a term of running the hotel at Grenville, New Mexico. In 1939 he was working for Roy Kendal on a ranch near Mt. Dora; thus Devers withstood the hard years by finding work on numerous ranches and through various occupations.[25]

W. D. Ross and his neighbors raised nearly everything they needed on their farms. Part of the sorghum crop was pressed and cooked into syrup. Grain was taken to town where the feed mills would grind it into flour. By putting finer screens in the mill the flour was satisfactory for baking and could be cooked as a hot cereal. Mrs. Mildred Ross and other housewives modified their recipes or developed new recipes that worked well with home-grown crops. Milk, cheese, eggs, lard, and whole grain flour were the major staples used in cooking.

During the extremely dry years when livestock feed was scarce, some families gathered soap weed. Farmers who could afford it took the soap weed to a mill where it was ground into silage. Other folks chopped the broad coarse plants into fine silage with a hand ax. It was a slow, laborious process, but it provided feed when it was most needed. In New Mexico and other areas where prickly pear cactus was plentiful, stockmen used a torch to scorch the spines off the plants, while the stock followed along eating the cactus. And the famous tumble weed was stacked and fed to livestock, especially milk cows.[26]

The methods used to survive the depression occasionally resulted in tragedy. Floyd Yorum who farmed near Springfield, Colorado, climbed down a windlass into a silo filled with thistles. While he was working, the silage caught fire and burned the windlass rope, trapping Yorum in the pit. His death left behind a widow and small children. Another man was killed near Boise City when the feed mill he had helped build fell apart during operation and shot nuts, bolts, and gears all over the grinding room.[27]

As equipment began wearing out and repairs were made with anything available, accidents increased. One farmer near Liberal was run over by a one-way plow when his tractor slipped into gear while he was working on the plow. A farm hand near Hugoton, Kansas, was dragged a mile and a half when his clothing was caught by a moving tractor plow; and Bobby Gardner, while working near Keyes, was killed by a one-way plow.

One of the most unusual accidents of the depression years occurred near Grenville, New Mexico. George Trembly stepped from the door of his ranch house to see what was disturbing the dog when, unsuspectingly, he was attacked and gored by a stray bull. There were other accidents including tragic fires, horses running away and killing the driver, men being thrown from horses, and windmills knocking men from the platform. Yet, the worst accident did not happen in the heartland of the dust bowl. At New London, Texas, between Tyler and Kilgore, school officials economized when installing gas lines to the school. In March 1937, the school exploded, taking the lives of 425 children. The impact and sorrow of the disaster was felt deeply by the residents of the eighteen dust bowl counties. Although accidents were not necessarily caused by the dust bowl, the tragic events added to the difficulty of the years.[28]

The area's residents could cope with depressions for they had seen harder times when the region was settled. They were the first to recognize that conservation technology lagged far behind other developments in agriculture. Because they were the ones who lived, coughed, and struggled through the dust storms, they were the most enthusiastic supporters of conservation practices that would work. It was residents of the area who developed new technology and new ways of controlling the erosion. They were the ones who went out into the blinding storms to chisel and lister to stop the blowing dirt. The people who lived in the region were among the strongest supporters of controlling true "wild lands."

What hurt knowledgeable residents of the area were some of the biased reports about the dust bowl. It was agreed that conditions were bad, and the first federal propaganda movie, "The Plow That Broke the Plains," did show that part of the story. When Department of Agriculture officials were asked why the film did not present a total picture by describing the better conditions, the federal authorities replied that to have shown anything else would have prevented Congress from approving the new agriculture bill. And Walter Davenport's story in *Collier's Magazine*, "Land Where Our Children Die," was yellow journalism at its very worst. The editor of the *Elkhart Tri-State News* replied to "Land Where Our Children Die." He realized, "[Davenport's] pen dripping with vitrol, with fangs as poisonous as a rattlesnake's he strikes at the high plains, knowing full-well that they cannot retaliate."[29]

In September 1937, Congressman Clifford Hope stopped in Elkhart. He "reported he found conditions here 'so much better than he had expected'—probably after reading all the damaging publicity and seeing all of the news photos, news reels and 'March of Times' releases that have been made."[30]

While the national press was painting a bleak picture of a region of dying paupers, James and Elsie Smalt, who rented their first farm in 1926 with $16 and credit for seed, were going about their daily chores of saving the land. They "suffered all the hardships that come to those who dedicate their lives to building up a new country."[31] And they did their share to build a new country.

Another couple who dedicated their lives to the region was Floy "Hoss" Yates and his wife Robbie. Hoss had driven to Stratford to see his sweeheart on April 14, 1935. Returning home he was caught in the famous roller and was forced to spend the night in an open car. In spite of the horrors and the bleakness of the continuing storms, when the young couple was married in April 1937, they did not look for new areas to begin their lives together. Floy and Robbie purchased the Wonder Drug at Stratford and began building their tomorrows in the stricken region.[32]

Chorla "Chloe" Basset was already a grandmother when she lost her husband in 1934. At her age one would expect her to seek refuge in another area where the hard years of the depression, drought, and death could be laid aside. After the estate was settled, she left the farm and moved to Boise City and Keyes where she nursed an elderly woman who had broken her hip. After the woman had sufficiently recovered, Chloe sold Avon products in Keyes until 1938 when she opened a variety store. She was not running or seeking refuge; Mrs. Basset was building a new life during the dust bowl days.[33]

During those drought years the Nash brothers of Guymon expanded their business. In Moore County, Texas, Sunray became a boom town with the development of gas, oil, and smelting. Guymon, Liberal, Hugoton, and Ulysses took on a renewed sense of hope with the increase in gas development and manufacturing carbon black. The dust bowl days were hard years, but they were years of building toward a happier future. The hardy pioneers who dedicated themselves to building up a new country knew it would rain at the end of the dry spell.

During the blowing seige of 1935, a Texas County farmer told a reporter for the *Oklahoma Farmer-Stockman* about the early days when he first homesteaded. He lost his first five crops, and it looked like he was going to lose his sixth crop. "When the tide turned, it turned quick and was awful good. The panhandle has done just that thing so many times during its short agriculture history."[34] When things turned at the end of the 1930s dry spell they turned quickly and were "awful good."

The dust bowl is one of those mysterious episodes in American history. History has accepted Oklahoma as the source of the terrific wind erosion. The high plains portion of Oklahoma, however, is only a narrow strip of land in the dust bowl. The worst effects of those tragic years were felt to the north of Oklahoma in Kansas and Colorado, and to the west of Oklahoma in New Mexico.

Despite the fame of the dust bowl, scholars have generally followed the pattern of Theodore Saloutos who believed: "The disasters that overtook the Great Plains have been recounted in dramatic fashion by columnists, feature writers, and others; hence it would be belaboring the obvious to repeat what others have stated."[35] The 1930s stories in national magazines are accepted without questioning the writer's zeal. Of the two major works written on the dust bowl, Vance Johnson's *Heaven's Table Land* and Fred Floyd's doctoral dissertation, "A History of the Dust Bowl," neither considered the importance of the oil and gas industry in the chain of events, nor did they closely view the business conditions. Both center their studies on the Soil Conservation Service without fully considering the broader ramifications of land-use planning. The report of the Great Plains Committee was accepted at face value, and the government's motives were not questioned.

The story of the Great Plains is one of extremes in weather. During the dry years dying grass, plagues of insects and rodents, overgrazing, and raging fires left the ground barren and subject to severe wind erosion. The mute sand hills stand as reminders of the aeons of wind erosion. The loess soil speaks of its birth. It is within the realm of reason to assume that terrific dust storms might have occurred on the Great Plains during the drought of the 1930s even if a plow had not touched the soil. Without doubt the plowed soil added to the intensity of the storms, but it did not cause dust storms.

With the advancement of technology, men with plows ventured onto the treeless land. As they went they developed a new farming method called dry land farming. The farmers worked to conserve moisture and protect the soil with cover crops. Dry land farming became a science closely studied by farmers, scientists, and government men. With the development of the tractor, combine, one-way plow, and truck, magnificent opportunity came to the frontier region. But with the new technology came a new set of standards. To achieve a higher standard of living it was necessary to abandon subsistence farming and become commercial farmers. The new technology and wheat farming promised happy days. But commercial farming required larger acreage and fewer farmers. Larger sums were required for equipment and land. The region's economy became badly maladjusted as farmers overproduced on farms that were too small and taxed the land. Although the adjustment was already begun before the depression struck, many farmers were trapped and could not escape. For them the dirty thirties were especially harsh.

Despite the hard years of the depression, the economy of the region was no worse than that of other areas of the nation, and in many respects was better. Railroads and the oil and gas industry provided money and employment for the area. Land value held up better in the dust bowl than it did in the humid areas.

With the development of more new technology and new methods of farming, farmers were able to battle the blowing dirt and reduce the margin between the know-how for raising a crop and preventing wind erosion. Thus the continual process of adapting men and culture advanced on the Great Plains.

The overall view of the government's activities was woeful, a story of oscillating, procrastinating, and deceiving while attempting to remove the residents from their land and homes. The heartland of the dust bowl was a place the scientists on the Potomac designated as their laboratory and America's Next Year People were often victims of the experiment. Even in the area of soil conservation the government did not introduce any new methods, implements, or concepts for controlling wind erosion on cultivated land. It was the local farmers who took the lead in controlling wind erosion. The primary goals of the Soil Conservation Service were to return the region to grass and prevent the planting of wheat. The total failure of the federal government's understanding of the region was vividly illustrated when the government began replanting the grasslands. They did not know how, nor had they made any serious studies beforehand. It took the government fifteen years from the time it purchased its first land to learn how to raise native grass. Even nature, when left alone, was ahead of that time schedule.

Relief efforts did complete many projects, and through the course of the depression, large sums were spent. Relief aid however, was designed to maintain the economic status quo and make the residents more dependent on federal assistance. When the federal authorities were ready to play their trump for removal of the people and establishment of the land-use plan, relief was reduced and farmers eliminated from local make-work projects. Thus folks were removed by "starving them out."

In the final analysis, the story of the dust bowl was the story

of people, people with ability and talent, people with resource-
fulness, fortitude, and courage, people like *Hanna* in the recent
book by Robert L. Osmunson. Hannah Kraft had a vision and the
internal strength to make that dream come true. The people of
the dust bowl were not defeated, poverty-ridden people without
hope. They were builders for tommorrow. During those hard
years they continued to build their churches, their businesses,
their schools, their colleges, their communities. They grew
closer to God and fonder of the land. Hard years were common
in their past, but the future belonged to those who were ready
to seize the moment. It was the people who stayed in the country who did their share in furnishing food to a hungry world
during World War II; and since then they have continued to
supply enough food to fight famine in various parts of the world.
From beneath their soil came the natural gas that heated the
cold cities and fueled the factories of the humid areas. Because
they stayed during those hard years and worked the land and
tapped her natural resources, millions of people have eaten better, worked in healthier places, and enjoyed warmer homes. Because those determined people did not flee the stricken area
during a crisis, the nation today enjoys a better standard of living.

Mrs. Edith Lewis summed up the feelings of most of the folks
who lived through those hard years. "Those were hard times. I
remember that the shortest crop we ever raised was during that
time. It was only 700 bushels of grain. A lot of people left while
the storms were going on, but E. P. and I decided to stay.
We're glad that we did."[36]

Notes

Chapter 1

1. Interview, Vernon L. Hopson; *Texhoma Times,* March 7, 1935.

2. *Rocky Mountain News,* March 23, 24, 26, 1935; Springfield *Democrat-Herald,* March 28, 1935; *Hugoton Hermes,* March 22, 1935, May 3, 1935; Brown, Gottlieb, and Laybourn, "Dust Storms and Their Possible Effect on Health," pp. 1369–83.

3. Interview, Robert Murphy; Dale, *An Oklahoma Lawyer; Panhandle Herald,* April 15, 1935.

4. Interview, Mrs. Emma Love.

5. Floyd, "A History of the Dust Bowl," pp. 17–18.

6. Saloutos, "The New Deal and Farm Policy in the Great Plains," p. 345.

7. Trombley, *The Life and Times of a Happy Liberal,* p. 116.

8. Saloutos, "The New Deal and Farm Policy in the Great Plains," p. 345.

9. Ibid.

10. *Panhandle Herald,* April 15, 1935.

11. *Hooker Advance,* April 18, 1935; Texhoma Genealogical and Historical Society, comp. and ed., *Panhandle Pioneers,* I, 9-10.

12. "Prehistoric Man on the High Plains," pp. 60-61; Watson, "The Optima Focus of the Panhandle Aspect," pp. 7-60; "Ancient Irrigation," p. 14.

13. Leighton, "Geology of Soil Drifting on the Great Plains," p. 25. For detailed discussion of the soils and terrain, see the current soil survey maps of Hamilton, Stanton, Grant, Morton, Stevens, and Seward counties, Kansas; Cimarron, Texas, and Beaver counties, Oklahoma; Dallam, Sherman, Hansford, Ochiltree, and Moore counties, Texas; and Prowers and Baca counties, Colorado.

14. U. S. Department of Agriculture, Soil Conservation Service, *Soil Survey, Seward County, Kansas,* p. 46. See also soil survey maps of counties listed above.

15. Weaver and Albertson, *Grasslands of the Great Plains,* Chapter 7: "Vegetation at the End of Drought" and also pp. 97-98; Savage, *Drought Survival of Native Grass Species in the Central and Southern Great Plains, 1935.*

16. Weaver and Albertson, *Grasslands of the Great Plains,* p. 79.

17. Ibid., p. 100; McCarty, *Maverick Town,* p. 240.

18. Precipitation records from the current county soil surveys; Schoff, *Geology and Ground-Water Resources of Texas County, Oklahoma;* Precipitation records from the Panhandle State University Experiment Station.

19. U.S. Department of Agriculture, Soil Conservation Service, *Soil Survey, Cimarron County, Oklahoma,* p. 2; U.S. Department of Agriculture, Soil Conservation Service, *Soil Survey, Baca County, Colorado,* p. 1.

20. U.S. Department of Agriculture, Soil Conservation Service, *Soil Survey, Stanton County, Kansas*, p. 5; U.S. Department of Agriculture, Soil Conservation Service, *Soil Survey, Hamilton County, Kansas*, p. 16; U.S. Department of Agriculture, Soil Conservation Service, *Soil Survey, Morton County, Kansas*, p. 44; U.S. Department of Agriculture, Soil Conservation Service, *Soil Survey, Grant County, Kansas*, p. 47.

21. Weaver and Albertson, *Grasslands of the Great Plains*, p. 78.

22. Gibson, *Oklahoma*, p. 71.

23. Ford, ed., *The Writings of Thomas Jefferson*, VIII, 192-202, 241-49; Malin, "Dust Storms," Part I, 132.

24. Malin, "Dust Storms," Part I, 134.

25. "The Awful Drouth of 1854," p. 10.

26. *Boise City News*, July 30, 1936.

27. Malin, "Dust Storms," Part I, 135, 137-38.

28. Bonnifield, "The Choctaw Nation on the Eve of the Civil War," p. 60.

29. Malin, "Dust Storms," Part II, 267.

30. Ibid., 269.

31. Ibid.

32. Ibid., 271.

33. Dean and Carpenter, comp., "History of Morton County."

34. Baugh, "Freedom on the Prairies."

35. *Hugoton Hermes*, Centennial Anniversary Edition, Section B.

36. *Gate to No Man's Land*, p. 3.

37. Summation from *Elkhart Tri-State News*, 50th Anniversary Edition; *Hugoton Hermes*, Centennial Anniversary Edition; *Gate to No Man's Land*; and several editions of the *Old Timers News*.

38. McCarty, *Maverick Town*, pp. 240-43.

39. Ibid., p. 241.

40. Malin, "Dust Storms," Part III, 406.

41. Ibid., 408.

42. Ibid., 409.

43. Interview, Charles Berends.

Chapter 2

1. Mullen, "Greatest Country I Ever Saw!" p. 3.

2. U.S. Department of Agriculture, Soil Conservation Service, *Soil Survey, Cimarron County, Oklahoma*, p. 2.

3. Nall, "Panhandle Farming in the 'Golden Era' of American Agriculture," pp. 68-93. See also numerous county and community histories.

4. Interview, Bill and Vi Kraft.

5. Ibid.

6. Fite, *The Farmers' Frontier, 1865-1900*, p. 200.

7. Nall, "Panhandle Farming in the 'Golden Era' of American Agriculture," p. 77.

8. Ibid., p. 75.

9. Ibid., pp. 79-80. See also McDaniel, *God, Grass & Grit*, pp. 78-80.

10. Interview, Bill and Vi Kraft.

11. Hofsommer, *Katy Northwest*; *Gate to No Man's Land*; Malin, *Winter Wheat in the Golden Belt of Kansas*.

12. Dean and Carpenter, comp., "History of Morton County."

13. Ibid.

14. Ibid.; *Hugoton Hermes*, Centennial Anniversary Edition.

15. *Hugoton Hermes*, Centennial Anniversary Edition; Myers, "Old Timer Recalls Prairie Fire," p. 91; Interview, Mrs. Gerald Davison.

16. David, "Point Rocks Flood," p. 42.

17. Tucker, "The Big Snow of 1918-19," p. 15.

18. Stanley, *The Perryton, Texas Story*, p. 5; *Ochiltree County Herald*, August 13, 1936 (Anniversary Edition); *Wheatheart of the Plains*; Jones, *A Search for Opportunity; Guymon Herald*, August 28, 1919.

19. *Johnson Pioneer*, September 4, 1930. See also Springfield *Democrat-Herald*, March 15, 1929.

20. See Hofsommer, *Katy Northwest; Eva;* Thomas, *The Windswept Land;* Minor, "The History of Moore County, Texas, Stressing Education"; *Boise City News*, Historical Edition, Summer 1968; *Texhoma Times*, April 1, 1927; Jones, *A Search for Opportunity*.

21. *Boise City News*, Historical Edition, Summer 1968; "History File," Boise City Library; also numerous articles appear in *Boise City News* for 1930 and 1931.

22. Strasner, "Moonshine Madness," p. 22.

23. Springfield *Democrat-Herald*, January 8, 1931; *Ochiltree County Herald*, September 3, 1936, June 8, 1939; *Clayton News*, April 29, 1936; *Lamar Register*, October 15, 1930; *Texhoma Times*, September 17, 1931, October 8, 1931, January 25, 1934; *Morton County Farmer*, July 15, 1932, July 29, 1932. See county newspapers for coverage of numerous violent crimes.

24. Springfield *Democrat-Herald*, July 9, 1931, July 16, 1931.

25. Moore, "Oil Creates an Industrial Frontier, West Texas, 1917-1937," pp. 341-351; Porter, *Memory Cups of Panhandle Pioneers*, p. 588; *Boise City News*, Historical Edition, Summer 1968.

26. Gould, "The Beginning of the Panhandle Oil and Gas Field," pp. 21-36; Cartwright, "History of Pioneer Natural Gas Company," pp. 60-86.

27. "The Roaring Twenties," p. 45.

28. *Guymon Herald*, September 4, 1919.

29. *Texhoma Times*, March 21, 1919, November 25, 1919, November 24, 1922; Texhoma Genealogical and Historical Society, comp. and ed., *Panhandle Pioneers*, IV, 29; *Guymon Herald*, September 11, 1919, January 15, 1920, January 29, 1920, October 28, 1921; Furbush, "Hugoton Field, Kansas," p. 55.

30. *Wheatheart of the Plains*, pp. 100-101.

31. Cartwright, "History of Pioneer Natural Gas Company," pp. 64-65.

32. Stanley, *The Phillips, Texas Story.* For impact on other counties see "Oil News" on the front page of *Texhoma Times*, 1925-27 and the *Guymon Herald*, 1925-27.

33. Minor, "The History of Moore County, Texas, Stressing Education," pp. 49-50.

34. *Morton County Farmer*, February 11, 1927.

35. *Boise City News*, December 25, 1930 (last story of test). Numerous references appear in earlier editions of the paper.

36. *Hugoton Hermes*, Centennial Anniversary Edition, Section E.

37. "Great Quantities of Natural Gas"; Schoff, *Geology and Ground-Water Resources of Texas County, Oklahoma*, p. 37.

38. *Oil and Gas Journal*, January 28, 1958, pp. A58-59, D36-37, E44.

39. *Hugoton Hermes*, Centennial Anniversary Edition, Section E.

40. Furbush, "Hugoton Field, Kansas," p. 59. See also numerous oil and gas references in local newspapers 1927-1931.

41. *Boise City News*, February 21, 1931. For growth and development see local newspapers 1929-1932. Papers often had a summary of the past year's growth and development in a January issue. See also *Nation's Business* maps representing business conditions until July 1931.

Chapter 3

1. Harris and Henderson, "Letters of Two Women Farmers, I," p. 238.

2. Kansas City (Mo.) *Times*, May 16, 1935.

3. Cady, "Is the Rainfall in Kansas Increasing?" pp. 132-33.

4. Bennett, *Soil Conservation*, p. 736. See also Campbell, *Campbell's 1907 Soil Culture Manual;* Malin, *Winter Wheat in the Golden Belt of Kansas;* Malin, "The Soft Winter Wheat Boom and the Agricultural Development of the Upper Kansas River Valley, I," p. 370.

5. Campbell, *Campbell's 1907 Soil Culture Manual*, p. 125.

6. Ibid., p. 178.

7. See Campbell, *Campbell's 1907 Soil Culture Manual;* Call and Aicher, *A History of the Fort Hays (Kansas) Branch Experiment Station, 1901-1962*, pp. 77-82.

8. Call and Aicher, *A History of the Fort Hays (Kansas) Branch Experiment Station, 1901-1962*, p. 77.

9. Drake, "Wind Erosion and Its Control," p. 197.

10. Call and Hallsted, *The Relation of Moisture to Yield of Winter Wheat in Western Kansas*, pp. 8, 11.

11. Chilcott and Cole, "Subsoiling, Deep Tilling, and Soil Dynamiting in the Great Plains"; Finnell, "The Moisture-Saving Efficiency of Level Terraces Under Semi-Arid Conditions"; Hallsted, "A Preliminary Report of the Relation Between Yield of Winter Wheat and Moisture in the Soil at Seeding Time."

12. Bennett, "Land Impoverishment by Soil Erosion," pp. 171-77+; Riley, "Sandstorms in Texas," pp. 30-31.

13. U.S. Department of Agriculture, *Yearbook of Agriculture 1934*, pp. 78-79.

14. Finnell, "The Moisture-Saving Efficiency of Level Terraces Under Semi-Arid Conditions," p. 523.

15. Drummond, "Dust Bowl," p. 39.

16. Ibid.

17. *Morton County Farmer*, June 3, 1927; Beaver *Herald-Democrat*, March 9, 1936.

18. Finnell, "The Plowup of Western Grasslands and the Resultant Effect Upon Great Plains Agriculture," p. 94. See also Berryman, "Early Settlement of Southwest Kansas," pp. 561-70; Fitzpatrick and Boatright, *Soil Survey of Texas County, Oklahoma*, pp. 7-11.

19. Cole and Hallsted, *Methods of Winter-Wheat Production at the Fort Hays Branch Station*, p. 2.

20. *Guymon Herald*, January 8, 1920.

21. *Texhoma Times*, July 1, 1921, January 1, 1926.

22. U.S. Department of Agriculture, *Yearbook of Agriculture 1930*, p. 574.

23. Tucker, "The Big Snow of 1918-19," p. 15; Nall, "Specialization and Expansion: Panhandle Farming in the 1920's," p. 55; U.S. Department of Agriculture, *Yearbook of Agriculture 1930*, p. 579.

24. *Oklahoma Farmer-Stockman*, March 10, 1922, p. 7.

25. Ibid., November 25, 1920, p. 7.

26. Ibid., January 10, 1923, p. 5.

27. Ibid., February 10, 1921, p. 41.

28. Ibid., April 25, 1920, p. 51.

29. *Texhoma Times*, June 10, 1921, June 24, 1921.

30. Hoover, *Kansas Agriculture After 100 Years*, p. 47.

31. *Panhandle Herald*, Pictorial Section, 1928.

32. *Texhoma Times*, June 29, 1928, September 21, 1928.

33. *Panhandle Herald*, Pictorial Section, 1928.

34. Kansas State Board of Agriculture, *Twenty-Seventh Biennial Report*, p. 192.

35. Hoover, *Kansas Agriculture After 100 Years*, p. 47.

36. Pennington, "The Inventor of the First Angell One Way Disc Plow," p. 33. See also numerous ads for one-way plows in local papers, 1927-1929.

37. Morton, *Snowstorms, Dust Storms and Horses' Tails*, p. 40.

38. Drake, "Wind Erosion and Its Control," p. 198.

39. Interview, Ed Tucker.

40. Fitzpatrick and Boatright, *Soil Survey of Texas County, Oklahoma*, p. 10.

41. Ibid., p. 7.

42. Morton, *Snowstorms, Dust Storms and Horses' Tails*, p. 40.

43. Springfield *Democrat-Herald*, May 8, 1930.

44. Ibid., May 11, 1930.

45. U.S. Department of Agriculture, *Yearbook of Agriculture 1931*, p. 1; *Texhoma Times*, "Market Reports," 1930-1932; Local newspapers June-August, 1931; Kansas State Board of Agriculture, *Twenty-Seventh Biennial Report*, p. vii.

46. *Morton County Farmer*, May 27, 1932.

47. *Texhoma Times*, July 7, 1932.

48. *Boise City News*, September 29, 1932.

49. Harris and Henderson, "Letters of Two Women Farmers, I," pp. 239-40.

Chapter 4

1. *Boise City News*, September 26, 1930.

2. Ibid., September 26, 1930, October 3, 1930; *Texhoma Times*, September 12, 1930.

3. *Boise City News*, November 21, 1930; *Lamar Register*, November 26, 1930.

4. *Lamar Register*, April 1, 1931; *Texhoma Times*, April 2, 1931; *Southwest Daily Times*, March 27, 1938.

5. *Texhoma Times*, April 6, 1932, March 17, 1932, April 28, 1932.

6. *Morton County Farmer*, June 10, 1932; Springfield *Democrat-Herald*, June 9, 1932; *Texhoma Times*, June 9, 1932; *Boise City News*, June 9, 1932, June 23, 1932.

7. *Texhoma Times*, June 23, 1932, July 7, 1932, August 4, 1932. See also other local newspapers for June and July, 1932.

8. *Morton County Farmer*, September 9, 1932.

9. Ibid., September 16, 1932.

10. *Texhoma Times*, January 26, 1933.

11. *Boise City News*, February 9, 1933.

12. *Grant County Republican*, April 20, 1933.

13. *Texhoma Times*, December 21, 1933.

14. *Hooker Advance*, March 30, 1933.

15. *Texhoma Times*, May 25, 1933.

16. Ibid., May 11, 1933.

17. Ibid., July 20, 1933.

18. Ibid., September 7, 1933.

19. Ibid., May 4, 1933. See also local newspapers for harvest, June and July and September and October, 1933.

20. Interview, Bill and Vi Kraft.

21. *Grant County Republican*, October 13, 1933.

22. *Hooker Advance*, January 22, 1931, February 5, 1931. Also interviews with residents of the area and winter newspaper listings of rabbit drives, 1929-1939.

23. Mattice, "Dust Storms, November 1933 to May 1934," p. 53.

24. Ibid., p. 54.

25. Langham, *Fertility Losses From High Plains Soils Due to Wind Erosion*, p. 13.

26. *Texhoma Times*, June 7, 1934, June 28, 1934; *Clayton News*, September 7, 1939; *Ochiltree County Herald*, January 6, 1938; Reeves, "Rainfall Data from 1911-1974, Goodwell, Oklahoma."

27. *Texhoma Times*, April 12, 1934.

28. *Morton County Farmer*, June 15, 1934.

29. Ibid., August 24, 1934; *Texhoma Times*, "Market Reports," June-September, 1934; Brown, "Dust Storms and Their Possible Effect on Health," p. 1369.

30. Interview, Vernon Hopson; *Texhoma Times*, March 7, 1935.

31. *Texhoma Times*, March 21, 1935.

32. *Boise City News*, March 21, 1935.

33. *Rocky Mountain News*, March 24, 25, 26, 1935.

34. Springfield *Democrat-Herald*, March 28, 1935.

35. Ibid.

36. Ibid.

37. *Morton County Farmer*, April 12, 1935.

38. Local newspapers contain dozens of dust pneumonia stories, March-May, 1935.

39. *Morton County Farmer*, February 1, 8, 22, 1935, April 12, 1935.

40. Springfield *Democrat-Herald*, April 18, 1935.

41. Interview, Mrs. Lee King.

42. *Texhoma Times*, April 18, 1935.

43. Interview, Mr. and Mrs. Arthur N. Howe.

44. Interview, Mrs. Cleo Rainey.

45. *Texhoma Times*, April 18, 1935.

46. Springfield *Democrat-Herald*, May 2, 1935, May 9, 1935.

47. *Boise City News*, May 30, 1935; Interview, Mrs. Clarene Keenen.

48. Brown, "Dust Storms and Their Possible Effect on Health," p. 1369; *Morton County Farmer*, June 7, 1935.

49. *Lamar Register*, July 17, 1935.

50. Ibid., August 28, 1935.

51. *Texhoma Times*, September 12, 1935.

52. Ibid., December 5, 1935.

53. Ibid., July 4, 1935.

54. *Hooker Advance*, July 11, 1935.

55. Ibid.; *Texhoma Times*, "Market Reports"; Floyd, "A History of the Dust Bowl," pp. 269-70.

56. *Clayton News*, January 8, 1936.

57. *Texhoma Times*, January 9, 1936.

58. *Spearman Reporter*, January 30, 1936.

59. *Texhoma Times*, April 19, 1936.

60. "Climatological Data: Oklahoma Section," 1930-1940; Reeves, "Rainfall Data from 1911-1974, Goodwell, Oklahoma"; "Precipitation Chart from Records Kept by U.S. Forest Service (Comanche Grasslands)"; *Clayton News*, September 7, 1939; *Ochiltree County Herald*, January 6, 1938. Also useful are the county Soil Surveys.

61. *Lamar Register*, June 3, 1936; *Texhoma Times*, June 4, 25, 1936; *Ochiltree County Herald*, September 17, 1936.

62. *Hooker Advance*, May 28, 1936.

63. Ibid., June 25, 1936.

64. *Spearman Reporter*, June 11, 1936; Floyd, "A History of the Dust Bowl," pp. 269-70. See also Chapter V.

65. *Spearman Reporter*, July 16, 1936.

66. *Ochiltree County Herald*, January 21, 1937; *Texhoma Times*, January 28, 1937.

67. Beaver *Herald-Democrat*, February 4, 1937, February 8, 1937; *Ochiltree County Herald*, February 11, 1937.

68. *Texhoma Times*, April 1, 1937.

69. See local newspapers, June-July, 1937; Floyd, "A History of the Dust Bowl," pp. 269-70.

70. Kansas State Board of Agriculture, *Biennial Reports*, 1933-1939.

71. *Texhoma Times*, "Market Reports" for 1937.

72. *Stratford Star*, June 10, 1937, June 17, 1937.

73. *Southwest Daily Times*, June 9, 10, 1937; *Johnson Pioneer*, June 10, 1937; *Clayton News*, September 8, 1937.

74. *Texhoma Times*, October 7, 1937.

75. *Clayton News*, July 7, 1937.

76. *Texhoma Times*, September 23, 1937.

77. "April, 1938 'Snuster'," p. 9; *Southwest Daily Times*, April 7-8, 1938; Beaver *Herald-Democrat*, April 14, 1938.

78. Floyd, "A History of the Dust Bowl," pp. 269-70; *Texhoma Times*, "Market Reports" for 1938.

79. *Stratford Star*, June 9, 1938.

80. *Clayton News*, May 18, 1938, June 8, 15, 22, 1938, August 10, 24, 1938; *Stratford Star*, June 2, 9, 16, 30, 1938, July 7, 1938, August 18, 1938; Interview, Vernon Hopson.

81. *Stratford Star*, August 4, 1938.

82. *Ochiltree County Herald*, January 12, 1939.

83. *Elkhart Tri-State News*, March 31, 1939.

84. *Stratford Star*, April 6, 1939.

85. *Texhoma Times*, August 8, 1939.

Chapter 5

1. Interview, Bill and Vi Kraft.

2. Harris, "Letters of Two Women Farmers, II," p. 351.

3. *Boise City News*, January 15, 1930, December 25, 1930, August 6, 13, 1931, November 12, 1931, January 14, 21, 28, 1932; *Texhoma Times*, August 6, 20, 27, 1931. See also numerous other local newspaper articles.

4. *Texhoma Times*, May 5, 1932. See also *Texhoma Times* March 3, 1932; *Boise City News*, April 28, 1932, September 8, 1932.

5. *Texhoma Times*, December 21, 1933.

6. Springfield *Democrat-Herald*, July 20, 1933.

7. *Texas County News*, September 10, 1933; Interview, Paul Schnabel.

8. Harris, "Letters of Two Women Farmers, I," p. 239; Interview, Mr. and Mrs. Charles M. Bonnifield; *Morton County Farmer*, February 5, 1932, September 16, 1932.

9. *Johnson Pioneer*, January 5, 1933; *Grant County Republican*, March 16, 1933; *Boise City News*, March 16, 1933; Springfield *Democrat-Herald*, March 16, 1933; *Texhoma Times*, November 9, 1933; *Hooker Advance*, December 11, 1930; Interview, Mrs. Emma Love (she was in the banking business); *Rocky Mountain News*, March 25, 1935. Author was unable to find any other bank closings for 1930-1939.

10. *Clayton News*, June 3, 1936.

11. *Elkhart Tri-State News*, December 1, 1939. See also bank financial reports in local newspapers for depression years.

12. *Texhoma Times*, July 11, 1930, July 16, 1931, July 14, 1932, July 13, 1933, July 12, 1934, July 11, 1935, July 16, 1936, July 15, 1937, July 14, 1938, July 13, 1939.

13. Information provided by Kansas State Historical Society. See also *Morton County Farmer*, August 20, 1937.

14. *Spearman Reporter*, January 6, 1938, February 2, 1939.

15. *Ochiltree County Herald*, January 6, 1938.

16. Shirk, "The Post Offices of Oklahoma, Nov. 26, 1907-Dec. 31, 1965," pp. 31-90.

17. Information provided by Kansas State Historical Society.

18. *Hardesty*; Information on Panhandle A & M College provided by Mrs. Kathryn A. Sexton, English Department, Panhandle State University, Goodwell, Oklahoma.

19. Springfield *Democrat-Herald*, May 20, 1937; *Texhoma Times*, June 22, 1939; Beaver *Herald-Democrat*, April 27, 1939; *Stratford Star*, June 22, 1939.

20. Beaver *Herald-Democrat*, January 26, 1939.

21. *Dalhart Texan*, January 14, 1936.

22. *Ochiltree County Herald*, March 11, 1937.

23. Ibid., March 11, 18, 1937.

24. *Guymon Daily News*, January 2, 1935; "Nash Brothers in 45th Year," p. 66; *Elkhart Tri-State News*, October 14, 1938; *Texhoma Times*, February 24, 1938.

25. Beaver *Herald-Democrat*, August 20, 1936.

26. Otto, *Trends in Land Values in Kansas*, p. 5.

27. *Morton County Farmer*, February 12, 1932.

28. Ibid., February 9, 1934; Minor, "The History of Moore County, Texas, Stressing Education," p. 52; *Texhoma Times*, November 1, 1934; Hemsell, "Geology of Hugoton Gas Field of Southwestern Kansas," p. 1056; *Hugoton Hermes*, Centennial Anniversary Edition, Section E; *Hugoton Hermes*, July 19, 1935.

29. Springfield *Democrat-Herald*, January 2, 1936; *Clayton News*, April 22, 1936, January 1, 1936, February 2, 1936, September 9, 1936; *Texhoma Times*, June 4, 1936, August 13, 1936, December 17, 1936; *Boise City News*, December 10, 1936; *Stratford Star*, June 11, 1936.

30. *Dalhart Texan*, January 18, 1936; February 5, 6, 27, 1936, March 6, 1936, June 1, 5, 1936, July 14, 1936. See also Minor, "The History of Moore County, Texas, Stressing Education," pp. 49-55; Weeks, "Developments in North-Central Texas and the Panhandle, 1936-1937," pp. 1031-33.

31. Weeks, "Developments in North-Central Texas and the Panhandle, 1936-1937," p. 1033.

32. Interview, Vernon Hopson.

33. *Boise City News*, May 21, 1936; *Guymon Daily News*, March 25, 1936; *Dalhart Texan*, February 29, 1936, April 4, 7, 1936, July 17, 1936; *Texhoma Times*, July 13, 1939.

34. *Elkhart Tri-State News*, January 21, 1937.

35. Hemsell, "Geology of Hugoton Gas Field of Southwestern Kansas," p. 1056; *Hugoton Hermes*, Centennial Anniversary Edition, Section E. See also dozens of local newspaper articles.

36. *Wheatheart of the Plains*, pp. 100-101. See also local newspaper.

37. *Clayton News*, June 16, 1937.

38. *Elkhart Tri-State News*, October 10, 1938. See also local newspapers especially the *Stratford Star*, January to May, 1938.

39. Furbush, "Hugoton Field, Kansas," p. 59.

40. Minor, "The History of Moore County, Texas, Stressing Education," p. 46.

41. Interview, Bill and Vi Kraft.

42. Interview, Mr. and Mrs. Cecil Grable.

43. Modrick, "A Yugoslavian Thanksgiving."

44. Interview, Mr. Gordon Grice.

45. See Chapter 4 and 10.

46. *Clayton News*, June 3, 1936.

47. *Texhoma Times*, August 19, 1937.

48. See *Nation's Business* maps of economic and business conditions of the nation.

Chapter 6

1. *The Future of the Great Plains*, p. 1.

2. Saarinen, *Perception of the Drought Hazard on the Great Plains*, pp. 138-40.

3. Webb, *The Great Plains*, p. 507.

4. Ford, *The Writings of Thomas Jefferson*, VIII, 200.

5. Ibid., pp. 192-203, 241-49.

6. Commanger, *Documents of American History*, p. 140.

7. Bonnifield, "The Choctaw Nation on the Eve of the Civil War," p. 63.

8. *Report of the Great Plains Drought Area Committee*, p. 4.

9. See Smith, *Virgin Land*.

10. Guttenberg, "The Land Utilization Movement of the 1920s," p. 477.

11. Ibid., p. 490. See also Gray, "The Utilization of Our Lands for Crops, Pasture, and Forests," pp. 415-506.

12. U.S. Department of Agriculture, *Yearbook of Agriculture 1930*, p. 36.

13. Springfield *Democrat-Herald*, May 8, 1930.

14. Freidel, *Franklin D. Roosevelt*, IV, 79.

15. Ibid., IV, 79-80.

16. Ibid., IV, 78-79.

17. National Resources Board, *A Report on National Planning and Public Works . . .* , p. 162.

18. "Chronological History of National Grasslands."

19. Hargreaves, "Land-Use Planning in Response to Drought: The Experience of the Thirties," pp. 565-66.

20. *Boise City News*, September 6, 1934.

21. *Hooker Advance*, November 2, 1933.

22. *Morton County Farmer*, November 3, 1933.

23. *The Future of the Great Plains*, p. 7.

24. National Resources Board, *A Report on National Planning and Public Works . . .* , p. 105.

25. Webb, *The Great Frontier*, p. 293.

26. *Ochiltree County Herald*, January 23, 1936.

27. Freidel, *Franklin D. Roosevelt*, IV, 82.

Chapter 7

1. Interview, Bud Troutman.

2. "Notes and Excerpts from McMillan Report on Baca County [Colorado] 1936," p. 1.3.

3. FitzGerald, *Livestock Under the AAA*, p. 29.

4. Ibid., p. 31.

5. U.S. Department of Agriculture, *Yearbook of Agriculture 1935*, p. 46.

6. *Texhoma Times*, August 3, 1933; *Hooker Advance*, August 4, 1933.

7. *Morton County Farmer*, September 29, 1933; *Boise City News*, September 28, 1933; Springfield *Democrat-Herald*, August 10, 1933; and other news articles, July to December 1933; U.S. Department of Agriculture, *Yearbook of Agriculture 1934*, pp. 34-35, 371-72.

8. U.S. Department of Agriculture, *Yearbook of Agriculture 1934*, pp. 371-72.

9. U.S. Department of Agriculture, Agricultural Adjustment Administration, *Participation Under A. A. A. Programs 1933-35*, pp. 4-5.

10. National Resources Board, *A Report on National Planning and Public Works . . .* , p. 105.

11. "Chronological History of National Grasslands."

12. A check of numerous records failed to reveal any extensive effort by the federal government to prevent wind erosion of allotment land before 1935.

13. FitzGerald, *Livestock Under the AAA*, pp. 175-76.

14. Ibid., p. 203.

15. See also Lambert, "The Drought Cattle Purchase, 1934-1935," pp. 85-93 and Lambert, "Drought Relief for Cattlemen; The Emergency Purchase Program of 1934-35," pp. 21-35.

16. *Boise City News*, July 19, 1934.

17. Ibid., July 26, 1934.

18. Ibid., August 2, 1934.

19. Ibid., August 9, 1934.

20. Ibid., August 16, 1934.

21. Ibid., August 30, 1934.

22. FitzGerald, *Livestock Under the AAA*, pp. 192-216; *Morton County Farmer*, August 3, 1934; *Texhoma Times*, August 2, 9, 1934, October 4, 1934, December 13, 1934; *Guymon Daily News*, January 2, 1935.

23. Lambert, "The Drought Cattle Purchase, 1934-1935," p. 86.

24. *Texhoma Times*, April 2, 1936.

25. Interview, Bud Troutman. The delay in announcing refinancing is verified by a check of local newspapers. Also useful Springfield *Democrat-Herald*, October 10, 1935. See Chapter 8.

26. *The Future of the Great Plains*, p. 7.

27. Ibid., p. 9.

28. Ibid., p. 7.

29. National Resources Board, *A Report on National Planning and Public Works . . .* , pp. 201-202.

30. *Texhoma Times*, July 12, 1934.

31. U.S. Department of Agriculture, *Yearbook of Agriculture 1934*, p. 21.

32. U.S. Department of Agriculture, *Yearbook of Agriculture 1935*, p. 46.

33. *Stratford Star*, March 19, 1936, January 14, 1937.

34. Ibid., April 28, 1938.

35. *Elkhart Tri-State News*, May 13, 1938.

36. Ibid.

37. *Stratford Star*, January 14, 1937.

38. Ibid.

39. Dreier, "The Coordinated Program for the Southern High Plains," p. 16.

40. See Chapters 8 and 9.

41. Dreier, "The Coordinated Program for the Southern High Plains," p. 17.

42. *Spearman Reporter*, April 22, 1937.

43. Ibid.

44. *Hooker Advance*, November 2, 1933.

45. *Boise City News*, December 14, 28, 1933, January 4, 25, 1934.

46. Texhoma Times, January 11, 1934, February 8, 1934.

47. Ibid., January 18, 1934, March 15, 1934.

48. *Hooker Advance*, May 3, 1934.

49. *Grant County Republican*, May 3, 1934.

50. *Hooker Advance,* May 3, 1934.

51. Ibid., July 26, 1934.

52. *Texhoma Times,* November 1, 1934.

53. *Morton County Farmer,* September 7, 1934, October 19, 1934, November 2, 9, 13, 1934.

54. Springfield *Democrat-Herald,* February 28, 1935.

55. Ibid., July 18, 1935.

56. *Texhoma Times,* April 5, 1934, August 23, 1934, February 21, 1935, May 9, 1935, October 31, 1935; Information on Panhandle A & M College provided by Mrs. Kathryn A. Sexton, English Department, Panhandle State University, Goodwell, Oklahoma.

57. Beaver *Herald-Democrat,* January 23, 1936.

58. *Texhoma Times,* January 23, 1936; *Clayton News,* May 13, 27, 1936; *Dalhart Texan,* January 23, 1936, June 8, 1936.

59. *Morton County Farmer,* August 20, 1937.

Chapter 8

1. "Chronological History of National Grasslands."

2. Ibid.

3. *The Future of the Great Plains,* p. 2.

4. National Resources Board, *A Report on National Planning and Public Works . . . ,* p. 182.

5. Ibid., p. 16.

6. *Hugoton Hermes,* March 15, 1935, May 17, 24, 1935, July 19, 1935, August 9, 1935.

7. U.S. Department of Commerce, Bureau of the Census, *United States Census of Agriculture: 1935,* pp. 358, 361; Otto, *Trends in Land Values in Kansas;* Ramsbacher, *Trends in Land Values in Kansas;* "Chronological History of National Grasslands"; Interview, Bud Troutman.

8. Interview, Bud Troutman.

9. *The National Grasslands Story,* p. 15.

10. *Better Land for Better Living.*

11. National Resources Board, *A Report on National Planning and Public Works . . . ,* p. 182.

12. U.S. Department of Agriculture, Agricultural Adjustment Administration, *Mills Land Use Adjustment Project New Mexico Proposal A-4: Resettlement Plans,* pp. 2-3.

13. U.S. Department of Agriculture, Agricultural Adjustment Administration, *Mills Land Use Adjustment Project New Mexico Proposal A-4: Final Plan,* p. 4.

14. Ibid., p. 5.

15. *Clayton News,* July 8, 1936.

16. Ibid.

17. *Boise City News,* August 20, 1936.

18. *Texhoma Times,* March 15, 1934; *Morton County Farmer,* April 6, 1934; *Johnson Pioneer,* April 12, 1934.

19. U.S. Department of Agriculture, *Yearbook of Agriculture 1934,* pp. 78-79.

20. *Texhoma Times,* February 15, 1934.

21. Bennett, *Soil Conservation,* p. 940.

22. Water conservation emphasis taken from dozens of federal statements in publications and newspapers. The file at the Texas County Soil Conservation Office, Guymon, Oklahoma, is filled with hundreds of pictures of efforts to conserve water by water erosion prevention methods.

23. Beaver *Herald-Democrat*, March 3, 1936; *Texhoma Times*, August 13, 1936.

24. *Elkhart Tri-State News*, January 29, 1939.

25. *Report of the Great Plains Drought Area Committee*, p. 5.

26. Ibid., p. 10.

27. Drake, "Wind Erosion and Its Control," p. 197.

28. Savage, *Methods of Reestablishing Buffalo Grass on Cultivated Land in the Great Plains*, p. 2.

29. Savage, *Drought Survival of Native Grass Species in the Central and Southern Great Plains, 1935*, p. 39.

30. *Texhoma Times*, September 26, 1935.

31. Henderson, "Letters from the Dust Bowl," p. 547.

32. *Spearman Reporter*, February 20, 1936.

33. *Ochiltree County Herald*, May 21, 1936.

34. Springfield *Democrat-Herald*, July 7, 1937.

35. Joel, *Soil Conservation Reconnaissance Survey of the Southern Great Plains Wind-Erosion Area*, p. 45.

36. Ibid.

37. National Resources Board, *A Report on National Planning and Public Works . . .* , p. 70.

38. Ibid.

39. Joel, *Soil Conservation Reconnaissance Survery of the Southern Great Plains Wind Erosion Area*, p. 20. See also *The Future of the Great Plains*, pp. 74-75.

40. *The Future of the Great Plains*, p. 63.

41. Ibid.

42. Ibid., p. 105.

43. U.S. Department of Agriculture, *Yearbook of Agriculture 1935*, p. 46.

44. National Resources Board, *A Report on National Planning and Public Works . . .* , p. 175.

45. Stein, *California and the Dust Bowl Migration*, p. 15.

46. U.S. Department of Agriculture, *Yearbook of Agriculture 1935*, p. 60.

47. Interview, Bill Kraft.

Chapter 9

1. Henderson, "Letters from the Dust Bowl," p. 546.

2. U.S. Department of Agriculture, *Yearbook of Agriculture 1935*, p. 111.

3. For discussion of farm production and land use see *Yearbook of Agriculture 1934, 1935, 1936, 1937, 1938*.

4. Hargreaves, "Land-Use Planning in Response to Drought: The Experience of the Thirties," pp. 561-82; Guttenberg, "The Land Utilization Movement of the 1920s," pp. 477-90; National Resources Board, *A Report on National Planning and Public Works . . . ;* Beaver *Herald-Democrat*, September 2, 1937.

5. *Stratford Star*, June 17, 1937.

6. *Morton County Farmer*, August 20, 1937.

7. See Chapter 7.

8. *Elkhart Tri-State News*, February 4, 1937.

9. Interview, Ed Tucker.

10. *Stratford Star*, July 8, 1937.

11. *Boise City News*, January 21, 1937.

12. *Texhoma Times*, February 25, 1937; *Boise City News*, February 18, 1937; Dean

and Carpenter, comp., "History of Morton County"; *Southwest Daily Times*, May 20, 1937; *Elkhart Tri-State News*, May 6, 1937; *Spearman Reporter*, June 17, 1937.

13. Beaver *Herald-Democrat*, September 2, 1937.

14. *Elkhart Tri-State News*, November 26, 1937.

15. U.S. Department of Agriculture, Bureau of Agricultural Economics, "Land Acquisition Plan: Mills Project," p. 5.

16. *Elkhart Tri-State News*, November 26, 1937.

17. U.S. Department of Agriculture, Bureau of Agricultural Economics, "Land Acquisition Plan: Tri-State Land Utilization and Land Conservation Project, Part I," p. 7.

18. *The Future of the Great Plains*, p. 7.

19. U.S. Department of Agriculture, Bureau of Agricultural Economics, "Land Acquisition Plan: Tri-State Land Utilization and Land Conservation Project, Part I," p. 1.

20. U.S. Department of Agriculture, Bureau of Agricultural Economics, "Land Acquisition Plan: Mills Project," p. 12.

21. Ibid., p. 20.

22. Ibid., p. 22.

23. Ibid., p. 19.

24. Ibid.

25. Cimarron National Grasslands, Base Map Tabular Record, LU-KA-21-256.

26. U.S. Department of Agriculture, Bureau of Agricultural Economics, "Land Acquisition Plan: Tri-State Land Utilization and Land Conservation Project, Part I," p. 2.

27. Ibid., p. 5.

28. Ibid., p. 8.

29. Ibid.

30. "Notes and Excerpts from McMillan Report on Baca County [Colorado] 1936," p. 1.3.

31. *Elkhart Tri-State News*, February 11, 1938.

32. Ibid., January 20, 1939, January 27, 1939.

33. *Texhoma Times*, February 23, 1939.

34. Schumacher and Atkins, *Reestablishment and Use of Grass in the Morton County, Kansas, Land Utilization Project*, p. 4.

35. Ibid.

36. Ibid.

37. Atwood and Johnson, *Oneways, Airplanes and Sand Lovegrass in Southwest Kansas*.

38. Finnell, *Land Use Experience in Southern Great Plains*, pp. 4-5.

39. Ibid., p. 4.

40. Hemphill, *Autobiography: Historical Data*.

Chapter 10

1. *Weekly Kansas City (Kansas) Star*, September 30, 1936, p. 8. Also numerous interviews and conversations with local residents.

2. Dean and Carpenter, comp., "History of Morton County."

3. Interview, Mrs. Edna Barnes; Interview, Mr. W. D. Ross.

4. Dougherty, "The John C. Dougherty Family," p. 69.

5. Henderson, "Letters from the Dust Bowl," pp. 542-43.

6. Stein, *California and the Dust Bowl Migration*, p. 81.

7. Henderson, "Letters from the Dust Bowl," p. 544.

8. See Stein, *California and the Dust Bowl Migration;* Slater, comp., *Directory and Manual of the State of Oklahoma, 1973*, pp. 252, 256, 285.

9. Beaver *Herald-Democrat,* January 23, 1936.

10. Interview, Bill and Vi Kraft.

11. Springfield *Democrat-Herald,* April 4, 1930.

12. *Boise City News,* Historical Edition, Summer 1968, Section D.

13. The *Guymon Daily Herald* ran a series of articles on the history of Panhandle churches in 1976-1977.

14. "Spradlin, From a Family History, 1968, Sent to Dorothy S. Jacobs," p. 11.

15. Interview, Gordon Grice.

16. Interview, Bill and Vi Kraft; Interview, Mr. and Mrs. Cecil Grable.

17. Interview, Jud Strain; Interview, Vernon Hopson.

18. *Stratford Star,* April 30, 1936.

19. Beaver *Herald-Democrat,* February 2, 1937.

20. Clingan, "Sharing the Years Together," p. 29.

21. Dale, *An Oklahoma Lawyer.*

22. Strasner, "Moonshine Madness," p. 22.

23. *Morton County Farmer,* September 21, 1934.

24. Interview, Gordon Grice.

25. "The Devers of Ochiltree County," p. 9. The chronicle of George Devers is only one of numerous pioneer profiles which appears in the *Old Timers News* (monthly) and the *Old Timers News Year Book* (annual).

26. Interview, Gordon Grice; Interview, Ed Tucker.

27. Springfield *Democrat-Herald,* February 16, 1933; *Boise City News,* April 19, 1933.

28. Accounts of accidents taken from numerous local newspaper articles.

29. *Elkhart Tri-State News,* September 7, 1937.

30. Ibid.

31. Hill, "The Land of Enchantment," p. 96.

32. David, "Floy 'Hoss' Yates," p. 58.

33. "Life of a Pioneer School Marm; The Life and Times of Chloe Bassett, Retired Pioneer Schoolteacher," p. 24.

34. Mullen, "Greatest Country I Ever Saw!" p. 3.

35. Saloutos, "The New Deal and Farm Policy in the Great Plains," p. 345.

36. David, "Mrs. E. P. Lewis - Elkhart," p. 5.

Bibliography

Books and Articles

Aicher, L. C. "Curbing the Wind." *Twenty-Ninth Biennial Report* of the Kansas State Board of Agriculture (Topeka: 1935):67-71.

———. "The Fort Hays Damming Attachment for Listers." *Thirtieth Biennial Report* of the Kansas State Board of Agriculture (Topeka: 1937):78-82.

Albertson, F. W. "Man's Disorder of Nature's Design in the Great Plains." *Annual Report of the Board of Regents of The Smithsonian Institution, 1950*, Pub. 4025 (Washington, D.C.: 1951):363-72. [Reprinted from *Transactions of Kansas Academy of Science* 52(June 1949)].

Alexander, Will W. "Report of the Administrator of the Farm Security Administration." (1939).

"Ancient Irrigation." *Oklahoma Today* 26(Winter 1975-76):14.

"April, 1938 'Snuster'." *Old Timers News Year Book, 1976*:9.

Arbingast, Stanley A. and Lorrin Kennamer. *Atlas of Texas* (Bureau of Business Research, The University of Texas, 1963).

Argow, Keith A. "Our National Grasslands: Dustland to Grassland." [Reprinted by the U.S. Forest Service for Official Use from *American Forests* (January 1962)].

Atwood, George S. and Leslie E. Johnson. *Oneways, Airplanes and Sand Lovegrass in Southwest Kansas* [Typescript] (Historical Data File, Cimarron National Grasslands Office, Elkhart, Kansas).

"The Awful Drouth of 1854." *Illustrated Weekly* 9 (August 29, 1901):10.

Baker, Bill. "Dust Bowl Blues." [Unpublished poem] (No Man's Land Historical Museum, Goodwell, Oklahoma).

Baldwin, C. B. "Report of the Administrator of the Farm Security Administration." (1940).

Baugh, Jay B. "Freedom on the Prairies." *Elkhart Tri-State News* (50th Anniversary Edition, 1913-1963).

Bennett, Hugh Hammond. "Land Impoverishment by Soil Erosion." *Twenty-Seventh Biennial Report* of the Kansas State Board of Agriculture (Topeka: 1931):171-77+.

———. *Soil Conservation* (New York: McGraw-Hill Book Company, Inc., 1939).

Berryman, J. W. "Early Settlement of Southwest Kansas." *Collections of the Kansas State Historical Society* 17(1926-28):561-70.

Bessire, Mrs. Roy, *Glimpses of Grant County* (The Ulysses [Kansas] News, 1973).

Better Land for Better Living [Brochure] (Washington, D.C.: Resettlement Administration, n.d.).

Black, William M. and Lowell H. Harrison. "C. O. Keiser and the Farmers' Settlement of Randall County." *Panhandle-Plains Historical Review* 43(1970):51-70.

Bonnifield, Mathew P. "The Choctaw Nation on the Eve of the Civil War." *The Civil War Era in Indian Territory* edited by LeRoy H. Fischer (Los Angeles: Lorrin L. Morrison, Publisher, 1974):58-73.

Box, Thadis W. "Range Deterioration in West Texas." *Southwestern Historical Quarterly*, 71(July 1967):37-45.

Brink, Wellington. *Big Hugh: The Father of Soil Conservation* (New York: MacMillan, 1951).

Brown, Earle G., Selma Gottlieb, and Ross L. Laybourn. "Dust Storms and Their Possible Effect on Health." *Public Health Reports* 50(October 4, 1935):1369-83.

Cady, Hamilton Perkins. "Is the Rainfall in Kansas Increasing?" *Collections of the Kansas State Historical Society* 12(1911-1912):132-33.

Call, Leland E. and Louis C. Aicher. *A History of the Fort Hays (Kansas) Branch Experiment Station, 1901-1962* (Kansas Agricultural Experiment Station Bulletin, No. 453. Manhattan, 1963).

Call, Leland E. and A. L. Hallsted. *The Relation of Moisture to Yield of Winter Wheat in Western Kansas* (Kansas Agricultural Experiment Station Bulletin, No. 206. Manhattan, 1915).

Campbell, Hardy Webster. *Campbell's 1907 Soil Culture Manual* (Lincoln, Nebraska: H. W. Campbell, 1907).

Cartwright, Thomas F. "History of Pioneer Natural Gas Company." *Panhandle-Plains Historical Review* 32(1959):60-86.

Chilcott, E. C. and John S. Cole. "Subsoiling, Deep Tilling, and Soil Dynamiting in the Great Plains." *Journal of Agricultural Research* 14(1918):481-521.

"Chronological History of National Grasslands." (Base Map Tabular Record, Comanche and Cimarron Grasslands).

Cimarron National Grasslands. (Base Map Tabular Record, LU-KA-21-256).

Clark, Everett R. *A Preliminary Report of the Growth and Effectiveness of Windbreaks in the High Plains Area of Oklahoma* (Panhandle [Oklahoma] Agricultural Experiment Station Bulletin, No. 55. Goodwell, 1934).

"Climatological Data, Oklahoma Section." (U.S. Department of Agriculture, Weather Bureau, 1930-1942).

Clingan, Vickie. "Sharing the Years Together." *Old Timers News Year Book*, 1977:29-30.

Cole, John S. and A. L. Hallsted. *Methods of Winter-Wheat Production at the Fort Hays Branch Station* (U.S. Department of Agriculture Bulletin, No. 1904. Washington, D.C., 1922).

Colorado Emergency Relief Administration. *Bulletin on Social Statistics* 1(1934) and 2(1935).

———. *News Bulletin* 2(1935).

Commanger, Henry Steele, ed. *Documents of American History*, 8th edition (New York: Appleton-Century-Crofts, 1968).

"The Crop Outlook in Oklahoma." *Oklahoma Farmer-Stockman* (August 15, 1934):17.

Dale, F. Hiner. *An Oklahoma Lawyer* (Guymon, Oklahoma: Guymon Publishing Company, 1961).

Daniel, Harley A. *Calculated Net Income Resulting from Level Terraces on Richfield Silt Loam Soil and Suggested Lines of Defense Against Wind Erosion* (Panhandle [Oklahoma] Agricultural Experiment Station Bulletin, No. 58. Goodwell, 1935).

———. *A Study of Certain Climatic Factors that May Affect Crop Yields in the High Plains of Oklahoma* (Panhandle [Oklahoma] Agricultural Experiment Station Bulletin, No. 57. Goodwell, 1935).

Davenport, W. "Land Where Our Children Die." *Collier's* 100(September 18, 1937):12-13.

David, Carol. "Floy 'Hoss' Yates." *Old Timers News Year Book*, 1976:59-60.

———. "Mrs. E. P. Lewis - Elkhart." *Old Timers News* 2(December 1975):5+.

———. "Point Rocks Flood." *Old Timers News Year Book, 1976:*42.

Dean, E. M. and Bertha Carpenter, comps. "History of Morton County." *Elkhart Tri-State News* (50th Anniversary Edition, 1913-1963). [Original manuscript in the library at Elkhart, Kansas].

"The Devers of Ochiltree County." *Old Timers News* 2(June 1976):9+.

"Documented Dust." *Time* 27(May 25, 1936):47-48.

Doerr, Arthur H. "Dry Conditions in Oklahoma in the 1930's and 1950's as Delimited by the Original Thornthwaite Climatic Classification." *Great Plains Journal* 2(Spring 1963):67-76.

———. "Oklahoma's Climate: The 'Dirty Thirties' and 'Filthy Fifties'—Climatic Analogue, Prologue or Epilogue?" *Proceedings of the Oklahoma Academy of Science* 41(1961):169-72.

——— and Stephen M. Sutherland. "Humid and Dry Cycles in Oklahoma in the Period 1930-1960." *Great Plains Journal* 5(Spring 1966):84-94.

Dougherty, Nellie. "The John C. Dougherty Family." *Old Timers News Year Book, 1977:*68-69.

Drake, Raymond R. "Wind Erosion and Its Control." *Agricultural Engineering* 18(May 1937):197-200.

Dreier, John. "The Coordinated Program for the Southern High Plains." *Land Policy Circular* (June 1937):15-18.

"Drouth Area Covers Entire Middle West." *Oklahoma Farmer-Stockman* (July 15, 1936):6.

"Drouth is Ended." *Oklahoma Farmer-Stockman* (August 15, 1938):4.

Drummond, W. I. "Dust Bowl." *Review of Reviews* 93(June 1938):37-40.

"Dust-Storm Film: U.S. Pictures Processes on Plains Leading to Tragedy." *Literary Digest* 121(May 16, 1936):22.

"Dust-Storm Forecasts." *Literary Digest* 120(July 13, 1935):19.

"Dust-Storms' Aftermath." *Literary Digest* 120(November 2, 1935):15.

"Dust Storms and Their Possible Effect on Health." *American City* 52(March 1937):19.

"Dust Storms, April 1935." *Monthly Weather Review* 63(April 1935):148.

Eva. (Place and Publisher unknown, circa. 1976).

Federal Emergency Relief Administration. *Monthly Report* (December 1 to December 31, 1933).

"Federal Movie Furor." *Business Week* (July 11, 1936):14.

Finnell, H. H. *Depletion of High Plains Wheatland* (U.S. Department of Agriculture Circular, No. 871. Washington, D.C., 1951).

———. *Dust Storms Come from the Poorer Lands* (U.S. Department of Agriculture Leaflet, No. 260. Washington, D.C., 1949).

———. *Land Use Experience in Southern Great Plains* (U.S. Department of Agriculture Circular, No. 820. Washington, D.C., 1949).

———. "The Moisture-Saving Efficiency of Level Terraces Under Semi-Arid Conditions." *Journal of the American Society of Agronomy* 22(June 1930):522-29.

———. "The Plowup of Western Grasslands and the Resultant Effect Upon Great Plains Agriculture." *The Southwestern Social Science Quarterly* 32, No. 2(1951):94-100.

Fite, Gilbert C. *The Farmers' Frontier, 1865-1900* (New York: Holt, Rinehart and Winston, 1966).

FitzGerald, D. A. *Livestock Under the AAA* (Washington, D.C.: The Brookings Institution, 1935).

Fitzpatrick, E. G. and W. C. Boatright. *Soil Survey of Texas County, Oklahoma* (U.S. Department of Agriculture, Series 1930, No. 28. Washington, D.C., 1930).

Flood, Francis A. "The Dust Bowl is Being Tamed." *Oklahoma Farmer-Stockman* (July 1, 1937).

Floyd, Fred. "A History of the Dust Bowl." Ph.D. Dissertation (University of Oklahoma, 1950).

———. "The Struggle for Railroads in the Oklahoma Panhandle." *The Chronicles of Oklahoma* 54(Winter 1976-1977):489-518.

Fly, C. L. *A Preliminary Report of the Chemical and Mechanical Analyses of Dust Deposited by Wind at Goodwell, Oklahoma* (Panhandle [Oklahoma] Agricultural Experiment Station Bulletin, No. 57. Goodwell, 1935).

Ford, Paul Leicester, ed. *The Writings of Thomas Jefferson*, Vol. 8 (New York: G. P. Putnam's Sons, 1897).

Forsythe, James L. "Clifford Hope of Kansas: Practical Congressman and Agrarian Idealist." *Agricultural History* 51(April 1977):406-20.

Freidel, Frank. *Franklin D. Roosevelt*, Vol. 4 (Boston: Little, Brown and Company, 1973).

Furbush, Malcolm A. "Hugoton Field, Kansas." *Kansas Oil and Gas Fields* (Kansas Geological Society, 1959):2:55-60.

The Future of the Great Plains (The Report of the Great Plains Committee to the House of Representatives, 75th Congress, 1st Session. Doc. No. 144. Washington, D.C., 1937).

Gaines, Stanley H., comp. *Bibliography on Soil Erosion and Soil and Water Conservation* (U.S. Department of Agriculture Miscellaneous Publication, No. 312. Washington, D.C., 1938).

Gate to No Man's Land ([Gate, Oklahoma]: GATEway to the Panhandle Museum Association, 1976).

Getty, R. E. *Experiments with Forage Crops at the Fort Hays Branch Station, Hays, Kansas, 1913-1928* (U.S. Department of Agriculture Technical Bulletin, No. 410. Washington, D.C., 1934).

Gibson, Arrell M. *Oklahoma: A History of Five Centuries* (Norman: Harlow Publishing Corporation, 1965).

Gould, Charles N. "The Beginning of the Panhandle Oil and Gas Field." *Panhandle-Plains Historical Review* 8(1935):21-36.

———. *The Geology and Water Resources of the Western Portion of the Panhandle of Texas* (U.S. Department of Interior, U.S. Geological Survey Water-Supply and Irrigation Paper, No. 191. Washington, D.C.,1907).

——— and John T. Lonsdale. *Geology of Beaver County Oklahoma* (Oklahoma Geological Survey Bulletin, No. 38. Norman, 1926).

——— and John T. Lonsdale. *Geology of Texas County Oklahoma* (Oklahoma Geological Survey Bulletin, No. 37. Norman, 1926).

Grasshoppers: A New Look at an Ancient Enemy (U.S. Department of Agriculture Farmers' Bulletin, No. 2064. Washington, D.C., 1954).

Gray, C. W. "Tractor Plowing." *Twenty-Seventh Biennial Report* of the Kansas State Board of Agriculture (Topeka, 1931):196-202.

Gray, L. C., et. al. "The Utilization of Our Lands for Crops, Pasture, and Forests." *Yearbook of Agriculture 1923* (U.S. Department of Agriculture. Washington, D.C., 1923):415-506.

"Great Quantities of Natural Gas." *Panhandle Herald* (Pictorial History, 1928).

Green, Donald E. *Land of the Underground Rain: Irrigation on the Texas High Plains, 1910-1970* (Austin: University of Texas Press, 1973).

Greenfield, G. "Unto Dust—; Great American Desert in the Making." *Reader's Digest* 30(May 1937):37-38.

Grimes, W. E. "Marginal and Submarginal Lands in Kansas." *Twenty-Ninth Biennial Report* of the Kansas State Board of Agriculture (Topeka, 1935):60-67.

Guttenberg, Albert Z. "The Land Utilization Movement of the 1920s." *Agricultural History* 50(July 1976):477-90.

Hallsted, A. L. "A Preliminary Report of the Relation Between Yield of Winter Wheat and Moisture in the Soil at Seeding Time." *Journal of Agricultural Research* 41(September 15, 1930):467-77.

―――― and O. R. Mathews. *Soil Moisture and Winter Wheat With Suggestions on Abandonment* (Kansas Agricultural Experiment Station Bulletin, No. 273. Manhattan, 1936).

Hambridge, Gove. "Soils and Men—A Summary." *Yearbook of Agriculture 1938* (U.S. Department of Agriculture. Washington, D.C., 1938):1-19+.

Hardesty (Place and Publisher unknown, 1976).

Hargreaves, Mary W. M. "Land-Use Planning in Response to Drought: The Experience of the Thirties." *Agricultural History* 50(October 1976): 561-82.

Harris, Evelyn and Caroline A. Henderson. "Letters of Two Women Farmers." *Atlantic Monthly* 152(August and September 1933):236-45 and 349-56.

Hemphill, Ernest C. *Autobiography: Historical Data* [Typescript] (Kiowa Grasslands Office, Clayton, New Mexico, dated December 11, 1964).

Hemsell, Clenon C. "Geology of Hugoton Gas Field of Southwestern Kansas." *Bulletin of the American Association of Petroleum Geologists* 23(July 1939):1054-67.

Henderson, Caroline A. "Letters from the Dust Bowl." *Atlantic Monthly* 157(May 1936):540-51.

―――― . "Spring in the Dust Bowl." *Atlantic Monthly* 159(June 1937):715-17.

Hill, Elsie Smalts. "The Land of Enchantment." *Old Timers New Years Book, 1977*:95-97.

Hofsommer, Donovan L. "Dirty Tricks of the Dust Bowl." *Orbit Magazine (Daily Oklahoman,* June 29, 1975):10.

―――― . *Katy Northwest: The Story of a Branch Line Railroad* (Boulder, Colorado: Pruett Publishing Company, 1976).

Holding, Vera. *Prairie Moods* (Dallas: American Poetry Association, Inc., 1938).

Holladay, Jeff. "The Great Panhandle 'Exodus' Furor." *Orbit Magazine (Daily Oklahoman,* June 19, 1977):6-8.

Hooker, Oklahoma: The Land of Opportunity (Hooker: Hooker Commercial Club, circa. 1920).

Hoover, Leo M. *Kansas Agriculture After 100 Years* (Kansas Agricultural Experiment Station Bulletin, No. 392. Manhattan, 1957).

―――― and John H. McCoy. *Economic Factors that Affect Wheat in Kansas* (Kansas Agricultural Experiment Station Bulletin, No. 369. Manhattan, 1955).

Hunger, Edwin A. "Kansas Outstanding Leader in Use of Combine." *Twenty-Seventh Biennial Report* of the Kansas State Board of Agriculture (Topeka, 1931):187-95.

Hunter, Lillie Mae. *The Book of Years: A History of Dallam and Hartley Counties* (Hereford, Texas: Pioneer Book Publishers, Inc., 1969).

Idso, Sherwood B. "Dust Storms." *Scientific American* 235(October 1976):108-14.

Isely, Bliss. "Unwhipped Dust Bowl Heroes Won't Budge." *Nation's Business* 29(November 1941):26-28+.

Joel, Arthur H. *Soil Conservation Reconnaissance Survey of the Southern Great Plains Wind-Erosion Area* (U.S. Department of Agriculture Technical Bulletin, No. 556. Washington, D.C., 1937).

Johnson, Vance. *Heaven's Tableland: The Dust Bowl Story* (New York: Farrar, Straus and Company, 1947).

Jones, Dotty. *A Search for Opportunity: A History of Hansford County* (Gruver, Texas: Jones Publishing Company, 1965).

Kansas State Board of Agriculture. *Twenty-Seventh Biennial Report* (Topeka, 1931).

―――― . *Twenty-Ninth Biennial Report* (Topeka, 1935).

————. *Thirtieth Biennial Report* (Topeka, 1937).

Kansas Weather and Climate (Kansas Agricultural Experiment Station Bulletin, No. 302. Manhattan, 1942).

Lambert, C. Roger. "The Drought Cattle Purchase, 1934-1935: Problems and Complaints." *Agricultural History* 45(April 1971):85-93.

————. "Drought Relief for Cattlemen; The Emergency Purchase Program of 1934-35." *Panhandle-Plains Historical Review* 45(1972):21-35.

Land Policy Circular (U.S. Department of Agriculture publication).

Langham, Wright H. *Fertility Losses From High Plains Soils Due to Wind Erosion* (Panhandle [Oklahoma] Agricultural Experiment Station Bulletin, No. 63. Goodwell, 1937).

————, Richard L. Foster, and Harley A. Daniel. "The Amount of Dust in the Air at Plant Height During Wind Storms at Goodwell, Oklahoma, in 1936-1937." *Journal of the American Society of Agronomy* 30(February 1938):139-44.

Lauber, Patricia. *Dust Bowl: The Story of Man on the Great Plains* (New York: Coward-McCann, Inc., 1958).

Laude, H. H. and others. *Growing Wheat in Kansas* (Kansas Agricultural Experiment Station Bulletin, No. 370. Manhattan, 1955).

Leighton, Morris Morgan. "Geology of Soil Drifting on the Great Plains." *Scientific Monthly* 47(July 1938):22-33.

"Life of a Pioneer School Marm; The Life and Times of Chloe Bassett, Retired Pioneer Schoolteacher." *Old Timers News Year Book, 1976*:24.

Luebs, R. E. *Investigations of Cropping Systems, Tillage Methods, and Cultural Practices for Dryland Farming at the Fort Hays (Kansas) Branch Experiment Station* (Kansas Agricultural Experiment Station Bulletin, No. 449. Fort Hays Branch, 1962).

McCarty, John L. *Maverick Town: The Story of Old Tascosa* (Norman: University of Oklahoma Press, 1946).

————. "A Tribute to our Sandstorms." [Clipping] (Special Collections, Mary E. Bivins Memorial Library, Amarillo, Texas).

————. "A Tribute to our Sandstorms." [Letter, January 27, 1937] (Special Collections, Mary E. Bivins Memorial Library, Amarillo, Texas).

McDaniel, Marylou, comp. and ed. *God, Grass & Grit; History of the Sherman County Trade Area* (Hereford, Texas: Pioneer Book Publishers, Inc., n.d.).

McGinty, Brian. "The Dawn Came, But No Day: The Dust Bowl." *American History Illustrated* 11(November 1976):8-18.

Malin, James C. "Dust Storms, 1850-1900." *The Kansas Historical Quarterly* 14(May, August, and November 1946):129-44; 265-96; 391-413.

————. "Man, the State of Nature, and Climax: As Illustrated by Some Problems of the North American Grassland." *Scientific Monthly* 74(January 1952):29-37.

————. "The Soft Winter Wheat Boom and the Agricultural Development of the Upper Kansas River Valley." *The Kansas Historical Quarterly* 11(November 1942):370-98 and 12(February and May 1943):58-91; 156-89.

————. "Soil, Animal, and Plant Relations of the Grassland, Historically Reconsidered." *Scientific Monthly* 76(April 1953):207-20.

————. "The Turnover of Farm Population in Kansas." *The Kansas Historical Quarterly* 4(November 1935):339-72.

————. "Wheat, Geology, and 'Professor' W. Foster." *Transactions of the Kansas Academy of Science* 59, No. 2(1956):240-48.

————. *Winter Wheat in the Golden Belt of Kansas: A Study in Adaption to Subhumid Geographical Environment* (Lawrence: University of Kansas Press, 1944).

Martin, Robert J. "Duststorms of 1938 in the United States." *Monthly Weather Review* 67(January 1939):12-15.

———. "Duststorms of January-April 1937 in the United States." *Monthly Weather Review* 65(April 1937):151-52.

———. "Duststorms of May 1936 in the United States." *Monthly Weather Review* 64(May 1936):176.

———. "Duststorms of May-December 1937 in the United States." *Monthly Weather Review* 66(January 1938):9-12.

Mattice, W. A., comp. "Dust Storms." *Monthly Weather Review* 63(March 1935):113-15.

———. "Dust Storms, November 1933 to May 1934." *Monthly Weather Review* 63(February 1935):53-54.

May, Irvin J. "Marvin Jones: Agrarian and Politician." *Agricultural History* 51(April 1977):421-40.

Minor, M. D. "The History of Moore County, Texas, Stressing Education." M. A. Thesis (West Texas State College, 1949).

Modrick, Ed. "A Yugoslavian Thanksgiving." *Guymon Daily Herald* (November 19, 1976).

Moore, Richard B. "Oil Creates an Industrial Frontier, West Texas, 1917-1937." *Texana* 8, No. 4(1970):341-51.

Morton, W. J., Jr. *Snowstorms, Dust Storms and Horses' Tails* (Dumas, Texas, 1966).

Muehlbeier, John. "Land-use Problems in the Great Plains." *Yearbook of Agriculture 1958* (U.S. Department of Agriculture. Washington, D.C., 1958):161-66.

Mullen, C. W. "Driving in the Rain." *Oklahoma Farmer-Stockman* (October 1, 1936).

———. "Farmers Will Boost Wheat Acreage." *Oklahoma Farmer-Stockman* (November 1, 1936):3.

———. "Greatest Country I Ever Saw!" *Oklahoma Farmer-Stockman* (April 15, 1935):3.

Myers, Cal D. "Old Timer Recalls Prairie Fire." *Old Timers News Year Book, 1976:*3.

Nall, Garry L. "The Farmer's Frontier in the Texas Panhandle." *Panhandle-Plains Historical Review* 45(1972):1-20.

———. "Panhandle Farming in the 'Golden Era' of American Agriculture." *Panhandle-Plains Historical Review* 46(1973):68-93.

———. "Specialization and Expansion: Panhandle Farming in the 1920's." *Panhandle-Plains Historical Review* 47(1974):46-67.

"Nash Brothers in 45th Year." *Old Timers News Year Book, 1976:*66.

The National Grasslands Story (U.S. Department of Agriculture, Forest Service. PA-607. Washington, D.C., 1964).

National Resources Board. *A Report on National Planning and Public Works in Relation to Natural Resources and Including Land Use and Water Resources with Findings and Recommendations* (Washington, D.C., December 1, 1934).

The Nation's Soil and Human Resources, Soil Improvement and Human Impoverishment (Resettlement Administration Publication, n.d.).

"Notes and Excerpts from McMillan Report on Baca County [Colorado] 1936." [Typescript] (File 1680, History Comanche Grasslands. Comanche Grasslands Office, Springfield, Colorado).

Oil and Gas Fields of the Texas and Oklahoma Panhandles (Panhandle Geological Society, 1961).

Osmunson, Robert L. *Hannah: True Story of a Spirited Oklahoma Girl's Struggle for Life, Love, and Peace with God* (Mountain View, California: Pacific Press Publishing Company, 1976).

Otto, M. L., H. L. Collins, and W. H. Pine. *Trends in Land Values in Kansas* (Kansas Agricultural Experiment Station Circular, No. 341. Manhattan, 1956).

Pennington, Alberta Lawson. "The Inventor of the First Angell One Way Disc Plow." *Old Timers News Year Book, 1977:*33.

Porter, Millie Jones. *Memory Cups of Panhandle Pioneers* (Clarendon, Texas: Clarendon Press, 1945).

"Precipitation Chart from Records Kept by U.S. Forest Service (Comanche Grasslands)." [Mimeographed] (Comanche Grasslands Office, Springfield, Colorado, 1976).

"Prehistoric Man on the High Plains." *Old Timers News Year Book, 1976*:60-61.

Ramsbacher, Harold H., Wilfred H. Pine, Merton L. Otto, and J. E. Pallesen. *Trends In Land Vaues in Kansas* (Kansas Agricultural Experiment Station Bulletin, No. 422. Manhattan, 1960).

Reed, Erik K. "Population Shifts in the Pre-Spanish Southwest." *Bulletin of the Texas Archeological and Paleontological Society* 21(1950):90-96.

Reeves, H. Eugene, comp. "Rainfall Data from 1911-1974, Goodwell, Oklahoma." [Mimeographed] (Panhandle State University Research Station and U.S. Weather Bureau. Goodwell, 1976).

Regional Map of a Portion of Oklahoma, Kansas and Texas (Oklahoma Geological Survey Bulletin, No. 40, Vol. II, Pt. 2, maps. Norman, 1930).

Report of the Great Plains Drought Area Committee (Submitted to the President, August 27, 1936, by Hugh H. Bennett, et. al.).

Riley, John A. "Sandstorms in Texas." *Monthly Weather Review* 59(January 1931):30-31.

Rister, Carl Coke. *No Man's Land* (Norman: University of Oklahoma Press, 1948).

———. *Oil! Titan of the Southwest* (Norman: University of Oklahoma Press, 1949).

"The Roaring Twenties." *Oil and Gas Journal* 57(January 28, 1959):45.

Rothrock, E. P. *Geology of Cimarron County Oklahoma* (Oklahoma Geological Survey Bulletin, No. 34. Norman, 1925).

Rowell, Edward J. "Drought Refugee and Labor Migration to California in 1936." *Monthly Labor Review* 59(December 1936):1355-61.

Rule, Glenn K. *Emergency Wind-Erosion Control* (U.S. Department of Agriculture Circular, No. 430. Washington, D.C., 1937).

Russell, W. M. "Development of Land Use Adjustment Projects." *Land Policy Circular* (June 1937):10-14.

Saarinen, Thomas Frederick. *Perception of the Drought Hazard on the Great Plains*, Department of Geography Research Paper No. 106 (Chicago: University of Chicago, 1966).

Saloutos, Theodore. "The New Deal and Farm Policy in the Great Plains." *Agricultural History* 43(July 1969):345-55.

Savage, D. A. *Drought Survival of Native Grass Species in the Central and Southern Great Plains, 1935* (U.S. Department of Agriculture Technical Bulletin, No. 549. Washington, D.C., 1937).

———. *Methods of Reestablishing Buffalo Grass on Cultivated Land in the Great Plains* (U.S. Department of Agriculture Circular, No. 328. Washington, D.C., 1934).

Schoff, Stuart L. *Geology and Ground Water Resources of Cimarron County, Oklahoma* (Oklahoma Geological Survey Bulletin, No. 64. Norman, 1943).

———. *Geology and Ground-Water Resources of Texas County, Oklahoma* (Oklahoma Geological Survey Bulletin, No. 59. Norman, 1939).

Schumacher, C. M. and M. D. Atkins. *Reestablishment and Use of Grass in the Morton County, Kansas, Land Utilization Project* (U.S. Department of Agriculture, Soil Conservation Service, SCS-TP-146. Washington, D.C., 1965).

Schuyler, Michael W. "Drought and Politics 1936: Kansas as a Test Case." *Great Plains Journal* 14(Fall 1975):2-27.

Sears, Paul B. *Deserts on the March* (Norman: University of Oklahoma Press, 1935).

Shirk, George H. "The Post Offices of Oklahoma, Nov. 26, 1907—Dec. 31, 1965." *Chronicles of Oklahoma* 44(1966):31-90.

Six, Ray L. *Oil and Gas in Oklahoma; Beaver, Texas and Cimarron Counties* (Oklahoma Geological Survey Bulletin, No. 40, Vol. 2. Norman, 1930): 461-91.

Slater, Lee, comp. *Directory and Manual of the State of Oklahoma, 1973* (Oklahoma City: Oklahoma State Election Board, 1973).

Smith, Henry Nash. *Virgin Land: The American West as Symbol and Myth* (New York: Vintage Books, 1957).

Smith, R. C. "Upsetting the Balance of Nature; With Special Reference to Kansas and the Great Plains." *Science* 75(June 24, 1932):649-54.

"Some Outstanding Blizzards, 1857-1961." [Mimeographed] (U.S. Department of Commerce, Weather Bureau, L. S. 6107. Washington, D.C., 1961).

"Spradlin, From a Family History, 1968, Sent to Dorothy S. Jacobs." *Old Timers News* 2(February 1976):2+ .

Stanley, Francis Louis Crocchiola. *The Perryton, Texas Story* (Nazareth, Texas, 1975).

————. *The Phillips, Texas Story* (Nazareth, Texas, 1975).

————. *The Skellytown, Texas Story* (Nazareth, Texas, 1974).

Stein, Walter J. *California and the Dust Bowl Migration* (Westport, Connecticut: Greenwood Press, Inc., 1973).

Strasner, Don. "Moonshine Madness." *Old Timers News Year Book, 1976*:22-23.

Svobida, Lawrence. *An Empire of Dust* (Caldwell, Idaho: The Caxton Printers, Ltd., 1940).

Taeuber, Conrad and Charles S. Hoffman. "Recent Migration from the Drought Areas." *Land Policy Circular* (September 1937):16-20.

Texhoma Geneological and Historical Society, comp. and ed. *Panhandle Pioneers*, 4 vols. (Texhoma, Oklahoma: The Texhoma Times, 1970).

Thomas, Myrna Tryon. *The Windswept Land: A History of Moore County, Texas* (Dumas, Texas: Myrna Tryon Thomas, 1967).

Thompson, Mrs. Harry (Goldianne) and William H. Halley. *Clayton, the Friendly Town in Union County, New Mexico* (Denver: The Monitor Publishing Company, 1962).

Throckmorton, R. I. "Regional Land Use for the Hard Red Winter Wheat Belt." *Thirtieth Biennial Report* of the Kansas State Board of Agriculture (Topeka, 1937):69-77.

Tinsley, J. D. "Agricultural Development of the Texas Panhandle." *Panhandle-Plains Historical Review* 8(1935):54-64.

Tolley, H. R., Mordecai Ezekial, and others. "What's New in Agriculture." *Yearbook of Agriculture 1935* (U.S. Department of Agriculture. Washington, D.C., 1935):111-19.

Trombley, Kenneth E. *The Life and Times of a Happy Liberal: A Biography of Morris Llewellyn Cooke* (New York: Harper and Brothers, Publishers, 1954).

Tucker, Lee. "The Big Snow of 1918-19." *Old Timers News Year Book, 1977*:15-16.

Tugwell, Rexford Guy and Howard C. Hill. *Our Economic Society and its Problems: A Study of American Levels of Living and How to Improve Them* (New York: Harcourt, Brace and Company, 1934).

U.S. Department of Agriculture. *Yearbook of Agriculture 1923* (Washington, D.C.: GPO, 1923).

————. *Yearbook of Agriculture 1930* (Washington, D.C.: GPO, 1930).

————, *Yearbook of Agriculture 1931* (Washington, D.C.: GPO, 1931).

————. *Yearbook of Agriculture 1932* (Washington, D.C.: GPO, 1932).

————. *Yearbook of Agriculture 1933* (Washington, D.C.: GPO, 1933).

————. *Yearbook of Agriculture 1934* (Washington, D.C.: GPO, 1934).

————. *Yearbook of Agriculture 1935* (Washington, D.C.: GPO, 1935).

————. *Yearbook of Agriculture 1936* (Washington, D.C.: GPO, 1936).

————. *Yearbook of Agriculture 1937* (Washington, D.C.: GPO, 1937).

————. *Yearbook of Agriculture 1938* (Washington, D.C.: GPO, 1938).

————. *Yearbook of Agriculture 1958* (Washington, D.C.: GPO, 1958).

————. Agricultural Adjustment Administration. *Agricultural Adjustment: A Report of Administration of the Agricultural Adjustment Act May 1933 to February 1934* (Washington, D.C.: GPO, 1934).

————. Agricultural Adjustment Administration. *Agricultural Adjustment in 1934* (Washington, D.C.: GPO, 1935).

————. Agricultural Adjustment Administration. *Mills Land Use Adjustment Project New Mexico Proposal A-4: Final Plan,* submitted by D. R. W. Wager-Smith, Fleming J. Rigney, and J. B. Gilmer (Mills, New Mexico, May 15, 1935).

————. Agricultural Adjustment Administration. *Mills Land Use Adjustment Project New Mexico Proposal A-4: Resettlement Plans,* submitted by D. R. W. Wager-Smith, Fleming J. Rigney, and J. B. Gilmer (Mills, New Mexico, May 15, 1935).

————. Agricultural Adjustment Administration. *Participation Under A. A. A. Programs 1933-35* (Washington, D.C.: GPO, 1938).

————. Bureau of Agricultural Economics. "Land Acquisition Plan: Tri-State Land Utilization and Land Conservation Project, Part I." Project Symbol: LU-NM-38-21 (Kiowa Grasslands Office, Clayton, New Mexico, prepared March 23, 1938).

————. Bureau of Agricultural Economics. "Land Acquisition Plan: Mills Project." Project Symbol: LA-NM-38-5 (Kiowa Grasslands Office, Clayton, New Mexico, revised June 3, 1938).

————. Soil Conservation Service. *Soil Survey of Baca County, Colorado* (Washington, D.C.: GPO, 1973).

————. *Soil Survey of Beaver County, Oklahoma,* Series 1959, No. 11 (Washington, D.C.: GPO, 1962).

————. *Soil Survey of Cimarron County, Oklahoma,* Series 1956, No. 11 (Washington, D.C.: GPO, 1960).

————. *Soil Survey of Dallam County, Texas* (Washington, D.C.: GPO, 1975).

————. *Soil Survey of Grant County, Kansas* (Washington, D.C.: GPO, 1969).

————. *Soil Survey of Hamilton County, Kansas,* Series 1958, No. 10 (Washington, D.C.: GPO, 1961).

————. *Soil Survey of Hansford County, Texas,* Series 1957, No. 3 (Washington, D.C.: GPO, 1960).

————. *Soil Survey of Moore County, Texas* (Washington, D.C.: GPO, 1975).

————. *Soil Survey of Morton County, Kansas,* Series 1960, No. 8 (Washington, D.C.: GPO, 1963).

————. *Soil Survey of Ochiltree County, Texas* (Washington, D.C.: GPO, 1973).

————. *Soil Survey of Prowers County, Colorado,* Series 1960, No. 28 (Washington, D.C.: GPO, 1966).

————. *Soil Survey of Seward County, Kansas,* Series 1961, No. 28 (Washington, D.C.: GPO, 1965).

————. *Soil Survey of Sherman County, Texas* (Washington, D.C.: GPO, 1975).

————. *Soil Survey of Stanton County, Kansas,* Series 1958, No. 15 (Washington, D.C.: GPO, 1961).

————. *Soil Survey of Stevens County, Kansas,* Series 1958, No. 13 (Washington, D.C.: GPO, 1961).

————. *Soil Survey of Texas County, Oklahoma,* Series 1958, No. 6 (Washington, D.C.: GPO, 1961).

U.S. Department of Commerce. Bureau of the Census. *United States Census of Agriculture: 1935* (Washington, D.C.: GPO, 1936).

Van Doren, M. "Further Documents, Film Produced by Resettlement Administration." *Nation* 142(June 10, 1936):753.

Ver Wiebe, W. A., G. E. Abernathy, J. M. Jewett, and E. K. Nixon. *Oil and Gas Developments in Kansas During 1947* (State Geological Survey of Kansas Bulletin, No. 75. Lawrence, 1948).

Wadley, Mrs. Dan T. "Highlights of Pioneering." [Typescript] (Possession of author, April 16, 1968).

Watson, Virginia. "The Optima Focus of the Panhandle Aspect: Description and Analysis." *Bulletin of the Texas Archeological and Paleontological Society* 21(1950):7-68.

Weaver, John E. *North American Prairie* (Lincoln, Nebraska: Johnsen Publishing Company, 1954).

————. *Prairie Plants and their Environment: A Fifty-Year Study in the Midwest* (Lincoln: University of Nebraska Press, 1968).

———— and F. W. Albertson. *Grasslands of the Great Plains: Their Nature and Use* (Lincoln, Nebraska: Johnsen Publishing Company, 1956).

Webb, Walter Prescott. *The Great Frontier* (Austin: University of Texas Press, 1952).

————. *The Great Plains* (Boston: Ginn and Company, 1931).

Weeks, Albert W. "Developments in North-Central Texas and the Panhandle, 1936-1937." *Bulletin of the American Association of Petroleum Geologists* 21(August 1937):1015-33.

Wehrwein, George S., et. al. "The Remedies: Policies for Private Lands." *Yearbook of Agriculture 1938* (U.S. Department of Agriculture. Washington, D.C., 1938):241-56+.

Wheatheart of the Plains: An Early History of Ochiltree County, 1st ed. (The Ochiltree County [Texas] Historical Survey Committee, 1969).

Wickard, Claude R. "Report of the Administrator of the Farm Security Administration." (1941).

Wickens, J. F. "Colorado in the Great Depression: A Study of New . . ." Ph.D. Dissertation (University of Denver, 1964).

Williams, A. J. "A Drainage Change Involving the North and South Canadian Rivers." *Proceedings of the Oklahoma Academy of Science* (1935):76-77.

Wilson, R. R. and Ethel M. Sears. *History of Grant County, Kansas* (Wichita Eagle Press, 1950).

Woodruff, N. P., W. S. Chepil, and R. D. Lynch. *Emergency Chiseling to Control Wind Erosion* (Kansas Agricultural Experiment Station Technical Bulletin, No. 90. Manhattan, 1957).

Newspapers and Magazines

Beaver (Oklahoma) *Herald Democrat*.

Boise City (Oklahoma) News, 1931-1939.

Boise City News, Historical Edition, Summer 1968.

Cimarron News (Boise City, Oklahoma), 1930.

Clayton (New Mexico) News.

Dalhart Texan.

Denver News.

Elkhart (Kansas) Tri-State News.

Elkhart Tri-State News, 50th Anniversary Edition, 1919-1963, April 25, 1963.

Grant County Republican (Ulysses, Kansas).

Guymon (Oklahoma) Daily News.

Guymon (Oklahoma) Herald.

Hooker (Oklahoma) Advance.

Hugoton (Kansas) Hermes.

Hugoton Hermes, Centennial Anniversary Edition, 1861-1961, August 1961.
Johnson (Kansas) Pioneer.
Lamar (Colorado) Daily News.
Lamar (Colorado) Register, 1929-1937.
Morton County Farmer (Rolla, Kansas).
Nation's Business.
Ochiltree County Herald (Perryton, Texas).
Oil and Gas Journal.
Oklahoma Farmer-Stockman.
Old Timers News (Keyes, Oklahoma).
Old Timers News Year Book, 1976.
Old Timers News Year Book, 1977.
Panhandle Herald (Guymon, Oklahoma).
Rocky Mountain News (Denver, Colorado).
Southwest Daily Times (Liberal, Kansas).
Spearman (Texas) Reporter.
Springfield (Colorado) *Democrat-Herald*, 1929-1938.
Stratford (Texas) Star.
Texas County News (Guymon, Oklahoma).
Texhoma (Oklahoma) Times.
Times (Kansas City, Missouri).
Ulysses (Kansas) News.

Interviews and Letters

Albert, Mrs. V. P., Librarian, Kansas State Historical Society. Letter, Topeka, December 22, 1976, to author.

Barnes, Mrs. Edna. Hugoton, Kansas, July 28, 1976.

Berends, Charles. Gate, Oklahoma, April 16, 1977.

Bonnifield, Mr. and Mrs. Charles M. Phippsburg, Colorado, June 20, 1976.

Davison, Mrs. Gerald. Texhoma, Oklahoma, May 26, 1977.

Grable, Mr. and Mrs. Cecil. Eva, Oklahoma (Interviewed at Goodwell, Oklahoma), January 25, 1976.

Grice, Gordon. Guymon, Oklahoma, February 3, 1976.

Hopson, Vernon. Goodwell, Oklahoma, February 5, 1976.

Howe, Mr. and Mrs. Arthur. Wichita, Kansas (Interviewed at Goodwell, Oklahoma by Mrs. Joan Kachel), May 23, 1976. No Man's Land Historical Museum, Goodwell, Oklahoma.

Keenen, Mrs. Clarene. Goodwell, Oklahoma (Interviewed by Ellen Bonnifield), June 9, 1977.

King, Mrs. Lee. Goodwell, Oklahoma, May 26, 1977.

Kraft, Mr. and Mrs. Bill [and Vi]. Goodwell, Oklahoma, January 23, 1976 and August 14, 1976.

Love, Mrs. Emma. Goodwell, Oklahoma, January 29, 1976.

Murphy, Robert. Goodwell, Oklahoma, October 23, 1975.

Rainey, Mrs. Cleo. Goodwell, Oklahoma (Interviewed by Ellen Bonnifield), February 16, 1977.

Ross, Mr. W. D. Texhoma, Oklahoma, February 2, 1976.

Schnabel, Paul. Goodwell, Oklahoma, March 17, 1976.

Strain, Jud. Goodwell, Oklahoma, April 9, 1976.

Troutman, Bud. Elkhart, Kansas, July 29, 1976.

Tucker, Ed. Elkhart, Kansas, July 7, 1976 and July 23, 1976.

INDEX

229